HUMOUR IN SOCIETY

Humour in Society

Resistance and Control

Edited by
Chris Powell
West Glamorgan Institute of Higher Education

George E. C. Paton
University of Aston, Birmingham

St. Martin's Press   New York

© Chris Powell and George E. C. Paton 1988

All rights reserved. For information, write:
Scholarly & Reference Division,
St. Martin's Press, Inc., 175 Fifth Avenue, New York, NY 10010

First published in the United States of America in 1988

Printed in Hong Kong

ISBN 0–312–00933–X

Library of Congress Cataloging-in-Publication Data
Humour in society: resistance and control/edited by Chris Powell,
    George E. C. Paton.
        p. cm.
    Bibliography: p.
    Includes index.
    ISBN 0–312–00933–X: $35.00
    1. Wit and humor—Social aspects.   2. Laughter (Psychology)
I. Powell, Chris.   II. Paton, George E. C.
PN6149.S62H85 1988
302.2—dc19
                                                        87–23261
                                                            CIP

Contents

12   In Search of Literature on the Sociology of
     Humour: A Sociobibliographical Afterword   260
     George E. C. Paton

Notes on the Contributors

Gregor Benton works in anthropology at the University of Amsterdam. He normally writes on China, but once co-authored a joke book – *The Big Red Joke Book*.

Christie Davies is Professor of Sociology at the University of Reading. One-time member of Cambridge Footlights Revue, he has written, broadcast and lectured extensively on the sociology of humour, as well as writing humorous pieces under a variety of pseudonyms. He is the author of *Jokes are about Peoples* (Indiana Press, forthcoming).

Gail Dines-Levy studied sociology at the University of Salford and since 1981 has been part-time doctoral student at the same university studying the images of women in *Playboy* cartoons. After emigrating to Israel in 1979 she became involved in rape crisis counselling and the setting up of a research institute concerned with images of women in the mass media. She teaches at Wheelock College, Boston, Massachusetts.

Alan Dundes is Professor of Anthropology and Folklore at the University of California, Berkeley. He has written a number of articles on joke cycles.

Thomas Hauschild is a leading German ethnologist who studied anthropology and folklore from 1973–78 and his 1979 dissertation on 'evil eye' beliefs was published under the title *Der Böse Blick* (Berlin, 1982). He carried out extensive fieldwork in southern Italy between 1982 and 1984 and was Professor at the Institute for Oriental Studies in Naples. Recently assistant at the Anthropological Institute of the University of Cologne.

Simon Holdaway worked for eleven years as a police officer before taking up his present post as Lecturer in Sociology at the University of Sheffield. He has published widely on various aspects of police work including *Inside the British Police* (Basil Blackwell, 1983). He is a worker priest in the Anglican Church.

Charles Husband is Senior Lecturer in Social Psychology in the Postgraduate School of Studies in Social Analysis, University of Bradford. His main interests are in race relations, communications, policy and inter-group theory.

Steve Linstead is Principal Lecturer in Organisational Behaviour at Middlesex Business School. After graduating in English and American Studies from Keele University in 1974, he worked in a number of skilled and unskilled manual jobs in a variety of industries. Completed postgraduate studies at Leeds University and Sheffield City Polytechnic, being awarded his PhD from the latter institution in 1984. He has published widely on various aspects of management and organisational studies.

John L. Oldani is Professor of Folklore and English, and Director of the Programme in American Studies at Southern Illinois University at Edwardsville. He has published articles on humour, especially the relationship of humour to religion, has delivered papers to many national conferences, and has spoken on Catholicism and humour at the International Conference on Humour.

George E. C. Paton is Lecturer in Sociology at the Management Centre of Aston University, Birmingham. His strictly *sub rosa* activity of lecturing on the sociology of humour has, to date, been at his own institution and other British universities and he has broadcast locally on various aspects of humour.

Chris Powell is Lecturer in Sociology at the West Glamorgan Institute of Higher Education, South Wales. As well as undertaking postgraduate research in the sociology of humour, he was a contributor to the first International Conference on Humour and Laughter, Cardiff, Wales, 1976 and founder and convenor of the BSA Sociology of Humour Group since 1983.

Gregory W. H. Smith is Lecturer in Sociology at the University of Salford. Apart from the academic study of cartoons, his other research interests include ethnography and ethnomethodology, the work of Goffman and the sociology of sport.

Paul Taylor completed his doctoral thesis at the University of Leicester on theories of laughter and the production of television comedy. He lives in London, working in public-sector housing.

Acknowledgements

First and foremost we must thank our contributing authors, far too many of whom have had to wait a long time for their work to reach the light of day. Their forbearance, not to mention their sense of humour, has been stretched to the limit and has not been eased by the editors' inexperience, on the one hand, and their determination to attract the widest possible range of the best contemporary work in the field, on the other. One contributor in particular, Christie Davies, has been particularly supportive and made invaluable suggestions for improving the style and readability of the editors' introduction. He is, of course, exempt from any responsibility for the views of the authors expressed therein, although one insertion brought a 'toothy' grin from one of the editors! We are particularly grateful to a bevy of Aston University secretaries, who over the years have maternally gestated a number of threatened abortive drafts into immaculate conceptions: Julia Cox, Monika Chamberlain, Beryl Marston and Helen Ruff. We wish to acknowledge the permission of the Managing Editor of the journal *Western Folklore* to reproduce the paper by Dundes and Hauschild. Lastly, whilst one of the editors is the eternal optimist, he acknowledges the necessary balance of his colleague who is inclined, on his own admission, towards a more pessimistic and negativistic interpretation of the world – probably the product of several years of relatively deep immersion in the works of the Frankfurt School! Thus he would like to thank the people who managed to avoid disturbing and annoying him too much during the course of the project. A particularly fond word should also be reserved for Sherup – his dachsund – who, as a representative of her breed has been the target for much ridicule. We regret, as sociologists, that we still feel incapable of informing the world as to whether dogs laugh, or indeed can resist laughter – perhaps they and she should have the last laugh!

Chris Powell
George E. C. Paton

Preface

Why should a sociologist want to or need to study humour? In the case of one of the editors, the stirring of the sociological imagination was occasioned over a decade ago by an occurrence on a balmy (and barmy!) July night at an Open University Summer School. Coming to the brow of a hill at the entrance to the campus his ears were greeted by the sound of collective laughter which drowned even the sounds of loud music emanating from the Students' Union Building. Fats Waller's classic witty song 'The Joint is Jumpin' ' flashed into his mind to be succeeded by the more sober realisation that whatever the nature of the pleasantries provoking the laughter they were clearly being enjoyed together as sociological acts of humorous communion over and above, as the psychologists would have it, each individual's release of psychic tension. Here then was a phenomenon worthy of research and explanation, firstly, as to what if anything sociologists had up to then had to say on the subject and, secondly in the likely event that this had not excited much professional attention, to explore and expand this further, using the more sophisticated range of sociological tools now available to the researcher.

For the other editor over much the same period of time, initial inquiry and curiosity led him to consider the sociological neglect of humour and the strange range of responses to his professed serious interest in this obvious and central human activity. He had been invited to give a talk to the sociology staff at a Scandinavian university. The convention was for such talks to take place at lunchtime over coffee and cake. After hearing an altogether too-short list of the areas he felt competent to discuss, his contact opted for 'the sociology of humour'. 'The context', he declared, 'requires something light, a kind of diversion'. The host was not being especially Philistine; his attitude is one all too frequently expressed.

One typical response by both lay members of the public and by sociologists on hearing that 'humour' is someone's research topic, is a noticeable relaxation of the posture and a liberal permissive communication usually expressed by means of a joke. Another common response is to assume that the researcher is clearly totally lacking a sense of humour and to turn him or her into the butt of a joke. A final response is the converse of this, to expect the researcher to be the life and soul of a joke-telling sequence. All such

responses refuse to take the subject seriously, all can be seen as mildly invalidating and each deserving of consideration as to why this might be.

One common denominator for such responses is that humour is widely and essentially seen as an individualistic and spontaneous expression of sheer creativity and that the social structural and processual parameters to that creativity are much less tangible and hence not readily amenable to sociological conceptualisation and theorising. What is however, on the surface at least, a little surprising is that members of the profession itself seem in practice to sustain fears about intellectual creativity in certain areas. For them humour seems to be one aspect of human practice best left to the realm of free will. Despite this, sociologists, of all people, should surely never be *reasoning* that *any* human activity can be totally extracted from 'the social' as a mere residue of human interaction. The reality is of course that sociologists in practice do not so reason. The comparatively few sociological contributions to the field (or perhaps we should say contributions by sociologists) have all, albeit perhaps with varying degrees of adequacy, been products of reason.

In this connection it is perhaps also worth making a brief comparison with sociological approaches to formal literature as a sociocultural phenemenon. Clearly and understandably the majority of literary critics as non-sociologists have resisted the sociological analysis of literature (even the genre of comic literature!), but within the discipline itself the sociology of literature is now a respectable specialisation. Such a form of creativity is thus seen as problematic enough to be addressed whilst engaged in intellectual work and fears concerning it do not prevent the work from actually taking place. Residual fears about creativity are suspended because it is considered intellectually necessary to question the myth of spontaneous unfettered artistic genius believed and fostered by traditional literary critics. Furthermore, it is widely recognised that 'literature', unlike humour, is a *serious* subject and so sociologists in this field are prepared to hide their credentials – research and teaching – behind the academic fig-leaf of 'seriousness'!

Sport, too, provides us with an interesting point of comparison. It also has been seen in commonsense terms as an expression of human creative (or recreative) power. There have been years of relative academic neglect, where sport has been equated with 'play' and therefore not something to be a focus for serious study and research. As a school subject it was something to be enjoyed or endured rather

than thought about, a temporary cathartic suspension of the real everyday world of work and productivity. In the context, however, of high unemployment, the 'constructive' (or at least not 'destructive') use of 'leisure time' warrants more serious attention and research. People are becoming acutely aware of the social implications of sport and policy-makers are keen to harness and control its practice. Consequently, research becomes 'useful' and 'Sports Science' becomes an accepted degree subject, even at universities!

How does humour fit into this? If literature and sport are both seen as being 'creative' or 'recreative' aspects of human existence, so surely is humour. All share the commonsense presumption that they are in some important ways apart from 'the productive process', being rather to do with 'free' leisure or consumer space. Cultural and popular cultural forms are recreative expressions of the whole person where the person is seen as relatively autonomous of his/her means of survival. The only real professional fear is that social scientific work may encourage incursions into this 'free sphere' by external and exploitative agencies using its findings. It must, however, be emphasised that the 'compulsory'/'free'/'productive'/'consumptive' dichotomies whilst having an element of validity are not wholly convincing when applied to such creative activities.

Finally, it is interesting that the acceptance of a sociology of literature has increased within the discipline in terms of 'seriousness' whilst having decreased outside of it in terms of 'relevance'. With regard to sport, within the discipline there is a growing recognition of its 'seriousness' and without of its 'relevance'. Such options, where available in sociology degree courses, are popular; researchers in these fields do not have great difficulty in persuading potential publishers of their work as to its market viability. Humour unfortunately, by definition, is regarded within and without the discipline as non-serious/relevant. To our knowledge no sociology department in this country offers an option in the sociology of humour.

We want here, then, to suggest that this imbalance which neglects the social dimensions of humour needs to be rectified. The pioneering collection of papers presented here establishes the claim that humour is a serious matter, maybe even a relevant one, for society and the reader is accordingly invited to judge the truth of this for him or herself on the evidence presented by the contributors to this book.

Introduction

Any subject matter as ephemeral and evanescent as humour initially
requires some clear-sighted conceptual framework or typology to
convey to the reader the distinctly sociological sense of it. This is a
necessary intellectual preliminary to permit the sociological imagination to make a recognisable contribution to the understanding and
interpretation of humorous expression in a myriad of social contexts
and situations which will begin to rival those already achieved by the
psychologist and philosopher. This is particularly necessary in the
case of this diverse and pioneering collection of papers from a variety
of authors writing within the very broad guidelines of the central
theme of the book, viz. the use of humour by social actors as a means
of social control or resistance to such control. There is a particular
need to make explicit these common themes and the continuity of
thinking of scholars entering a new area of study from a variety of
positions and perspectives and using a wide range of methods of
gathering and analysing data.

The truism, well understood by practitioners, that sociology is a
multi-paradigmatic social science is not always appreciated by readers
who are not professional teachers or researchers. If it is an editor's
intention, as it is in this case, to bring to a wider audience of
intelligent laypersons, as well as colleagues, the significance of a
sociological approach to humour, both the sociologist of humour and
his readers must accordingly reconcile themselves to the basic
premise that there is no single approach to its study that we can label
the sociology of humour. At best there are a number of sociologies of
humour reflecting the different paradigms within the subject which in
turn encompass a variety of perspectives, dimensions, parameters,
methods, concepts, etc., adopted by and presented by sociologists
writing on humour. Humour is no different in this respect from other
social phenomena – it is simply that there is not yet a definitive body
of work within any one paradigm. For the more technically minded
this can include structural functionalism, conflict theories, Marxist
analyses, social action theory or symbolic interactionism, all of which
inform and highlight the continuing theme of this volume, i.e. the
employment of humour as both resistance and control mechanisms in
social relationships and societies of all kinds.

Readers will thus search in vain for a common perspective in our

authors and indeed we would argue that we do not as yet have sufficient grounds for adopting such a perspective on humour in society in general, let alone its resistance and control aspects. This volume accordingly represents a sample of current sociological work on humour and is justified in the first instance simply because such a collection has not been produced before. As editors we see ourselves more as pioneers than as established settlers. In other words we are exploring a series of routes in the hope of finding some roots! Although such an objective might sound rather modest there are other justifications for such broad parameters as are adopted here and the consequent eclecticism in the contents of this volume. We want to open up serious discussion of humour rather than to close it down and, with this end in view, we are here laying out sociologies of humour rather than a sociology of humour.

As noted above, sociology has a rich array of paradigms and attendant theories and research techniques, a number of which are represented or touched on in this volume. Indeed such an approach might be said to be predicated by the rich diversity of the types of humorous expression in the variety of societies, communities, organisations and groups referred to by our contributory authors. We would therefore expect the readership of this volume to initially find this both somewhat confusing and somewhat clarifying. Furthermore, we would expect (and indeed hope) in the best academic tradition to raise in the minds of the student of humour as many questions about its social ramifications as are hopefully clarified or resolved. This seems to us to be what all social scientific and especially sociological work should be about.

The most explicit theoretical perspective presented in this volume is that of Powell who, in advancing a phenomenological analysis of humour in society, not only illustrates the centrality of humour responses as important components of social resistance and control processes but paves the way for the kind of qualitative research in intracultural settings undertaken and reported here by Linstead and Holdaway.[1] Most of these paradigms are reflected in the work of the authors in this volume but, rather than imputing to them or inflicting on the reader an over-technical approach to humour, we have adopted a simplified typology of their approaches which embraces the different levels of analysis of humour and both the universal and specific social contexts of humorous expression. In this way we hope we have done justice to our authors who have presented both formal and informal analyses of, and both macro- and micro-level sociologi-

cal perspectives on, humour and given some indication of the connections between their work.

Both the universal and specific contexts of humour briefly referred to above require us to consider in more detail the main parameters within which the sociologist, as theoretician and/or investigator, may operate in making sense of and substantiating the relevance of humour in society. The parameters suggested here are broad enough to encompass the extant literature of sociological import (by non-sociologists as well as sociologists) without precluding future diversification in the sociology of humour. Thus even if much of the more extensive taxonomy suggested by Paton at the end of this volume can be seen as contiguous with this parametric framework, the latter does not constrict sociological inquiry.

The first parameters relate both to the scope of the social phenomenon, in this case humour, and to the levels of analysis being engaged in by the sociologist. The significance of humour may be studied at: (a) the societal level, i.e. for a particular society or type of society, e.g. the polity, religion, ethnic groups (see Benton, Oldani and Davies in this volume); and (b) the small group level where social processes of negotiating and constructing social reality predominate and where humour has a direct significance and function for its members (see Linstead, Holdaway in this volume). The first level of analysis permits the classification of humorous expression in various societies and the analysis of its societal functions for comparative purposes between both similar and different types of society. Social anthropological studies of humour at this level have greatly benefited the sociology of humour. Apart from the more obvious delineation of joking relationships in traditional societies, anthropological findings such as Handelman and Kapferer's distinction between 'setting specific' and 'category-routinised' joking frames can also profitably be used at a macro-level to distinguish the roles of professional comedians as mediators of cultural codes in advanced societies (see Paton in this volume for the British case).

At the micro-sociological level the overlap between sociology and social psychology in the study of humour (recognised in the extensive literature on humour and our authors' references) provides a focus for interdisciplinary cooperation in analysing, investigating and explaining it. In particular both sociologists and social psychologists have sought to empirically substantiate the social significance of humour and its universality for tension management between social actors in small group situations (industrial, occupational, etc.). The

choice of either one or the other of these two levels of analysis reflects the concerns of particular sociologists and whether they believe humour in society is best seen as and investigated as a top-down or a bottom-up phenomenon.

Parallel to the above categories are those more specific ones of formal and informal organisation when applied to the broad spectrum of forms of social organisation which sociologists and social anthropologists have identified. Humour can, in this connection, be analysed first in relation to formal organisation or institutionalised systems, e.g. comedy can, following Goodlad, be seen as 'institutionalised humour'. In the latter case the sociological significance of literary and theatrical forms of comedy can be established in societies from Ancient Greece to the present day. Similarly, the humorous expression permitted periodically in the carnivals of the Middle Ages in western European societies can be seen as a formal expression of popular culture exemplifying the cultural concept of 'The World Upside-Down'. Anthropologists and folklorists have similarly seen role-reversal and liminality or cultural play[2] in ceremonies and rituals of traditional societies as safety valves for the collective release of social tensions or, as we would prefer to term it, the social control or resistance function of 'tension management' in hierarchical social relationships. These are terms within which the most contemporaneous formal expression of institutionalised humour such as the 'sitcoms' of the world of television comedy (see chapters by Taylor and Husband) or the magazine cartoon (see chapter by Dines-Levy and Smith) can be analysed. This does not mean that there is an 'official' humour associated with a given society, nor to suggest that national characteristics determine whether or not people in a particular society have a sense of humour or decide what types or genres of humour will flourish in a given society. Rather it is to suggest that, *lèse majesté* notwithstanding, even the most sacred and exalted of man-made formal institutions (see Oldani's chapter on Catholic jokes) can be profaned as the butt of humorous expression which renders it more humane or accessible to even the humblest of understandings. Indeed, the exasperated and in consequence jokey remark, 'Is nothing sacred?!' bears eloquent testimony to this.

Within formal organisations as such, the humorous expression associated with informal organisation in its most developed form has been seen by organisational sociologists as being 'in' rather than 'of' the formal organisations in which it is expressed, or at best as an 'emergent property' of formal organisation. As it has been observed

and recorded as a small group phenomenon, humour has been regarded by sociologists as a form of spontaneous behaviour and expression of sub-cultural norms which reinforces social controls within the group and expresses its members' shared resistance to the social pressures and tensions created by the formal organisation of the wider environment with which the group interacts (see Linstead and Holdaway in this volume). At least since the Hawthorne Experiment studies of Elton Mayo *et al.* half a century ago, humorous expression in the form of joking, 'horse-play', etc., has been recorded in a wide variety of work situations as being a significant if not universal feature of the informal social processes within such groups. Our contributors here (Linstead and Holdaway) confirm that this is the case in the industrial and police force situations they have investigated, thus reaffirming this approach as a necessary one in the analysis and especially in the empirical investigation of humour in society. Humour in the most formal of organisations, far from being an unremarkable and superficial froth on social relationships, is symptomatic of the most profound inter-subjective needs of group members who employ humour to make sense of and to control the tensions in their social relationships.

Irrespective of the formal/informal and macro/micro parameters of humour in society, the central tension management function of humour in all forms of social relationships and societies relates back clearly to our central theme of social resistance and control. Zijderveld[3] and Davies[4], in their recent major overviews of the sociology of humour and laughter, have suggested that these mechanisms are very influential in conflict and solidarity, particularly in the demarcation and maintenance of group boundaries. Our original formulation though is preferred here, for it is broader and connects the resistance and control of group members with humour as a mechanism for coping with conflict situations and the maintenance of group solidarity.

The analyses of the social resistance functions of humour deployment emphasise the social distancing of members of one group *vis-à-vis* another social group, perhaps most noticeably in the kind of self-deprecatory humour developed by Jews in resistance to the threats of racial prejudice of host nations and persistent anti-Semitism as identified by Dundes and Hauschild in this volume. Zijderveld perceptively notes in this connection that joking stereotypes tend to be resisted when self-consciousness has grown among the members of a minority group. Social resistance at the macro/formal

level is particularly well illustrated in the contributions here by Christie Davies and Gregor Benton with regard to ethnic jokes in Western industrial societies and political jokes in Eastern Europe. In the former case these may be seen as humorous sign-vehicles resisting the non-rational or stupid actions or beliefs of groups perceived as outside the modern 'rational' world, and as social resistance to displays of over-rationality by particular ethnic groups such that their very 'rationality' is seen as irrational and hence risible. Benton has shown in detail that Soviet jokes, along with their counterparts in other East European countries such as Poland and Czechoslovakia, have become bywords for the citizens' resistance to the over-bureaucratised and over-standardised views officially encouraged by the regimes. As core elements in the contemporary popular culture of such societies they sustain resistance, if not dissidence, to such inhuman constraints. Political jokes become, as Benton reminds us, 'a powerful transmitter of the popular mood in societies where this mood can find no officially sanctioned outlet'. At the micro-level, Linstead has extended traditional studies of joking in the informal organisation of work groups by placing such mechanisms in the context of theories of humour, highlighting the way in which humour is developed and deployed by members of an operator culture to manage group boundaries and to resist the demands of much process technology and, in particular, the management's constant threat to their status and autonomy.

The use of humour to reinforce the social control of deviance from shared standards, both between groups and within groups, further suggests its deployment as a form of what Lazarsfeld and Merton,[5] in the context of mass media, long ago referred to as 'norm enforcement'. In this collection of papers we can see evidence of social control at work at a macro/formal level in the case of joking directed at European emigrants to the USA in the early part of this century as a feature of their socialisation into the American community (see Duncan, referred to in Paton's first paper). At a micro/informal level, the significance of joking as a form of social control was established by the work of Mayo and his associates in the Hawthorne Experiment and members of work groups have consistently been observed, then and since, exercising social controls in the form of horse-play, verbal sarcasm, etc., in maintaining the norms of that group. Whilst this 'put down' humorous response is often employed in resistance to other groups with which the group is in relationship, especially management, it is essentially an internal regulating

mechanism of social control used to pointedly ridicule or embarrass/ shame the norm-breaker. In this volume, Holdaway's ethnographic study of the use of humour in police work neatly illustrates the use of humorous narration as a control mechanism in helping the lower ranks of the police to sustain what they regard as normal policing and to reinforce team membership and discipline. The reader's attention should also be drawn here to Oldani's development of the esoteric and exoteric factors in what he calls 'jokelore', the latter relating especially to stereotypes, in this case of Catholics in American society. Thus social control, as well as resistance, functions of humour depend respectively on what one group thinks of itself and what it supposes others think of it (esoteric), or what one group thinks of another and what it thinks that other group thinks it thinks (exoteric).

These parameters and sub-themes inevitably stress the study of humour at a particular period in time, but our knowledge that humour has taken similar as well as different forms over time also suggests and requires historical studies of its social expression. Here again, as suggested in the bibliographical essay by Paton at the end of this volume, a social historical perspective on humour has been growing which we would wish to see informed increasingly by sociological concepts, i.e. a sociological history of humour. Although humour or comedy *per se* have not been explored as a component of the civilising process, we would see it as just this and, moreover, as an important social indicator of historical developments and social changes. One can see Norbert Elias's concept of 'figurations',[6] and their emergence over time and in 'civilisations' as significant here with the emergence and persistence of 'figures of fun' – archetypes which become butts of humour ('Amazons', 'matronly women', 'mothers-in-law', 'fat men', 'small men', 'mad scientists', to mention but a few) – often at the expense of a 'cherished' institution or 'revered' type of person which is rendered risible. As some contributors (notably Davies and to a lesser extent Benton) in this volume indicate, such a dimension illuminates the functions of humour at earlier periods of time in a given society. In particular it helps to identify forces for social change or stability and the way in which humour is employed by social actors (especially radical or conservative humorists and comedians, *pace* Paton) and groups to advance either objective. Not least, this indicates the sub-cultural aspects of humour in terms of its emergence and form of expression in particular historical periods and its deployment to control or resist

social pressures, both by and against significant groups (ethnic, religious, sex), in a society at different periods of time.[7]

In this connection in the context of contemporary history, we would point to the significant emergence of female humorists with a distinctive women's humour in the past two decades, in parallel with the women's movement in Western advanced industrial societies. The literature on humour in the humanities and the social sciences, as the keen-eyed reader of the footnotes and bibliographies of this book can confirm, has thus witnessed a welcome growth in egalitarianism in intellectual endeavours in that there are now many significant studies of humour by women. Whilst Gail Dines-Levy, in partnership with Greg Smith in this volume, clearly indicates the promise and significance of such contributions from female social scientists in enhancing our understanding of humorous expression, in this case the visual humour of cartoons, the editors would be the first to admit they have not been able to achieve the authorial balance between the sexes they would have wished to see. It is hoped that future volumes in the sociology of humour edited or co-edited by women studying humour will succeed in righting this imbalance.

One final remark by way of introduction is necessary for the guidance of the reader in making his or her way through this set of readings setting out parameters for the sociological study and understanding of humour and society. Whilst there are numerous examples of jokes cited by way of illustration throughout the readings, and joke-telling and joking frameworks are recurring themes in a number of the papers, this does not imply that the editors or authors equate humour solely with jokes and joke-telling or that readers should draw such conclusions. Whilst readily subscribing to the Goffmanesque view of jokes as sign-vehicles so far as the sociology of humour is concerned, we would also agree with Waters in Trevor Griffiths' play *Comedians* who comments, 'It's not the jokes. It's what lies behind 'em. It's the attitude.'[8] Shared attitudes and the expression of shared sentiments and beliefs of resistance to or social control over social situations and relationships through humour are the essence of the sociology of humour which can be discerned from the contributions to this volume. This shared and inter-subjective humorous expression takes richly diverse socio-cultural forms other than joke-telling for, as well as unintentional humour (Freudian slips, misprints, etc.), we have humour deriving from the tone of an expression be it satirical, ironical, sarcastic or a play on words such as punning. This again is reflected in a host of literary and

artistic genres using the written word or visual, non-verbal imagery (e.g. the cartoon, caricature), and informally in the popular cultural form of graffiti. Lastly, and by no means least, the plain or downright comical, as represented by the logic of children's humour, comic postures and gestures such as 'funny' walks, 'fingers of scorn', and the oral humour of sounds, which Goffman calls 'response cries',[9] all await serious sociological analysis and exposition which it is hoped this volume will inspire and future volumes of such readings will compile.

We present this first broad attempt to collate a representative sample of current work in the sociology of humour to demonstrate the significance of humour in and for society. The work of the authors not only confirms the intrinsic interest of the study of humour but also their conviction of its extrinsic relevance for the study and understanding of society and culture. If, however, humour is a counterpoint to or mirror of a society, as the Dutch sociologist Zijderveld plausibly suggests, we should also agree with him that, as well as being an essential part of the fabric of social life, humour and laughter are just as often playfully 'useless' and 'senseless'. Indeed, it is the shared recognition and communication of something as 'nonsense' that invariably evokes humorous expression and establishes jokelore. It is perhaps in this sense that humour as a unique expression of *Homo ludens* can best be seen as a liberating social force, even to the extent of the true comedian's joke, as Griffiths suggests, changing the situation. Thus, the otherwise publicly unthinkable or outrageous act or belief can often be referred to or touched on and expressed more appropriately and acceptably in humorous form than in other literary or journalistic forms of speech, or indeed may be most pointedly made in a non-verbal humorous form, such as a cartoon. The bisociation of sense and nonsense suggested in the old but still toothy saw that 'truth is stranger than fiction' is a fertile area for humour in contrasting a more staid, normatively controlled social reality with an alternative reality, however absurd or surreal, so long as the humorous enunciation can be recognised as containing a germ of truth as to its feasibility or possibility. If this volume demonstrates to the reader nothing else but this, then the fledgling sociology of humour will rapidly take flight liberating us all from the societal constraints of Max Weber's 'iron cage'!

NOTES

1. One of the most seminal discussions of qualitative research, albeit in the context of intercultural communication research, which in our view would significantly inform and augment the sociology of humour as a medium of both cultural and sub-cultural communication, is that of Stella Ting-Toomey, 'Qualitative Research: An Overview', in W. B. Gudykunst and Y. Y. Kim (eds) *Methods for Intercultural Communication Research* (Beverley Hills: Sage Publications, 1984).
2. See V. Turner, in B. Babcock (ed.) *The Reversible World: Symbolic Inversion in Art and Society* (Ithaca and London: Cornell University Press, 1978).
3. A. C. Zijderveld, 'The Sociology of Humour and Laughter', *Current Sociology*, vol. 31, no. 3, Winter 1983 (whole edition).
4. C. Davies, 'Commentary on Anton C. Zijderveld's Trend Report on "The Sociology of Humour and Laughter"', *Current Sociology*, vol. 32, no. 1, Spring 1984, pp. 142–57.
5. P. Lazarsfeld and R. Merton, 'Mass Communication, Popular Taste and Organized Social Action', in L. Bryson (ed.) *The Communication of Ideas* (New York: Harper, 1948).
6. N. Elias, *The Civilising Process. Vol. 1 The History of Manners* (Oxford: Basil Blackwell, 1978).
7. See, for example, K. Thomas, 'The Place of Laughter in Tudor and Stuart England', *Times Literary Supplement*, 21 January 1977, pp. 77–81.
8. T. Griffiths, *Comedians* (London: Faber, 1976) p. 20.
9. E. Goffman, *Forms of Talk* (Oxford: Basil Blackwell, 1981) pp. 78–122.

1 Stupidity and Rationality: Jokes from the Iron Cage[1]

Christie Davies

One of the most outstanding features of the jokes told in industrial societies is the enormous and universal popularity of jokes told at the expense of allegedly stupid groups of people. In the Western industrial countries these jokes are usually told about an ethnic group or minority, whilst in Eastern Europe the jokes are of a political nature. It is perhaps not surprising that, apart from jokes about sex, ethnic jokes of all kinds are perhaps the most popular and numerous of all jokes in the West whilst political jokes tend to dominate the popular humour of Eastern Europe. However, what is remarkable is the range, durability and popularity of jokes about stupidity in both types of industrial society. It is a phenomenon that calls for a sociological explanation. Why, for instance, do people in Western industrial societies prefer jokes about 'stupid' ethnic minorities to almost any other kind of joke? Why are they so fond of jokes like these:

A Polish couple decided to have a chicken farm. They bought two chickens, took them home, dug a hole in their backyard and buried the chickens head first. Next morning they discovered the chickens were dead.

They bought two more chickens, this time planting them in the yard feet down. By the next morning the fowl had died. They wrote to the Polish consulate explaining their problem. Within a week they received a prompt reply from the Polish consul. The letter said, 'Please send us a soil sample.'[2] (American)

Article in Irish medical journal: 'Are vasectomies hereditary?'[3] (British)

A Sabena (Belgian airlines) aeroplane was unable to land at Brussels airport. The Belgian pilot signalled to the control tower that the landing-strip was too short for him to land on. 'Your landing strip', he said in amazement, 'is only a few dozen metres long and several kilometres wide.'[4] (French)

1

Practically every Western industrial country has its own 'stupid' group about whom such jokes are told, as can be seen from Table 1.1.

Table 1.1

Country where jokes are told about a 'stupid' group or minority	Group or ethnic minority about whom such jokes are told
United States	Poles
Also locally:	
New Jersey	Italians
San Francisco	Portuguese
Minnesota	Swedes
Britain	Irish
Australia	Irish, Tasmanians
New Zealand	Irish, Maoris
Canada (Eastern)	'Newfies' (i.e. Newfoundlanders)
Canada (Western)	Ukrainians, Icelanders
Ireland	Kerrymen
France	Belgians
Holland	Belgians
Belgium	Flemings
Germany	Ostfrieslanders
Denmark	Århusiernes (citizens of Århus), Norwegians
Sweden	Norwegians, Finns
Norway	Lapps
Finland	Gypsies, Karelians
Austria	Carinthians
Italy	Southern Italians
Greece	Pontians (Black Sea Greeks)

The jokes are told in each case about a group living on the social or geographical periphery of the country where the jokes are told. The group is usually an ethnic minority but the jokes may well be applied to the inhabitants of a neighbouring country (such as the Belgians) or of a peripheral provincial town or district (such as Århus or Ostfriesland). Often identical jokes are to be found in different countries and it is sometimes clear that the jokes of one country have been adapted or translated for consumption in another. The joke-tellers may dislike, despise, feel indifferent towards, or feel affection for the group who are the butt of their jokes. In a sense the victims are unimportant and in general attempts to explain such jokes simply in terms of the relationships between particular ethnic groups are

mistaken. The key facts about these jokes is that they reflect a deep-seated need that people have to tell jokes about a group of stupid outsiders. By telling jokes about the stupidity of a group on the periphery of their society, people can place this despised and feared quality at a distance and gain reassurance that they and the members of their own group are not themselves stupid or irrational.

There have always been jokes about simpletons, noodles and village idiots and in many pre-industrial societies joke-tellers have fastened the label 'stupid' on the inhabitants of a particular village, town, region or country. Towns such as Abdera in Thrace, Chelm in Eastern Europe, Kampen in Holland and Sidon in Phoenicia were made the butt of jokes about the foolishness of their inhabitants[5] long before modern industrial societies came into being. However, in the pre-industrial world there was nothing to compare with the great flood of 'Polish jokes', 'Irish jokes', Ostfriesenwitze and other jokes about stupid outsiders that has characterised the industrial societies, particularly since the 1960s. In the pre-industrial world stupidity was just one among many despised traits that was mocked in jokes, whereas in the advanced industrial countries of Western Europe and North America, jokes about stupidity have become something of an obsession.

There certainly seems to be a correlation between the increased popularity of ethnic jokes about stupid minorities and the development and intensification of industrial society. Jokes about the alleged stupidity of the Irish first appeared towards the end of the seventeenth century and showed a steady growth in popularity during the eighteenth and early nineteenth centuries, the period when Britain was becoming the world's first industrial country.[6] Irish jokes have remained popular in Britain ever since and the Irish have also been the main butt of jokes about stupidity in Australia, New Zealand and until relatively recently, the United States.[7] Jokes about stupidity have, as one might expect, always been popular in the United States and have been pinned on a variety of immigrant groups – the Irish, the Italians, the Portuguese, the Swedes, as well as the Poles. The Polish jokes which have been so popular in the United States since the 1960s are only the most recent in a long tradition of American jokes about stupid ethnic outsiders. Since the Second World War countries as diverse as India, Mexico, Iran and South Africa have advanced considerably along the road to industrialisation and have also begun to produce large numbers of jokes about their own local 'stupid' minorities. We may now add the industrialising

countries of Table 1.2 to the list of industrial countries producing
jokes about stupidity cited earlier.

Table 1.2

Country where jokes are told about a 'stupid' group or minority	Group or ethnic minority about whom such jokes are told
India	Sardarjis (i.e. Sikhs)
Mexico	Yucatecos (people of Yucatan)
Iran	Azerbaijanis
South Africa	'Van der Merwe' jokes about Afrikaners

The reason for the enormous popularity of jokes about stupidity in
Western industrial societies must be sought in the antithesis between
the attitudes and behaviour displayed by the member of the 'stupid'
minority in the joke on the one hand and the intensely and
increasingly 'rational' character of industrial society on the other.
Modern industrial societies are dominated by a belief in technical and
economic efficiency, by the view that all institutions should be
'rationally' organised via the interplay of the key impersonal forces of
the market place, bureaucracy and modern science so as to maximise
the stated goals of these institutions from the means at their disposal.
At one level, then, we may see jokes about stupid outsiders as an
affirmation of the value of rationality, efficiency and applied
intelligence on the part of the joke-tellers, for any failure to live up to
and conform to these qualities is ascribed to outsiders and then
subjected to severe ridicule. It is *they* who are comically stupid and
irrational and *we* who are intelligent, skilled and organised. By
apportioning implicit praise and direct mockery in this way, the jokes
presumably act as a minor means of social control. They are one
more factor pressing individuals into conformity with the 'rational'
demands of modern organisations and society.

However, in order to provide a full explanation of the popularity of
these jokes, it is necessary also to consider the negative impact of
rational social organisation on the individual. The key question that
must be asked is: 'What aspect of such a rational social order is likely
to make an individual anxious about his position in the rational world
in which he lives and want to indulge in jokes about stupid outsiders
as a release from this anxiety?' The answer to this question probably

lies in the high degree of specialisation and division of labour imposed on him by the market, bureaucracy and modern science. The mass market encourages individuals to become specialists who sell their particular skills in the market place and thus take advantage of the enhanced over-all efficiency and profitability created by their market-coordinated division of labour.[8] Modern bureaucratic organisations of all kinds are, almost by definition, organised around the principle of the division of labour. As Weber put it, 'bureaucracy rests upon expert training, a functional specialisation of work and an attitude set for habitual and virtuoso-like mastery of single, yet methodically integrated functions'.[9] Modern science, even where it is not organised along bureaucratic and market-oriented lines (which it usually is),[10] also demands a high degree of specialisation from those who become scientific workers of all kinds simply because of the enormous and increasing body of scientific knowledge[11] that now exists. No one can know and understand more than a fraction of it or keep up with the torrent of new research findings except within a severely limited area of study.

The extreme division of labour that characterises Western industrial society has produced a situation where everyone, including even the most highly skilled and intelligent of individuals is aware that he is a minor part of a system (be it a market, a bureaucracy or a science) that contains far more skill and knowledge than he can ever master. We are all specialists whose individual efforts in isolation might amount to very little.

Each individual specialist knows that he is perpetually dependent on innumerable other specialists whose work and skills he cannot reproduce and possibly cannot even comprehend. Under these circumstances even the most knowledgeable and skilled person is aware of how little he knows and how little he can do in a world that puts an enormous emphasis on skill and knowledge. In such a world everyone needs to be reassured that they are not really stupid and that real stupidity is safely restricted to the ranks of the Poles, the Irish, or whoever is the butt of the local ethnic joke. It is significant in this context to note how many of the jokes about a stupid minority have as their setting an aeroplane, a submarine[12] or a space rocket where everyone is locked in a technically sophisticated artificial environment and dependent for survival on the intelligent behaviour of highly skilled specialists. The situation of people caught up in such a scientifically controlled and constructed but potentially dangerous situation is an extreme metaphor[13] of the anxious and dependent

position of anyone trapped like Weber's bureaucrat as 'a single cog in an ever-moving mechanism which prescribes to him an essentially fixed route of march'. The introduction of a stupid outsider into the artificial situation of the joke has disastrous, but comic, results:

> Pokorski got a job as a test pilot. He took a helicopter up to 5000 feet ... 10 000 feet ... 15 000 feet. All of a sudden it crashed. Pokorski woke up in the hospital ward. His boss was there asking him what had happened. 'It got too cold', said the Polish pilot, 'so I turned off the fan.'[15] (American)

> 'How do you sink a Belgian submarine?'
> 'You knock on a port-hole and wait for someone to come and open it.' (French. See also earlier French example about the Belgian airline Sabena)

> Van was a wealthy Free State farmer with his own aeroplane. One day while on a holiday in the Cape his friend Van Tonder asked Van if he would like to fly his seaplane. Van gratefully accepted and did a perfect take-off from the bay accompanied by Van Tonder as his co-pilot. After flying around for some time Van began letting down over the aerodrome much to Van Tonder's alarm.
> 'Hey, Van'! he said. 'This is a seaplane not an aeroplane. You must land on water not on land.'
> Van thanked Van Tonder for his timely advice, pushed forward the throttle and flew off to the bay where he did a graceful landing. He then turned to Van Tonder and said: 'I cannot thank you enough for reminding me not to land on that aerodrome. If you had not pointed it out it would have been the end of us.'
> With these words he stepped out of the plane into the water.[17] (South African 'Van der Merwe' joke)

> The pilot of a plane approaching Heathrow airport asked the control tower for a time check. The control tower replied: 'If that's Quaint-arse the Australian airline, well the time is now three o'clock. If it's Air France, well the time is now fifteen hundred hours. And if you're Aer Fungus the Irish airline, well the big hand is on the twelve and the little hand is on the three.'[18] (British)

> Aer Fungus the Irish airline introduced a completely automatic plane on their flight from Dublin to London. As the plane took off

from Dublin airport a deep voice announced on the loudspeaker: 'This is your computer control speaker. You are now travelling in the world's first pilotless completely computerised and automatic aircraft. Everything has been carefully programmed by the very best Irish engineers and you can rest assured that nothing can possibly go wrong, go wrong, go wrong, go wrong . . .'[19] (British)

In 1990 the Swedes sent their first rocket up into outer space with a crew consisting of a chimpanzee and a Norwegian. On the control panel in front of them was a red light and a green light. When the red light flashed it indicated that instructions were about to come through for the Norwegian and when the green light showed it signalled an imminent instruction for the chimpanzee. Ten minutes after blast-off the green light flashed and the chimpanzee was instructed to alter the course of the rocket slightly, to take infra-red photographs of Sweden and to repair the radio transmitter. Half an hour later the green light flashed again and the chimpanzee was told to calculate the rate of fuel consumption, adjust the computer and make observations in connection with the earth's magnetic field.

By this time the Norwegian was getting restless at having nothing to do and resentful of the busy chimpanzee. Then one hour later the red light flashed and the Norwegian eagerly awaited his instructions. A minute later came the order: 'Feed the chimpanzee.'[20] (Swedish)

Thus far there has been an emphasis on one aspect of the rational society that in one way or another impinges on everyone – everyone at some time feels inadequate as a lone individual faced with the complexity of modern technology and social organisation and likes to feel superior to the comic outsider who cannot cope with it. However, in a society with a high degree of occupational specialisation and division of labour, people are divided into highly diverse and unequal groups differentiated by the degree of skill, training and acumen demanded by their work. At one extreme we have highly skilled specialists who must regularly undertake complex tasks involving a high degree of intelligence, knowledge, judgement or dexterity. A surgeon, a pilot, an electrical engineer, a barrister, a bank manager, a dealer in grain futures, simply must get it right most of the time if they are to survive in their chosen business or profession. For such people jokes about stupid outsiders are a

release from the strain of having to exercise a perpetual intelligent vigilance, of having to live by one's wits. Jokes about other people's stupidity can serve to dissipate any anxiety about losing their skill or intellectual powers at a crucial moment. It was probably for a similar reason that in the pre-industrial world jokes about stupidity seem to have been most popular in trading and commercial communities such as those of the ancient Athenians – with their gibes at nearby peasant societies such as Boetia or their trading rivals from Sidon[21] – and of the Jews of Eastern Europe with their jokes about Chelm or Schlemiels.[22] Where a community has to live by its wits stupidity is likely to be a despised, feared and widely mocked characteristic.

At the other extreme of a society characterised by a very high degree of division of labour are those who perform extremely simple, repetitive tasks that are but a fragment of some complex industrial or bureaucratic process and which require the exercise of hardly any skill or intelligence at all. The effect of such a job on the person who does it was clearly outlined by Adam Smith, one of the earliest observers of the introduction of modern division of labour:

> The understandings of the greater part of men are necessarily formed by their ordinary employments. The man whose whole life is spent in performing a few simple operations of which the effects too are perhaps always the same or very nearly the same has no occasion to exert his understanding or to exercise his invention in finding out expedients for removing difficulties which never occur. He naturally loses, therefore, the habit of such exertion and generally becomes as stupid and ignorant as it is possible for a human creature to become.[23]

People of this kind are also likely to be anxious about stupidity. They are anxious about their own low status in a society which prizes skill, intelligence and rationality, and are anxious lest the complex and baffling society in which they live should make unexpected demands on them which they will not know how to fulfil. Such anxieties are relieved by jokes about ethnic groups reputedly so stupid that they cannot even reach the level of social and economic competence attained by the least skilled of the occupational groups created by the division of labour. For such people perhaps the one remaining source of intellectual self-esteem that they have is the belief that they are more sophisticated than the newly arrived immigrant from the provinces, the countryside or a technically-backward country. An

unskilled person may well feel over-awed by the complexity of the world in which he works, but his very familiarity with its complexity enables him to feel superior to the ignorant newcomer. Hence the fund of stories about immigrant bumpkins who have not yet learned to master even the simplest task.

Did you hear about the Polack who lost his elevator operator's job because he couldn't learn the route?[24] (American)

A Toronto woman called a firm which was renowned for its landscaping and interior decorating. A man from the company soon arrived and the lady showed him round the house. Every time she asked what colours he would recommend for a particular room he used to go to the window, raise it and call out 'Green sides up!' before answering her. This happened several times and the woman's curiosity got the better of her. 'Is this some kind of a ritual?' she asked. 'No', he replied, 'its simply that I've got two Newfies next door laying sod.'[25] (Canadian)

A Sardarji (Sikh) working on a building site was trying to knock a nail into the wall head first. Another Sardarji seeing that his efforts were unavailing said to him, 'You're using the wrong kind of nail. That nail is meant for the wall opposite.'[26] (Indian)

Perhaps, then, the universal appeal of jokes about stupid outsiders lies in the fact that they have the power to relieve and defuse the various forms of anxiety experienced by the citizens of a rational society. Such anxieties may be generally experienced or specific to those occupying a particular niche in the division of labour with its own level of skills and intellectual demands and attendant fears. Different people may well laugh at jokes involving stupid ethnic minorities for widely differing mixtures of reasons, but the nature of the modern rational world is such that everyone will have *some* reason to feel anxious, some reason to need ethnic jokes of this kind. The feelings of anxiety and of an accompanying need for humorous release engendered by a rational society may not be homogenous but they are probably pretty universal.

Thus, the predominant ethnic jokes of the Western industrial societies serve the cause of rationality by denigrating its opposite – stupidity – and by defusing the various anxieties of those who live in the modern rational world. As such, they constitute a minor form of

social control. The Irish joke, the Polish joke, the Ostfriesenwitze, in some small way reconcile each trapped individual to his fate who, like Weber's 'individual bureaucrat, cannot squirm out of the apparatus in which he is harnessed'[27] or who is 'chained to his activity by his entire material and ideal existence'.[28] The jokes about stupid outsiders constitute part of that ideal existence – they are one small item helping to inculcate into people a secure belief in a 'rational' world devoted to the pursuit of 'precision, speed, unambiguity, knowledge of the files, continuity, discretion, unity, strict subordination, reduction of friction and of material and personal costs'.[29]

However, a careful study of the world of ethnic jokes reveals also an awareness that the rational world of 'rules, means ends and matter of factness'[30] that we have created is, at a deeper level, irrational. The successful pursuit of efficiency has created 'a joyless economy',[31] a world in which work is, for many people, tedious, monotonous and uncreative and where leisure is all too often simply a mirror-image of such work.[32] If this is what the pursuit of rationality has achieved then perhaps the pursuit was itself irrational. In a pessimistic mood, Max Weber wrote of the trap in which we now find ourselves:

The Puritan wanted to work in a calling; we are forced to do so. For when asceticism was carried out of monastic cells into everyday life and began to dominate worldly morality, it did its part in building the tremendous cosmos of the modern economic order. This order is now bound to the technical and economic conditions of machine production which today determine the lives of all the individuals who are born into this mechanism, not only those directly concerned with economic acquisition. Perhaps it will so determine them until the last ton of fossilised fuel is burnt. In Baxter's view, the care for external goods should lie on the shoulders of the 'saint like a light cloak which can be thrown aside at any moment'.

But fate decreed that the cloak should become an iron cage . . . in the United States the pursuit of wealth stripped of its religious and ethical meaning tends to become associated with purely mundane passions which often actually give it the character of a sport. No one knows who will live in this cage in the future or whether at the end of this tremendous development entirely new prophets will arise or there will be a great rebirth of old ideas and ideals or if neither, mechanised petrification embellished with a

sort of compulsive self-importance. For of the last stage of this cultural development it might truly be said: specialists without spirit, sensualists without heart; this nullity imagines that it has attained a level of civilisation never before achieved.[33]

Ethnic jokes protesting against the constraints of the iron cage are less popular, less numerous and less insistent than the jokes that pillory those groups too stupid to survive within its bars. Nonetheless, diverse ethnic jokes of this kind do exist and three types may be cited, each of which reveals one facet of the revolt against rationality. These are jokes about work-addicted Americans, jokes about rigid, pedantic, over-obedient Germans and jokes about stingy, over-rational, humourless Scotsmen. In each case the joke-tellers mock the members of another ethnic group for their excessive subordination to the world of work, money and duty. They are portrayed as senseless beings who have locked themselves in the iron cage and thrown away the key. Their very rationality is irrational, for their methodical manipulation of means towards ends robs their lives of the possibility of human joy and freedom.

An American businessman visiting in Mexico watched an Indian making pottery vases. He asked the price. Twenty centavos each. And for 100? The native thought it over and then answered: 'That will be 40 centavos each.' The American thought the Indian was making a mistake in his quotation of the price so he tried again. 'And if I bought 1000 all alike?' 'All alike?' he said. 'One thousand? Well, Senor, then they would cost you 60 centavos apiece.'
'Impossible! Why you must be insane!'
'It could be', replied the Indian, 'but I'd have to make so many and all alike and I wouldn't like that. So you see you would have to pay me for my boredom as well as for my work.'[34] (American)

An engineer was trying to put through a railroad project in one of the Latin American countries and he was seeking some local support for it.
'How long does it take you to get your goods to market on a burro?' he inquired of a native.
'Four days', he was told.
'See there', cried the engineer triumphantly, 'with our road you could get your goods to market and be back in one day.'

'But, Senor', protested the native, 'what would we do with the other three days?'[35] (American)

A couple of French tourists winding up an extensive trip around the United States passed an old folks' home. The inmates were rocking back and forth vigorously in their chairs on the porch. 'Regardez, Clarinda', remarked the French husband, 'these crazy Americans keep up their mad pace to the very end.'[36] (American)

An American teacher undertook the task of convincing an indolent native son of the Philippines that it was his duty to get out and hustle.
'But why should I work?' inquired the guileless Filipino.
'In order to make money', declared the thrifty teacher.
'But what do I want with money?' persisted the brown brother.
'Why, when you get plenty of money you will be independent and will not have to work any more', replied the teacher.
'I don't have to work now', said the native. And the teacher gave up in disgust.[37] (American)

Northern visitor (in Georgia): 'I see you raise hogs almost exclusively here. Do you find they pay better than corn and potatoes?'
Native (slowly): 'Wal no, but yer see, stranger, hogs don't need hoeing.'[38] (American)

In a South Carolina town a businessman beset by domestic and financial worries had blown his brains out. Naturally the tragedy, for the time being, was the main local topic of conversation. A resident who knew the suicide slightly was discussing the sad affair with his negro office servant.
'Joe', he said, 'speaking of such things, I've been struck by a curious circumstance. To the best of my recollection, I never heard of a member of your race deliberately killing himself because of private troubles and yet every day in the papers we see where white people have been taking their own lives. I wonder why this should be? You're a negro yourself, what are your theories on the subject?'
'Mista Barnwell', said Joe, 'yere's de way it tis: a white man gits hisself in a jam and he can't seem to see no way out of it and he sets down and thinks about it and thinks about it some mo' and after a

while he grabs up a pistol and shoots hisself. A black man, he gits snarled up in trouble the same way and he sets down and starts thinkin' and after a while he goes to sleep!'[39] (American)

These Yankee jokes, though at one level patronising about the lack of a work-ethic among Latin-Americans, Filipinos, blacks, white Southerners, etc., also reveal an uneasiness about their own work-obsessed society. There lurks in all these jokes a distinctly subversive message about the value and purpose of work and about the rationality of being a hustling American workaholic.[40]

There is a similar subversive message to be found in jokes about those dour, rational, stingy Scotsmen in whose Calvin-bounded lives the idea of duty in one's calling prowls about in a far from ghost-like way.[41]

An Aberdonian sat at the bedside of his friend who was a patient in a nursing home. 'Ye seem to be cheerier the day, John', said the visitor.
'Ay, man, I thocht I was going to dee but the doctor tells me he can save my life. It's to cost a hunner pounds.'
'Eh, that's terrible extravagance! Do ye think its worth it?'[42] (British)

A Deeside wife listened for a whole evening to the jokes and patter of Billy Connolly without a hint of a smile. Next day she confided to a friend, 'He's a great comic. It was all I could do tae keep from laughing.'[43] (British)

Wee Willie Deegan loved his game of golf but one bright sunny day his friends saw him sitting disconsolately in the club house, his clubs nowhere in sight.
'Why aren't you out playing, Willie?' asked the friend.
'Ach, I nae can play agin', sighed Willie.
'Why not?' asked his friend.
'Ach', said Willie, 'I lost me ball.'[44] (American)

An Aberdonian and his wife went to Rothesay for a holiday and went for a sail. Unfortunately the wife fell overboard and was drowned. The Aberdonian asked the pier-master to let him know if her body was found. Two weeks later he received a wire saying: 'Body recovered yesterday covered with crabs. Send instructions.'

The Aberdonian sent a wire back saying, 'Sell crabs; send on money; reset bait.'[45] (British)

An Aberdonian with a rotten molar went to his dentist who said he would charge £5 to pull it out.
Aberdonian: 'Couldn't you loosen it for a £1 so that I can pull it out myself?'[46] (British)

An undertaker at a Rotary dinner offered a free funeral to the first member of the club to die. Suddenly there was a shot from the back of the room. A Scotsman had shot himself.[47] (British)

A young Scotsman, methodical, painstaking, and sincere, as so many of his race are, had been a bachelor of long standing. Since coming to this country he had saved his money until now he felt he was qualified properly to support a domestic establishment. One day he went to a friend:
'I've about decided to get married', he said. 'In fact, I'm looking around now for a wife.'
'Where are you looking?' asked his friend.
'I'll tell you', said the Scot. 'It's my belief that the girls who work as clerks in the big department stores here in New York, are mighty fine types. As a rule, they are well dressed and tidy and good-looking and have nice ways. They must be self-reliant or they wouldn't be working. They have to be intelligent or they couldn't hold their jobs. They know how to make a dollar go a long distance, or they couldn't dress as well as they do on the modest wages most of them get. My notion is this: On pretext of wanting to buy something, I am going to tour the big shops until I see a girl behind a counter who seems to fill my requirements. Then I'm going to find out her name and make private inquiries as to her character and disposition, and if she answers all the requirements. I'll secure an introduction to her and if she seems to like me I'm going to ask her to marry me.'
Six months went by. The cautious Scot and the man to whom he had confided his plan of campaign met again. The latter thought his friend looked rather careworn and unhappy.
'How are you getting along?'
'Well', said the Scot, 'I'm a married man, if that's what you mean.'
'Well, did you follow the scheme you had in mind – I mean the one you told me about the last time I saw you?'

'Yes. I married a girl that worked at Macy's.'
'Congratulations. How's everything getting along?'
The Scot fetched a small sigh.
'Sometimes', he said, 'I can't help thinking that maybe I might
have done better at Gimbel's.'[48] (American)

Here it is thrift, self-control and rational calculation that are
comically undermined and subverted. The Scotsman's excessive
adherence to these three bars of the iron cage is shown as being self-
defeating and even self-destructive, for it is a world from which
warmth and enjoyment have been banished. A third example of an
ethnic joke 'against the cage' depicts the typical German's orderly
methodical, pedantic procedure-bound and obedient behaviour as
equally self-destructive.

A Stickler for the Code
A survivor of Mosby's Cavalry told me this one, years ago as
illustrative of the German's love for regularity and orderly routine
in all the affairs of life:
A Bavarian immigrant joined a Union regiment and in the third
year of the·(American Civil) war was sent to Virginia. One night
he imbibed too heavily of strong drink and fell asleep in a corn
crib. When he wakened he discovered that during the night a
negro camp follower had stolen his uniform, leaving behind a
ragged civilian outfit. The German clothed himself in these tatters
and set out to find his command.
Presently another and an even more disagreable circumstance
than the theft of his wardrobe impressed itself upon him. By
certain signs he was made aware that the Federal forces had
withdrawn from their old positions and the enemy had advanced
so that he was now inside the foe's lines. As he limped toward the
rear hoping to overtake the retreating force, a squad of ragged
gray troopers came whirling out of a thicket and surrounded him.
Quite frankly he told them who and what he was and they took
him prisoner.
Presently his captors halted him where a tree limb stretched
across the road, and one of the Southerners unlooping a plow line
from his saddle-bow, proceeded to fashion a slip-noose in one end
of it. The captive inquired of the lieutenant in command what the
purpose of all this might be.
'Why', said the lieutenant, 'we're going to treat you as we would

any Yank caught inside our lines in disguise. Under the laws of war
we're going to hang you as a spy.'
'Vell', said the German, 'votefer is der rule!'[49] (American)

On a Lufthansa flight from Heathrow to Berlin the captain's
speech to the passengers went something like this: 'Gut mornink,
ladies und jentlemen, ziss iss your captain shpeakink. Ve took off
from Heat'row precisely on time at 10.30 hours British Mean
Time, unt ve are now flyink at a height of fifteen thousand feet. In
two hours und forty three minutes ve shall descent to ten thousand
feet und sixteen minutes und fifteen seconds later ve shall descent
to five thousand feet. Ve shall remain at this height for seven
minutes and twenty-eight seconds and then ve shall land at 13.56
precisely. In the event of an emergency you vill all follow to the
letter the safety regulations printed on the cards in front of you.
There need be no panic or any casualties provided *you all do
exactly* AS YOU ARE TOLD!'[50] (British)

Lufthansa hostess: 'Good mornink, ladies and schentlemen. You
vill enjoy the flight.'[51] (British)

Two Germans in a bar in Mexico city see a third man coming in.
First German: 'That man is a police officer.'
Second German: 'How do you know?'
First German: 'He's wearing a uniform.'[52] (Mexican)

A small child walking down Ben Yehuda Street in Tel Aviv asked
an adult the time. 'It is precisely seventeen and a half minutes past
three', replied the adult.
'Are you a Yekke (German Jew)?' asked the child.
'Yes, but how did you know?'[53] (Israeli)

Easy for the trained mind
I was a reporter on the *New York Evening World*. The body of a
young woman, expensively dressed, was found in a thicket in a
lonely and remote part of Long Island. She had been murdered –
shot through the head. Harry Stowe of our staff, since deceased,
was the first reporter to reach the place. The body had not been
moved and in searching about it Stowe happened upon something
the local coroner had overlooked – a scrap of discoloured paper
bearing printed and written words in German upon it.

Stowe quietly slipped the paper into his pocket and caught the first train for town. He couldn't read German himself so he took his find to the office of the German consul. There he met an elderly, spectacled, exceedingly serious-looking under-secretary who translated the printed and written inscriptions for him.

Then the secretary wanted to know what it was all about. Stowe told him, explaining that the identity of the murdered woman was still a profound mystery – that nobody could guess who or what she was. He described her clothing in some detail.

'Pooh!' snorted the German. 'Stupid fools that these American policemen are! To the trained mind the whole thing is simplicity itself. By a process of elimination and deduction it is possible to ascertain beyond question exactly what manner of woman this was.'

'Could you do it?' asked Stowe, hopefully.

'In one little minute', said the under-secretary impressively.

'Go ahead then, please and do it', begged Stowe.

'Very well', said the German. 'My young friend, please follow me closely. This paper shows that some woman bought at a store in Leipzig certain small articles, kitchen utensils – a bread knife, a potato masher, a coffee grinder. No woman in Germany unless she was a housewife would buy such things. So! On the other hand, this woman, you tell me, wore forty-dollar corsets. No woman in Germany unless she was an actress would wear forty-dollar corsets. No actress would buy common household utensils. That would make her a housewife! No housewife would wear forty-dollar corsets. That would make her an actress. And there you are!'[54] (American)

Sign in a continental train:
E pericoloso sporgersi
Dangerous to lean out
Nicht Hinauslehnen![55] (British)

All these ethnic jokes about the 'rational' Americans, Scots and Germans are the mirror-image of the earlier jokes about stupid ethnic groups. The excessive devotion to work, money, order, rules, precision, rationality of the latter ethnic groups are also portrayed as forms of stupidity. Jokes which depict such an enthusiasm for the iron cage as stupid after its own fashion and which project such stupid traits safely on to other groups are a protest against the encroach-

ments of the bars. They also serve to dispel our anxiety that we too may become completely absorbed into a competitive and bureaucratic world. The comforting message of the jokes is that it is the others who are irrationally rational whilst we are wise enough not to be trapped in the constricting formal and technical rationality of the iron cage.

The jokes about stupidity and irrationality so far discussed have been mainly in relation to the ethnic jokes of the Western industrial capitalist societies. However, practically identical jokes about stupid groups are just as numerous and popular in the socialist countries of Eastern Europe. What is significant, though, is that in Eastern Europe such jokes are told about groups holding or exercising political power rather than about ethnic minorities. The people portrayed as stupid in East European jokes tend to be the leaders of the Communist Party, apparatchiks, official heroes and members of the militia (police). Thus the East European equivalent of Irish and Polish–American jokes are told about groups defined not in ethnic but political terms.

Why do Polish militiamen have a stripe round their elbows?
So that they can remember where to bend their arms.[56] (Polish)

A Polish militiaman took his car into the garage to have it serviced. 'There's something wrong with the indicator lights', he told the mechanic. The mechanic got into the car and turned them on.
'How are they now?' he asked.
'They're working. They're not working. They're working. They're not working ...' replied the militiaman.[57] (Polish)

Two Czech militiamen were on duty in Wenceslas Square in Prague. A foreigner came up to them and asked them in German how to get to the main railway station but he received no reply. The militiamen simply shrugged their shoulders so he tried in English. Again no reply. In French – still nothing. In Russian – not even then. Finally the foreigner also shrugged his shoulders and went away.
'You know, I think it would be a good idea to learn a foreign language', said one of the militiamen.
'Whatever for?' asked the other. 'Just look how many languages that chap spoke and it didn't help him one bit.'[58] (Czech)

A Czech militiaman went to see his doctor with severe burns on both his ears. 'How did this happen?' asked the doctor.
'Well, someone rang up while I was ironing', said the policeman.
'Yes, but how did you manage to burn both ears?' asked the doctor.
'Well, then I had to ring for an ambulance', said the militiaman.[59]
(Czech)

Why do Czech militiamen go round in groups of three?
One can read, one can write and the other is keeping an eye on the two intellectuals.[60] (Czech)

When Gierek was secretary of the Polish Communist Party he was renowned for making long, dull and boring speeches. After one particularly tedious three-hour speech, one of his colleagues hinted that a shorter speech might go down better with his audience. Gierek took the hint and told his secretary to limit his speeches to twenty minutes. At his next public appearance, however, he spoke for a full hour to the great irritation of his colleagues. The next day Gierek said angrily to his secretary: 'I gave you definite instructions that my speech was under no circumstances to be longer than twenty minutes.'
'But, Comrade Gierek', replied the secretary, 'I wrote you a twenty-minute speech just as you requested and as usual I gave you two carbon copies to go with it.'[61] (Polish)

The phone rang in the Kremlin one night. Brezhnev woke up, put on the light, put on his glasses, fumbled in his pyjama pocket for the appropriate scrap of paper, picked up the phone and read out carefully: 'Who is it?'[62] (Russian)

All Brezhnev's speeches at the Olympic games in Moscow carried as a heading the Olympic symbol, ⬯⬯⬯. As a result Brezhnev began all his speeches with the phrase 'Oh! Oh! Oh! Oh! Oh!'[63] (Russian)

Antonin Norotný (President of Czechoslovakia from 1957 to 1968) wanted to take his wife to the annual ball of the Academy of Sciences but his advisers tried to dissuade him. 'They are a nasty lot. They will ignore you.'
The Norotnýs went all the same.

The next day he bawled out his advisers: 'Ignore us my foot! Nobody took the slightest notice of us!'

At the same ball Mrs Norotný had noticed the beautiful complexion of some of the ladies. Norotný set his spies to work: 'Find out how they do it.'
They reported back within a few minutes: 'They use eau de toilette, Mr President.'
'Oh–de–what?'
'Toilet water, Mr President.'
When he comes home next evening his wife has a big bump on her head.
'What happened to you?' he asks.
'I tried this thing with the toilet water', says the first lady, 'but the lid dropped on my head.'[64] (Czech)

The fearless hero of the Civil War, Vasiliy Ivanovitch Chapaev, and his loyal orderly, Pyetka, were sky-diving.
'We're only 100 metres from the ground', said Pyetka, excitedly. 'It's time to pull the ripcord, Vasiliy Ivanovitch!'
'It's still kind of early', Chapaev answered calmly.
'It's only fifty metres now', screamed Pyetka. 'Pull the ring Vasiliy Ivanovitch!'
'Calm down, Pyetka', said Chapaev. 'There's still time before we hit.'
'Only three metres remaining!' cried Pyetka. 'Pull!'
'It's not worth it', answered Chapaev. 'From this height I can land without a parachute ...!'[65] (Russian)

After the successful Apollo–Soyuz space flight, Leonid Brezhnev called to congratulate the cosmonauts. However, he also reproached them with:
'The Americans are winning the space race. We must accomplish something to outdo them. They've already landed on the moon so we in the Politburo have decided to send you for a landing on the sun.'
The cosmonauts groaned: 'But, Comrade Brezhnev, we'll be burned alive.'
'What do you think', interrupted Brezhnev, 'that we don't understand anything? Don't worry, we've already planned all the details. First of all you are going to complete the landing at night.'[66] (Russian)

Why was Grechko made a Marshal of the Soviet Union?
Because he was too stupid to be a General.[67] (Russian)

Husak one day held a reception for Mrs Gandhi and the staff of the Indian Embassy in Prague. He and his wife arranged a curry buffet and had all the Czechs dress up in Indian costume. Half way through the reception, Husak's wife came over and said: 'Gustav, we've not dressed right.'
'What do you mean?' asked Husak.
'You've got to paint a red spot on your forehead like Mrs Gandhi', said his wife.
'Why?' said Husak.
'Well', said his wife, 'all the Indians are looking at you and tapping their foreheads with a finger.'[68] (Czech)

What is May 1st?
Socialist April Fools' Day.[69] (Czech)

The content of all these jokes about stupidity is the same as in the Western jokes cited earlier, but instead of the jokes being told about peripheral groups in the society they are told about groups at the very heart of the political order. What the jokes reflect is the awareness in the minds of the East Europeans who invent and tell them, of the unresolved tension in their societies between the pressures towards rationality inherent in any modern industrial economy and the dictates of their political system. The jokes are, as in the West, an expression of the values of rationality and of the anxieties engendered by modern forms of rational social organisation but they are also a protest against the perceived irrationality of the dominant modes of political authority and coercion. The jokes are a form of social control upholding the technostructure of society and yet also a means of subverting the legitimacy of the political order. The jokes exalt work and deny politics. East European jokes about stupidity underline the fundamental contradiction that exists in these societies between the rational outlook engendered by modern processes of production, administration and scientific enquiry, and the irrational, arbitrary, muddled and obstructive exercise of power that emerges from their political system.[70]

The politicisation of jokes about stupidity is a reflection of the general politicisation of society in Eastern Europe, a politicisation which can be both irrational in itself and productive of unforeseen

irrational consequences. At one level the irrationality can be seen simply as a result of continual arbitrary and irrelevant political interference with the workings of the basic 'rational' processes of modern society – the market, bureaucracy and science – for reasons of ideology or expediency to such an extent that the rational and routine functioning of these processes is perceptibly disrupted. At another and possibly more fundamental level, the irrational aspects of East European societies can be seen to be the inherent result of attempts to extend ostensibly rational forms of bureaucratic planning and control beyond what is possible and beyond what is rational to attempt. All societies, all economic and legal systems, all modes of production consist of a blend of two interacting and complementary forms of order, the specifically planned order of, say, a machine, a factory process or a bureaucracy, and forms of spontaneous order such as the market place or the advance of science. Any workable social, legal or economic system necessarily includes both forms of order. A rational social order is not one which seeks to maximise planned order (or, come to that, spontaneous order) but one which combines elements of planned and spontaneous order, of corporate and self-adjusting systems in an optimal way. The fundamental irrationality of the socialist societies of Eastern Europe[71] stems to a large extent from their excessive reliance on specifically planned order and in particular (a) their self-defeating 'attempts to exercise more specific control over the machinery of economic life than is compatible with the rules of an effectively functioning system of production';[72] (b) their failure to establish a fully workable and independent system of private law which can impartially enforce contractual obligations (e.g. between two state enterprises);[73] and (c) their attempts to predict and determine the advance of scientific knowledge.[74]

These East European attempts to impose massive constraints on the spontaneous form of order in society together with a failure to provide an institutional framework within which such forms of order can operate effectively would necessarily have horrendous irrational consequences even if the overriding specifically planned order were rationally designed.[75] In practice, of course, the pervasive, intrusive and irresponsible nature of East European politics ensures that even those smaller simpler social tasks that *can* be planned on a rational basis are subject to irrational pressures and distortions.[76]

East European jokes about stupidity do not only involve the ascribing of a lack of intelligence to those individuals and groups most

responsible for or most expressive of the irrational aspects of their social order. They also focus specifically on just those departures from the rational operations of the market, bureaucracy and science outlined above. With regard to the workings of science, the jokes tend to stress the stupidity of arbitrary political interference, though Polanyi noted on his various visits to scientific institutions in the USSR that attempts to plan the advance of science were themselves the subject of 'contemptuous jokes'.[77] The Lysenko affair[78] gave rise to many such jokes, the main butt of the jokes being the unfortunate horticulturalist Michurin who allegedly had produced wonderful hybrid fruit in defiance of the 'bourgeois' Mendelian laws of inheritance.[79]

Who invented barbed wire?
Michurin. He crossed earthworms with hedgehogs.[80]

Do you know how Michurin died?
No, how?
He broke his neck when he fell off one of his strawberries.[81]

Do you know how Michurin died?
How?
He crossed his legs and could no longer urinate.[82]

Professor Beckmann, a Czech electrical engineer who is something of a connoisseur of these jokes, has also recorded a number of true anecdotes about incidents involving the absurd exercise of political power to override scientific rationality:

> For example, in Ostrava an industrial town in north-east Moravia, a worker had proposed a machine that in essence was to throw rocks into the air and the rocks would then do work coming down. The chief engineer tried to explain the principle of the conservation of energy to him but to no avail; the worker turned to the Party, the engineer was fired and the proposal wandered all over the country, one expert handing it to another like a hot potato.[83]

Similar anecdotes and jokes arise from the conflict between the arbitrary exercise of political power and the rational operation of bureaucratic administration. A source of jokes about the irrationality and stupidity of political processes in Eastern Europe is the

contradiction between the 'rational' view that managers, officials, etc., should be appointed on the basis of ability, experience, skills and qualifications, and the Party view that political reliability and social background should take precedence.[84] Hence the jokes about the stupidity of those whose position depends mainly or entirely on political power or political loyalty.

By attempting to politicise management or science or civil administration and to make political power prevail over expertise in these areas, the politicians have sparked off a comic counter-attack in which rational expertise prevails over stupid politics. Similarly, the attempt to elevate men like Chapaev to hero status largely because of their unlettered origins has led to a counter-attack by the proponents of skill and education in which these erstwhile peasants and proletarians are made to look stupid. These processes are often mocked both directly and implicitly in East European jokes.

Two comrades met in the street. 'Heavens, you've changed!' said one. 'You've lost so much weight.'
'Well you see, I got married and my wife can't cook', replied the other.
'Why don't you send her on a state cookery course?' asked the former.
'That's exactly what I did just after we got married six months ago.'
'Well?'
'The course has only just reached the revolution of 1905.'[85] (Russian)

It was finally decided to introduce striptease into the Soviet Union, and since this was thought to be an extremely avant-garde concept it was decided only to employ women who had been members of the Party for at least 20 years. One day Brezhnev himself came along to watch the imported novelty. To ensure absolute ideological correctness a girl who had been a Party member since 1917 was the main star. Brezhnev watched her act for a while and when with palsied hand, she removed the last veil he said in a bored voice: 'I can't understand why those westerners are so enthusiastic about striptease.'[86] (Russian)

A Czech interview:
'What was your father's occupation?'
'I don't rightly know ... He used to mingle with the crowds in

market places and at soccer games and come back in the morning loaded with money.'
'In other words, a pick-pocket. And your mother?'
'I don't rightly know. She used to leave at night and come back in the morning loaded with money.'
'In other words, a prostitute. Anybody else in the family?'
'There was an uncle. He used to go from door to door selling combs and brushes.'
'A petit-bourgeois businessman! You fool, you could have been a first-class cadre but your uncle spoiled it all for you!'[87] (Czech)

The greatest number of Eastern European jokes directly concerned with the irrationality of the system deal with the failures of central economic planning, particularly in relation to agriculture and consumer goods. The queues, shortages and bottlenecks that result from the inability of a centrally directed system of prices and outputs to adjust rapidly to changing conditions of production and demand are probably the most popular theme of all in East European jokes. Their centrally directed economic plans aim to be rational, yet fundamentally they are irrational for they are often attempting to achieve something that is administratively impossible – 'impossible in the same sense in which it is impossible for a cat to swim the Atlantic'.[88] East European jokes mock both the irrational consequences of such a system and its ideological justifications.

Why do the Poles build their meat shops two miles apart?
So that the queues won't get mixed up.[89] (Polish)

At the May Day parade in Moscow, Leonid Brezhnev and other Russian officials watched as usual the long parade of Soviet military power – missiles, tanks, armoured cars and the like. At the end of the parade came a little truck with three middle-aged men sitting in it. Comrade Brezhnev turned to the Defence Minister and asked: 'Who are they?' The Defence Minister replied: 'Those are the economists. You would not believe the destructive power they possess.'[90] (Russian)

The Russians have absolute proof that the Bible is wrong. According to the Holy Book originally there was chaos and then there was order. The Russians know from experience that this is not so. *First* there was planning and then there was chaos.[91] (Russian)

When will the Cubans be certain that they have achieved socialism?
When they begin importing sugar.[92] (Ukrainian)

In Moscow in a café on Gorky Street, a comrade was boasting to his friends about the brilliant future of the regime:
'By 1987 every citizen of the Soviet Union will have his own personal aeroplane.'
'But why should I need an aeroplane of my own?'
'Well', said the other, 'to get from place to place. Suppose for example you learned that they were selling potatoes in Kiev; you could simply get in your aeroplane and fly there to get some.'[93] (Soviet)

A Russian economist gave a lecture in Moscow about a visit he had made to West Germany. 'The poverty to be seen in West Germany, comrades, is quite incredible. The shops everywhere are full of the finest goods and produce but no one can afford to buy them. There is not a single queue to be seen anywhere in the whole country.'[94] (Russian)

What do the Polish and American economies have in common?
In neither country can you buy anything with zloties.[95] (Polish)

Under capitalism you get discipline in production and chaos in consumption. Under socialist economic planning you get discipline in consumption and chaos in production.[96] (Polish)

There may be chaos in production but it is nonetheless disciplined chaos. The departures from rationality that are made fun of in East European jokes have not released anyone from the iron cage. They have merely ensured that everyone is caged twice – first in the familiar iron cage of rationality and secondly in an independent iron curtain cage whose bars are political, ideological, irrational. Neither cage encloses the other. Rather they are set at an angle to one another so that the hapless inmates are doubly constrained by some of the bars of each.

Today it is every bit as tedious to work on an assembly line in Togliattigrad, in a tractor factory in Budapest[97] or in an insurance office in Prague as in their Western equivalents. As the Czech economist Ota Šik guardedly noted: 'At the socialist stage of

development labour is still relatively onerous (long hours) and intensive. There is a relative lack of variety, work is monotonous and for most people offers little creative scope. There is still a fairly rigid division of labour binding the majority to one occupation for life.'[98] This fact, too, has been noted in the political jokes of East Europe[99] which thus provide a protest against the irrationality of rationality as well as the irrationality of irrationality.

CONCLUSIONS

In all industrial countries jokes about stupidity are immensely popular and this reflects the fact that the crucial institutions of these societies are organised along rational lines in the sense that they are designed to extract the maximum ends from given means. Jokes about stupidity are an affirmation of rationality and a release from the anxieties and tensions engendered by a zealously rational social organisation. As such they constitute a minor form of social control; but other jokes act as a protest against the iron cage of rational organisation and question the rationality of 'rationality'. Such jokes suggest that it is irrational for human beings to lead joyless, tedious lives spent in the pursuit of work or wealth.

In the Western capitalist countries the key vehicle for jokes about stupidity is the ethnic joke which places this despised quality at a safe distance by pinning it on to a peripheral ethnic minority. 'They are stupid but we and our society are rational' is the message of the jokes. In Eastern Europe jokes about stupidity are political and ascribe this quality to those holding or exercising political power at the core of society. In this way the political order itself is criticised for its perceived irrationality. Such jokes are a significant vehicle of protest in a type of society which lacks many such outlets.

NOTES

1. This article was written in the home of Mark and Janet Jenkinson in Leeds. I would like to thank them for their hospitality and the staff of the Brotherton library, University of Leeds, for their help. I wish to acknowledge also the assistance and advice of Michael Beckham, Dr B. Holbek, Christoph Jaffke, Lauri Lehtimaja, Dr W. M. S. Russell and a number of East European friends, colleagues and joke-tellers

who must remain anonymous. Finally I would like to thank the editor, Chris Powell, for encouraging me to write this article.

2. Larry Wilde, *The Complete Book of Ethnic Humour* (Los Angeles: Corwin, 1978) p. 176.

3. Garry Chambers, *The Second Complete Irish Gag Book* (London: Star, 1980) p. 94.

4. My translation.

5. See Evan Esar, *The Comic Encyclopaedia* (Garden City, New York: Doubleday, 1978) pp. 295–6; Leo Rosten, *The Joys of Yiddish* (London: W. H. Allen, 1970) pp. 85–6.

6. For a detailed history of the growth of the comic stereotype of the Irish during this period see J. O. Bartley, *Teague, Shenkin and Sawney* (Ireland: Cork University Press, 1954). For instances of eighteenth-century English jokes about the Irish see *Joe Miller's Jests or the Wit's vade-mecum* (New York: Dover Publications, 1963, facsimile reproduction of 1739 original).

7. For Australian Irish jokes see Wilbur G. Howcroft, *Black with White Cockatoos or Mopokes and Mallee Roots* (Melbourne, 1977) p. 105 *et seq.* The Americans also told jokes about Irish stupidity until the 1940s, see for example Bennett Cerf, *Laughing Stock* (New York: Gosset and Dunlap, 1945) which contains numerous jokes about stupid Irishmen (pp. 58, 82–3, 97, 108, 111, 140, 149, 159, 167, 106, 211, 214, 220, 237) but none about Polish Americans.

8. See Adam Smith, *An Inquiry into the Nature and Causes of the Wealth of Nations* (London: G. Bell, 1896) for one of the earliest accounts of this process.

9. Max Weber, in H. Gerth and C. W. Mills (translators and eds) *From Max Weber: Essays in Sociology* (London: Routledge & Kegan Paul, 1948) p. 229.

10. See for instance the comment in Arnold J. Toynbee, *A Study of History*, vol. 1, Humphrey Mitford under the auspices of the Royal Institute of International Affairs (Oxford University Press, 1934) p. 2. See also Weber (1948) pp. 223–4.

11. See Toynbee, p. 2.

12. See Stephane Steeman, *Raconte . . . une fois les vraies histoires Belges* (Paris: Editions Mengès, 1977) p. 95. 'The submarine seems to inspire our French friends and it is, with "chips", the most popular subject of Belgian jokes invented in France.'

13. The advantage of the metaphor is that everyone can readily understand the disastrous but comic consequences of introducing a stupid outsider into a plane or a submarine. One does not need any specialised knowledge to understand the physical and technical parameters of the situation depicted in the joke.

14. Weber (1948) p. 228.

15. Larry Wilde, *The Last Official Polish Joke-Book* (Los Angeles: Pinnacle Books, 1977) p. 135.

16. Steeman, p. 95.

17. John Carver, *Ag, shame, van der Merwe* (Hillbrow, South Africa: Lorton, 1980) p. 39.

18.　Told to me in England in the 1970s.
19.　Told to me in England in the 1960s.
20.　Told to me by a Swedish civil servant in the Swedish prison service in Salzburg, Austria, May 1977. For an American version see Larry Wilde, *The Official Polish Joke Book* (Los Angeles: Pinnacle Books, 1973) p. 22.
21.　See Esar, p. 295.
22.　See Henry D. Spalding, *A Treasure Trove of American Jewish Humor* (New York: Jonathan David, 1976) p. 119. 'The Jew had literally as a matter of survival been forced by circumstances to place a premium on intelligence.'
23.　Smith, Vol. II, Book V, Chapter I, Article 2nd, pp. 301–2. See also Karl Marx, *Capital, a Critical Analysis of Capitalist Production* (Moscow: Progress Publishers and London: Lawrence and Wishart, 1974) p. 342.
24.　Wilde (1977) p. 152.
25.　Gerald Thomas, 'Newfie Jokes', in Edith Fowke (ed.) *Folklore of Canada* (Toronto: McClelland and Stewart, 1976) p. 148.
26.　Told to me in Srinagar, Kashmir, in 1980.
27.　Weber (1948) p. 228.
28.　Ibid.
29.　Ibid., p. 214.
30.　Ibid., p. 244.
31.　See Tibor Scitovsky, *The Joyless Economy, an Enquiry into Human Satisfaction and Consumer Dissatisfaction* (New York: Oxford University Press, 1976).
32.　See for instance, Daniel Bell, 'Work and its discontents, the cult of efficiency in America', in Daniel Bell, *The End of Ideology* (New York: Free Press, 1960).
33.　Max Weber, *The Protestant Ethic and the Spirit of Capitalism* (London: Unwin University Books, 1930) p. 181.
34.　Jacob M. Braude, *Braude's Handbook of Humor for all Occasions* (Bombay: Jaico, 1976; original publication Englewood Cliffs: Prentice-Hall, 1958) pp. 38–9.
35.　George Q. Lewis and Mark Wachs, *The Best Jokes of All Time and How to Tell Them* (Bombay: Jaico, 1972; originally United States: Hawthorne, 1966) p. 255.
36.　Bennett Cerf, *The Laugh's on Me* (Garden City, New York: Doubleday, 1959) p. 195.
37.　Lewis and Faye Copeland, *10,000 Jokes, Toasts and Stories* (Garden City, New York: Garden City Books, 1939) p. 761. See also Lewis and Wachs, p. 352, for a similar story about a Red Indian in New Mexico, and Wilde (1978) p. 170, where the joke is told about a Mexican.
38.　J. Gilchrist Lawson, *The World's Best Humorous Anecdotes* (New York: Harper, 1923) p. 16.
39.　Irvin S. Cobb, *Many Laughs for Many Days* (Garden City, New York: Garden City Publishing, 1925) p. 233.
40.　These jokes are far from being a purely American phenomenon. The French tell similar jokes about lazy Corsicans, or people from the

South of France; the Dutch tell them about Surinamers; and even the lazy British have lazier Geordies like Andy Capp who has become popular all over the world.

41. Max Weber (1930): 'the idea of duty in one's calling prowls about in our lives like the ghost of dead religious beliefs'.
42. Graham Moffat, *The Pawky Scot* (Dundee: Valentine, 1928) p. 16.
43. Max Hodes, *The Official Scottish Joke-book* (London: Futura, 1978) p. 58.
44. Cerf (1945) p. 16.
45. From the archive of Scottish jokes at the House of Humour and Satire, Gabrovo, Bulgaria. These mainly date from 1968. There is also an American–Chinese version of the joke in Braude.
46. Bulgarian archives, 1968.
47. Bulgarian archives, 1968.
48. Cobb, p. 72.
49. Ibid., p. 201.
50. Michael Kilgarriff, *Best Foreigner Jokes* (London: Wolfe, 1975) p. 24.
51. Told to me in England in the 1960s.
52. Told to me in Mexico city in 1979.
53. Told to me in England in 1980.
54. Cobb, p. 238.
55. See in a continental train 1981. In fairness to the Germans it also said 'Défense de se dépender dehors'.
56. Anonymous Polish source, 1981 (via Michael Beckham of Granada Television).
57. Anonymous Polish source, 1981.
58. Anonymous Czech source, 1981.
59. Anonymous Czech source, 1981.
60. Anonymous Czech source, 1981.
61. Anonymous Polish source 1981. See also John Kolasky, *Look Comrade the People are Laughing* (Toronto: Peter Martins, 1972) pp. 38–9 for a similar story about Gomulka.
62. Anonymous Russian source, 1981.
63. Told to me in 1980, in England, by Emil Abramovitch Draitser, a former writer for *Krokodil* in Moscow, now teaching Russian at UCLA.
64. Petr Beckmann, *Whispered Anecdotes* (Boulder, Colorado: The Golem Press, 1969) p. 94. Professor Beckmann was a research scientist at one of the institutes of the Czechoslovak Academy of Sciences until 1963.
65. Emil Draitser, *Forbidden Laughter* (Los Angeles: Almanac Publishing, 1978) p. 50.
66. Draitser, p. 56.
67. Kolasky, p. 70.
68. Anonymous Czech source, 1981.
69. Anonymous East European source, 1981.
70. For a contemporary discussion of the nature of the contradiction see Maria Hirszowicz, *The Bureaucratic Leviathan: A Study in the Sociology of Communism* (Oxford: Martin Robertson, 1980) Chapter

4, 'The Limitations of Rationality in a Planning Society' and especially pp. 131–2.

71. See M. Polanyi, *The Logic of Liberty* (London: Routledge and Kegan Paul, 1951) p. 156.

72. Polanyi (1951) pp. 152.–3.

73. See Polanyi (1951) pp. 185–6.

74. See M. Ruhemann, 'Note on Science in the USSR', Appendix VII in J. D. Bernal *The Social Functions of Science* (London: Routledge, 1937) and especially 'The Planning of Research', pp. 445–7. See also Sidney and Beatrice Webb, *Soviet Communism: A New Civilisation* (London: Longman Green, 1944) pp. 769–73.

75. The problems the East European economies have encountered as a result of their inherent irrationality stemming from their attempts to suppress and control spontaneous forms of order were predicted well in advance by such far-sighted sociologists and economists as Vilfredo Pareto, Max Weber and Ludwig von Mises. See for instance Ludwig von Mises, *Socialism: An Economic and Sociological Analysis* (London: Jonathan Cape, 1974) pp. 211–20; Max Weber, *Economy and Society. An Outline of Interpretive Sociology* (London: University of California Press, 1968) pp. 81–113.

76. See Hirszowicz, pp. 127–67.

77. M. Polanyi, *The Contempt for Freedom, the Russian Experiment and After* (London: Watts, 1940) pp. 46–7.

78. For an account of the Lysenko affair see John Langdon-Davies, *Russia Puts the Clock Back. A Study of Soviet Science and Some British Scientists* (London: Victor Gollancz, 1949).

79. See discussion in Beckmann (1969) p. 78.

80. Petr Beckmann, *Hammer and Tickle* (Boulder, Colorado: Golem, 1980) p. 67. See also Kolasky, p. 111.

81. Kolasky, p. 110; and Beckmann (1980) p. 67.

82. Beckmann (1980) p. 67.

83. Beckmann (1969) p. 123. There is an interesting contrast to be made between this true anecdote and Evelyn Waugh's fictitious comic account of a mad inventor let loose on the British wartime bureaucracy in *Put Out More Flags* (London: Chapman and Hall, 1942).

84. See Hirszowicz, pp. 101–2.

85. Anonymous Russian source, 1981. See also Egon Larsen, *Wit as a Weapon* (London: Frederick Muller, 1980) p. 95.

86. Anonymous Russian source, 1981.

87. Beckmann (1980) p. 84.

88. Polanyi (1951) p. 126.

89. Anonymous Polish source, 1981.

90. Anonymous East European source, 1981.

91. Kolasky, p. 129.

92. Kolasky, p. 132.

93. Armand Isnard, *Raconte . . . Popov* (Paris: Editions Mengès, 1977) p. 79.

94. Anonymous Russian source, 1981. For a similar joke see also G.

Benton and G. Loomes, *The Big Red Joke Book* (London: Pluto, 1976) p. 98.

95.   Larson, p. 90.

96.   Benton and Loomes, p. 98.

97.   See Miklós Haraszti, *A Worker in a Worker's State* (Harmondsworth: Penguin, 1977).

98.   Ota Šik, 'Socialist Market Relations and Planning' in C. K. Feinstein (ed.) *Socialism, Capitalism and Economic Growth. Essays Presented to Maurice Dobb* (Cambridge: Cambridge University Press, 1967) p. 139. At that time Šik was Professor of the Czech Academy of Sciences in Prague. Section 3 of his article 'Labour under Socialism' is especially instructive.

99.   See for instance, Beckmann (1969) p. 102; Isnard, p. 95.

2 The Origins of the Political Joke

Gregor Benton

Political jokes run in the veins of modern dictatorships of all political sorts, but they are at their best and most plentiful in the Soviet Union, and it is with the Soviet joke and its close relatives that these pages will chiefly engage.

Political jokes are told by hundreds of thousands to an audience of hundreds of millions, but they are little known outside the dictatorships that produce them. They are a product of acute tension and inhibition – conditions under which good humour commonly thrives – and despite their specific grievances, they have a universal quality, carrying well even where their point does not directly apply. In the West, joke-telling is fast becoming the business of paid entertainers who serve an audience of television-viewers. Political jokes are not so handicapped: for obvious reasons they mainly circulate only outside official channels. Tellers and hearers develop a great appetite for them and are critical judges of the art, killing off any that do not meet the highest standards.

Political jokes are the citizens' response to the state's efforts to standardise their thinking and to frighten them into witholding criticism and dissent. Freud said that jokes are especially suited for ridiculing people in high places who we would otherwise fear to attack because of inner or outer inhibitions. The political joke perfectly illustrates this point. The politically powerless use it as a tribunal through which to pass judgements on society where other ways of doing so are closed to them.

Political jokes give a unique view into the problems of everyday living under dictatorships. They are peopled by all social types, from Party bosses and prima donnas to small-town bureaucrats and drunks. Most questions are reflected in them, from the price of tables to the rate of spending on space travel. They are a powerful transmitter of the popular mood in societies where this mood can find no officially sanctioned outlet. A good joke that hits the right wavelength with a topical issue will bounce from Brest to Vladivos-

33

tock and back at a speed that the Minister of Information would envy.

In itself, political humour is nothing new. Ever since there were states, philosophers and court clowns have poked fun at those holding the reins of power in society. The ancient Greeks and Romans saw mockery as a legitimate weapon in the political armoury, and sages of ancient China had a quick eye for folly and hypocrisy in high places, and a savage tongue. But humour of this sort was mainly for the elite. The people who supported the base of pre-modern societies had no real tradition of political humour as we now know it, for they knew little of high politics. No doubt local despots were the butt of some class-inspired laughter in the villages, but villagers lacked political distance from them, and without distance humour is not easy.

Not all people in lowly positions were as remote from the centres of power and decision. Flunkies, prostitutes, petty retainers, *yamen* runners, and the like, had a wider view of the political process, and if the seeds of an early popular political humour ever sprouted, it was surely among them. But whatever the case, there is little that can be said about it, since such oral culture went largely unrecorded across the centuries.

Modern societies in which the people have democratic freedoms also know political jokes – you could even say that the right to tell them is one of those freedoms. But most political jokes in bourgeois democracies are a bloodless strain, told by professionals. The reason is obvious: a society with the vote has no urgent need of political jokes, for it has more effective ways of easing political tensions.

It is only under modern dictatorships that political jokes come truly into their own and are part of the everyday life of all classes. Factory workers swap them; and so do bishops, brain surgeons, tractor drivers . . . and, of course, the dictators themselves. Such jokes are no longer about the foibles and idiosyncracies of this or that top politician, as are most political jokes in democracies: they take in the whole range of issues in politics and society as their subject matter.

To be sure, political jokes are not the only vehicle for non-official opinion in societies that forbid opposition, but they are probably the least dangerous. Joke-tellers, unlike the intellectuals who write *samizdats* or the activists who take their protests on to the street, need be neither book-trained nor especially brave: all they need is a sense of fun and timing, and humour can even defuse the wrath of some officials. Even so, it is wise to tell your most outrageous jokes in

parks and open fields, out of earshot of policemen and informers. In Hitler's Germany the very word for political joke was *Flüsterwitz* or 'whisper joke'. One anti-Hitler joke (based as usual on a Jewish original) tells it all:

> Five citizens of the Reich sit in a railway room. One sighs, another clasps his head in his hands, a third groans, and a fourth sits with tears streaming down his face. Says the fifth: 'Be careful, gentlemen. It's not wise to discuss politics in public.'

Folklore studies show that core themes of the various genres of folklore are common to widely different cultures on different parts of the globe, probably mainly as a result of cultural diffusion. What is true of traditional folklore is a hundred times truer of the political joke, which is the chief form of orally-transmitted folk wisdom today. There are countless cases where the same political joke is told in widely different countries and even on different continents. Often not only the substance but even the outer form is translated from one setting to another, even across oceans. Once a few inessential elements – name, place, style of address – are changed, such jokes cross instantly from one system to another. In 1973, refugees from the Pinochet coup in Chile arrived in exile telling the same jokes as opponents of the Third Reich in the thirties and the war years. In this example Jewish refugees who had left Nazi Germany to settle in Latin America were no doubt the chief carriers. This trade in humour is no respecter of political labels. It can flourish even between systems ideologically at war with one another, like Hitler's Germany and Stalin's Russia, stubbornly homing in on their common ground: camps, sealed borders, a chained press, queues and a corrupt bureaucracy.

Dictatorship is a necessary condition for a flourishing political humour, but not all dictatorships produce one. For example, military dictatorships rarely yield rich crops of humour. Most military regimes depend on brute force to achieve their political ends, and have no concern to 'reshape society's spirit' or 'create a new man'. However barbarous in other ways, they are seldom able to subject people to the spiritual meddling that characterises more subtle repressive systems. But experience suggests that it is not brute force but the special pain and outrage of spiritual violation that produces widespread political joke-telling.

Whereas most military juntas master only the flesh, dictatorships of

the latter sort demand the soul as well as the body. They are not content that the people should merely give in to them – they insist also on capitulation willingly, or at least with a convincing show of sincerity. To achieve such a conversion, ordinary political means are not enough. Such regimes therefore evolve a complex web of controls designed to stretch out into every area of human life. In practice such controls are hard to sustain, and the Soviet rulers have been forced to loosen their grip a little and allow small areas of individual freedom. But everyone is to some degree subject to the official machine, which controls the media, the schools and most public entertainment. In the cities, the pressure from this system remains great, and living under it creates tensions that would put society's collective sanity under intolerable strain if they could not quickly find some relief. Soviet society knows many such reliefs, ranging from vodka to vandalism. But among the commonest and the least troublesome in its consequences is the political joke.

The political joke can therefore be explained as a response to the nagging strain of everyday living under these dictatorships. People's public faces no longer match their private feelings. The gap between self and society, the widespread tension and ambiguity, the confrontation between two codes of meaning and behaviour, those of private and public life – these are the ingredients for an excellent humour.

But political jokers, if they are wise, will choose time and place with care before practising their art. Repression has its high tides and its low, and not to know which is which is to ask for trouble. Many people believe that political jokes thrive best on wars, revolutions and crises, but this is a romantic misunderstanding. In revolutions people have other things to do than tell jokes, and wars and crises are likely to lead to a general tightening of controls, so that laughter becomes dangerous. Political jokes are not a form of confrontation. People will only tell them when they are confident that their listeners will respond in fun. But in a society of permanent alert this confidence is confined to the smallest circles and political jokes can no longer circulate freely. In such periods one of the few places where political jokes can still be freely told is in the Party leadership. Stalin was a great fan of Karl Radek's Jewish jokes before he shot him in 1937, and he even let the writer Nicolai Virta tell jokes in the Politburo.

No states specifically outlaw political jokes. After all, to do so would make them look even more ridiculous. But states can and do use other laws – laws against economic sabotage, undermining

national morale, and so on – to silence joke-tellers. In Hitler's Germany the Catholic priest Josef Müller, hanged for telling a political joke to an electrician working in his house, was one of many such victims of the Nazi state; and in the Soviet Union so many jokers were sent to Stalin's camps that according to persistent rumour the White Sea Canal was built by them. But in the long run jokes cannot be stamped out by locking up or killing the tellers. On the contrary, to do so merely creates the occasion for an endless series of new jokes along the lines:

> Is it true that Comrade Stalin collects political jokes?
> Yes, but first he collects the people who tell them.

What of the concentration camps, that satanic apogee of Nazi intolerance? Gamm found in his study of the *Flüsterwitz* that jokes were not told in concentration camps, though jokes were sometimes told about them. One would have thought that he must be right. Political jokes thrive in the last inch of life, but in Hitler's camps the terror was so total that there was surely no longer any place for them. And yet they were told. Alexander Drozdzynski, for example, told jokes in Auschwitz, Buchenwald and Bergen-Belsen to keep up his own and his comrades' spirits. After the war Drozdzynski became famous throughout Warsaw as a teller of Jewish and political jokes. He even has tapes of satirical songs sung by prisoners in the Soviet camps. Life in Stalin's camps was harsh, but less so than in Hitler's. Only in the camps did people really feel free, says Drozdzynski. To judge by his and other accounts of Soviet camp life, telling political jokes is the Soviet political prisoners' main form of unofficial entertainment.

Salcia Landmann predicted in her book, *Der Jüdische Witz*, that the Jewish joke would become extinct in the Soviet Union through Stalin's terror. Others believed that in China, too, traditional forms of humour, especially political humour, had been killed off during Mao's last years, when the Gang of Four 'ran rampant' and when even the most innocent entertainments were burdened with a Party message. Happily both predictions were disproved. Khrushchev and Deng Xiaoping, who succeeded Stalin and Mao, were earthy men who peppered their talk with jokes and anecdotes and put right at least some of the worst abuses of their predecessors. Under Khrushchev the political joke prospered as never before and was enriched by new forms from Eastern Europe. Under Deng old

masters of the comic art returned to delight audiences with quick-fire jokes that tore into society's faults. Political humour had confounded the pessimists and shown that it remained indestructible as long as it was necessary.

Soviet scholars have shone at ethnographic and folklore research, but the same scholars who lovingly record the folkways of remote minority peoples must for obvious reasons turn a deaf ear to the hardiest strain of Soviet folklore: the political joke. They are not alone in this. Western social scientists too have largely ignored the role of political jokes. Studies or anthologies of political humour in the Soviet Union in the 1920s and under Stalin, or in Germany under the Nazis, are extremely rare (though in recent years Eastern European emigrés scattered round the world have published some anthologies of contemporary political humour). It is interesting to consider the reasons for this neglect in the West.

One criticism sometimes made of political jokes is that they trivialise the horrors of dictatorial regimes. During the Second World War, propagandists of the allied governments collected and published large numbers of anti-Hitler jokes to strengthen public morale at home, but people who brought out similar collections after the war were sometimes criticised. Others are unfriendly to the very idea of cataloguing and analysing jokes on the grounds that to write them down is to kill them. And to both these arguments there is some truth. Still others see popular humour as aesthetically and intellectually uninteresting, and look down especially on the joke as the lowest form of humour. It is of course true that political jokes, like any other jokes, cannot claim literary elegance or subtle psychological insight, and usually reach their climax quickly and in one go, unlike more refined forms of humour. Yet they do have some merits that we should not ignore: they are refreshingly economical, and are trite and pompous only at their peril; and they are a window on to the unlovely backside of dictatorships.

Today, when the art of political discourse in the Soviet Union has sunk below fathoming, it is hard to believe that the Soviet state was founded by men and women who could set crowds alight with their oratory. Stalin was a man of notoriously little rhetoric and his main stylistic trick was a debased version of the Socratic method. There is a joke that makes this point very well:

Stalin is standing on Lenin's mausoleum in the Red Square. 'Comrades!' he tells the crowd. 'An historic event! A telegram of

congratulations from Leon Trotsky!' The crowd hushes. Stalin reads: 'Joseph Stalin. The Kremlin. Moscow. You were right and I was wrong. You are the true heir of Lenin. I should apologise. Leon Trotsky.' The crowd roars. But in the front row a little Jewish tailor gestures to Stalin. Stalin leans over to hear what the tailor has to say. 'Such a message! But you read it without the right feeling.' Stalin raises his hands to still the crowd. 'Comrades! Here is a simple worker who says that I read Trotsky's message without the right feeling. I ask that worker to read it to us himself.' The Jew reads: 'Joseph Stalin. The Kremlin. Moscow.' Then he clears his throat and sings out: 'You were *right* and I was *wrong*? *You* are the true heir of Lenin? *I* should apologise?'

Most of Stalin's successors lack even his virtue of bluntness, and their political style is routinely deformed by clichés, euphemisms and deliberate imprecision. George Orwell, in a memorable essay, argued that ugliness, vagueness and question-begging are a necessary feature of modern political language, since if politicians revealed their true aims in a simple, straightforward way they would stand no chance of getting them accepted. 'In our time,' he wrote, 'political speech and writing are largely the defence of the indefensible . . . . Where there is a gap between one's real and one's declared aims, one turns as it were instinctively to long words and exhausted idioms, like a cuttlefish squirting out ink.'

Orwell was writing about England, but his comments apply even better to the political style of Soviet Stalinism. Under Stalinist systems there is little that is not directly or indirectly under political control, so that many more forms of Soviet speech and writing are tainted by politics than in Orwell's England. However, jokes, which are the main outlet for unofficial comment in the Soviet Union and the main rival of official language for the political ear of the Soviet people, match each vice of the official style with a virtue. In a society where official political language is poisoned at the source, the political joke is a universally recognised antidote and cure.

Jokes are short and pithy – brevity is their essence; official language is long-winded and involved. Jokes are scraped bare of inessential detail (unless inessential detail is their very point); official language is befogged by great blustering and vapouring. Jokes are vivid and sparkling; official language is tired and lustreless. Jokes are incorruptible, and true even when false; official language lies as a matter of necessity and routine.

Incongruity and zany logic – what Arthur Koestler pompously but accurately called the 'sudden bisociation of an idea or event with two habitually incompatible matrices' – lie at the very heart of the joke. The joke raises and dashes expectations which shatter into laughter. In the Soviet context this characteristic has a special meaning. In a system where the laws of the dialectic ensure that 'nothing is an accident', the joke rejoices in the basic contingency of life. It draws its whole force from 'defeating habit' and thus cocks a snook at the repressive determinism of state thought.

It is in the nature of jokes that they are not complete until grasped and digested by the listener, who must be listening by choice. The listener's role is indispensable in the creation of the laughter; the teller's main satisfaction is the pleasure had by the audience when it 'gets' the joke. Cooperation between teller and listener goes on throughout, as Koestler has observed. This is necessary because of the joke's characteristic implicitness. The audience cannot but take an active role if the joke is to succeed; it must 'fill the gaps, complete the hints, trace the hidden analogies'. Listener and teller must be in fun, and relaxed in one another's company. Without this the conditions for the release of tension will be lacking. The audience's cooperation is voluntary, but its response to the punch-line is involuntary and spontaneous; it is delighted and its feelings explode in laughter. With official speech everything is the other way around. The audience is not free; it is not expected to play any role in the events it sits through; it is tense or numbed; it responds routinely, without pleasure and delight; and its applause is measured and contrived.

George Orwell wrote in his essay 'Funny, but not Vulgar' that 'every joke is a tiny revolution', and that 'you cannot be memorably funny without at some point raising topics which the rich, the powerful and the complacent would prefer to see left alone'. It is clear that Orwell, who applauded obscenity as 'a kind of subversiveness', underestimated the strong element of racist and sexist aggression in humour, which frequently pokes fun not at the rich, the powerful and the complacent, but at the poor and the powerless and at women. Even some political jokes get their laughs by exploiting racist and sexist prejudices.

There was a flood of jokes in China shortly after the fall from power of Jian Qing, Mao's widow, that combined criticism of the Party with out-and-out misogyny. But on the whole political jokes fulfil Orwell's criterion better than most other kinds of joke, and

illustrate his theory rather well. They depend for their impact on puncturing the state's swollen pretensions and exposing the greed, stupidity, cruelty and hypocrisy of its leaders. So they contribute to the weakening of the state's authority and in that sense they play a subversive role.

But political jokes are revolutions only metaphorically. They are moral victories, not material ones. To be sure, officials whose pride is wounded will smart for a while and may lash out at those responsible for the hurt. But the more cynical and far-sighted among them know that political jokes and the other small freedoms that irritate some zealots are a useful means of dissipating tensions and of keeping people happy, and that it would be foolish to deal with them too harshly.

There can be no doubt that for getting society stable the 'liberal' tactic is the more effective one. The political joke is not a form of resistance. Revolutionaries and freedom-fighters are engaged in a serious and even deadly business, and are reluctant to make light of the enemy or to fritter away hatred through laughter. To permit jokes against the state is therefore a clever insurance against more serious challenges to the system.

The character of political humour can differ greatly even between countries with similar political systems, although these differences are nowadays being eroded by cross-cultural diffusion. Some nations, like Bulgaria and Albania, are not known to have much sense of political humour at all, and belong to what Drozdzynski has called the 'joke-free zone'. That cultural traditions influence political humour is clear from a comparison of the Soviet Union and China. The Chinese are not by nature a humourless people. On the contrary, they have a rich comic tradition, and since Mao's death are telling more and more political jokes (some based on Soviet originals). But compared to most Soviet-bloc countries China's political humour is still in its infancy. This can be partly explained by political factors. During its first ten years the People's Republic was shaken by frequent crises, but it managed to avoid sowing the extremes of cynicism and disillusion on which the Soviet joke feeds. It more effectively 'touched people's souls' than the Soviet system, so that there was less place in it for the hidden resentment that wells up in the political joke. Then, by the 1960s, China had entered a prolonged phase of 'mass mobilisation' when joke-telling could get you into big trouble. This goes some way toward explaining why political jokes are not yet widespread in China. But more important is the lack of a

strong Chinese tradition of popular humour with social and political themes. Russia and Eastern Europe have such a tradition in the Jewish joke. Even East Asian folk humour is not entirely without social criticism, especially criticism of official greed and corruption. But its chief preoccupations are those of peasant humour everywhere: sex, ghosts, farting and delight in the misfortunes of others. In China the sort of humour most likely to have a political theme cannot properly be called folk humour, since it is mostly literary, intellectual, or professional. Its forms include the *xiangsheng*, a comic stage dialogue or cross-talk between a wise man and a fool, which for a while degenerated into a form of Party didacticism following the Cultural Revolution, but which is now restored to vigour; the intricate pun; and the humorous literary allegory.

It is widely argued, particularly by joke-tellers, that there is no such thing as a new joke and that all jokes are simply rehashes of earlier ones. This is obviously wrong. Jokes may circulate anonymously, but someone must have thought them up in the first place, however many centuries ago. On rare occasions new formulas are added to the common stock by people who see connections where others never did. But such creative acts are few, and it is true that most 'new' jokes are quarried from the rich sediment left by centuries of telling.

Many influences went into producing the Soviet political joke, from Armenian riddles and Georgian drinking speeches to traditional peasant tales and proverbs. But to trace even a small part of them would require a superhuman effort of research, for political jokes change their ground more often than any other form of joke, and like all jokes are told in an infinite number of variants. But one influence that is so fundamental to Soviet political humour that it is immediately identifiable is the Jewish joke.

The Jewish joke as we now know it first developed in various national forms in nineteenth-century Europe during the movement for Jewish emancipation. It was renowned for its sarcasm and merciless irony, and also for its unique strain of self-irony. Paul Landau, writing in the early thirties, spoke of its 'passionate hatred for all falseness and hollowness, its irresistible urge to unmask all cheating and hypocrisy'. The Jewish joke has been analysed as a product of the acute self-consciousness and self-doubt of Jews who strove unsuccessfully to remake their personalities in ways acceptable to the broader community, and who ended up making enemies in both the community they were trying to leave and the one they were

trying to enter. But, for Jews, even questions of cultural identity were directly political in those days. Jews in Eastern Europe and Tsarist Russia were harried whichever way they turned by racial bigots in the majority community and in the state bureaucracy. They stood outside *goyish* society, but were unable to avoid contact with it. It is not surprising that they developed a strong tradition of social and political criticism. This tradition found its expression partly in humour, and it is to the Jews that the world owes the first modern political joke.

Jewish folklore and religion had influenced the traditional cultures of Slavic and Baltic peasants ever since Jewish settlement in Eastern Europe, and whole sentences out of the Talmud were incorporated as proverbs into the local languages. In Central Europe, Jewish jokes circulated widely in the radical movement in the period leading up to the Revolution of 1848 and, in the late nineteenth century, Jewish joke collections were popular with the non-Jewish public in Vienna and Berlin. The Jewish joke set the tone for the many humorous publications that started up in Germany and Austria around that time, and also found echoes on the stage, in cabaret and in literature. So there are strong historical precedents for the role that Jewish humour was to play in the twentieth century in the development of the Soviet political joke.

Jews, attracted by the uncompromising internationalism of the Bolsheviks, flocked to the Bolshevik Party and the October Revolution. Jews were also inevitably the Party's best political jokers. With a century of practice behind them, they were the driving force of the Soviet political joke in its Golden Age in the 1920s, before Stalin forced it underground. In this period the Jewish communist leader Karl Radek was notorious for his joke-telling and featured as a sort of 'Confucius he say' figure in popular humour of the day. Radek and others adapted many of the forms of the Jewish joke to articulate the feelings of bitterness and frustration that began to well up in Russia as socialist revolution gradually yielded to Stalinist dictatorship and nationalism. These jokes entered the repertoire of folk humour in the Soviet Union and, after 1945, in Eastern Europe. 'The typical Jewish joke', said Alexander Drozdzynski, 'acquired new features in the Soviet Union. It helped to overcome the hard times. It consoled not only Jews; it gave many people the courage to survive .... It seems paradoxical, but the Jewish joke survived the Jews in Eastern Europe, just as anti-Semitism did.'

Discrimination and persecution, and how to cope with them, are the subject of innumerable traditional Jewish jokes. When the Cossacks swept through the ghettos killing, raping and looting, Jews made the nightmare tolerable by joking about it, and especially joked about the Jewish victims who passively or with polite irony submitted to *force majeure*. One strategy that many a Jew followed in the hope of an escape from the horrors of the ghetto was to be baptised as a Christian. The *geshmat* whose Christianity was only skin-deep became a stock character in Jewish (and not only Jewish) humour. When you baptise a Jew, people said, hold him under water for at leave five minutes to make sure he does not revert. Other popular joke figures included Jews masquerading as Gentiles who inadvertently let their irrepressible Jewishness slip out, and (in a variant of the same joke) Jews who cleverly rescued themselves at the expense of some *goy* from a similar *faux pas*. Many jokes got their laughs by turning the tables on racial bigots and bullying officials, either by showing them up as fools or by tricking them into admitting their discrimination. Needless to say, in a society in which bigotry is widespread some people will sense it even where it is not and the Jewish joke, which excels at self-irony, also takes them as a favourite target.

All these forms of joke have close or direct parallels in the political joke. Three main sorts of discrimination feature in the political joke: discrimination by a minority, the Party, against the non-Party majority; discrimination by majorities against minorities (e.g. Russians against Uzbeks or Czechs against Slovaks); and discrimination by a strong nation (the Soviet Union) against weaker ones (Eastern Europe and China). In the last two categories, both victims and victimisers put their feelings into joke form. This results in two different sorts of joke corresponding to *jüdische Witze* (jokes told by Jews) and *Judenwitze* (jokes told about Jews).

Discrimination against the non-Party majority in the Soviet-bloc countries has produced many jokes based on Jewish originals. But this Soviet form of discrimination differs from anti-Semitism in that it is practised by a minority against a majority rather than the other way round. The Jewish discrimination joke is therefore vastly more poignant than the Soviet one, for it is the cry of protest of a bullied minority with few defences and many enemies.

The following discrimination jokes, one Jewish and the other Russian, show both the continuity between the two traditions and the change:

A butcher tells a waiting crowd: 'Jews can go home. They'll get no meat anyway.' Exit the Jews, grumbling. Hours later the butcher returns: 'I've just heard there'll be no meat at all today. You can all go home.' The crowd disperses. One to the other: 'Those Jews, they're always lucky.'

A long queue in front of a Moscow meat-store. The crowd has been waiting patiently for hours. The shop is closed. Suddenly the manager appears: 'OK, citizens, you can all go home. Only Party members need wait.' The crowd curses, but finally goes away. The manager: 'Comrades, now we're alone I can tell the truth. There *is* no meat.'

Baptism jokes also have their counterpart in Soviet humour. In the Soviet Union it is the Party that has a monopoly of power, so many join it to improve their prospects in life. But like the *geshmat*, their real nature stubbornly breaks through:

A peasant applies to join the Party. First the Party secretary asks him a few questions. 'Comrade, if the Party were to ask you for a donation of a hundred roubles, would you give it?' 'Yes.' 'And if the Party asked you to enlist your only son in the Red Army?' 'I'd enlist him.' 'What if the Party were to ask you to donate your cow to the state? Would you do so?' 'No.' 'Do you mean to tell me that you would give a hundred roubles or an only son, but not a cow?' 'But comrade, I *have* a cow.'

Jokes about dumb cops and hectoring bureaucrats are among the commonest forms of political joke, just as they were of the Jewish joke. These jokes are told in countless variants and turn up in different national dress all over the Soviet Union and Eastern Europe. Typical themes include the battle of wits with the obstructive official, adventures at the border while trying to go abroad, worsting a policeman, the self-seeking politician, elections with 99.8 per cent majorities, GPU men who torture bizarre confessions out of innocent people, bullying schools inspectors who make fools of themselves in classrooms, and the legendary stupidity of the Bulgarian policemen – these are just a few of the standard favourites that can be found in any collection. Most of them have parallels in the Jewish discrimination joke.

In the early days of Hitler's Reich, when Jewish children still

attended the same schools as other children (but sat at separate desks), Jews in Germany told this classroom joke, with its many layers of subtle humour:

> A teacher asks his pupils: 'Who wrote *Mein Kampf*? Put up your hand if you know.' No hands go up, apart from that of little Moritz Kohn in the Jewish row at the back. 'Well then, Moritz, who wrote it?' 'It wasn't me, Sir!' Teacher is furious, and calls old Kohn up to the school. Kohn considers the facts, and says stoutly: 'Herr teacher, believe me, my Moritz is a cheeky boy, but he never lies. If he says he didn't write it, then he didn't write it'. And then, indulgently: 'And even if he did, Herr teacher . . . I ask you, such a child. . .'

The Soviet Union knows several variants of the same joke. This one has a particularly savage twist to the irony:

> A school inspector visits a classroom. He sees a globe on the table and points to one of the children: 'You there, tell me why that globe is sloping to one side.' The boy cannot answer. Nor can any other child in the class. That evening the inspector meets the local Party secretary, and says: 'Not even your son could tell me why the globe was sloping to one side.' The Party secretary: 'But comrade, I know my son, I'm sure it wasn't him, he'd never do such a thing.' The next morning the local GPU chief rings the inspector. 'Don't worry about that globe any more, we've interrogated the teacher and cleared the matter up.' 'But comrade major, there was nothing to be cleared up, the globe has to be at a tilt.' 'Too late, he's confessed already.'

Finally, delusions of persecution and discrimination are themes common to the Jewish and the political joke. In the political joke it is the Party which, for a change, is wrongly accused:

> An old Czech peasant has used up all his savings and is in urgent need of money. He writes a letter to God: 'Dear God, I have prayed to you all my life. Winter is coming and I need a thousand crowns. Please help me.' The censor reads the letter and passes it on to the Party committee. The Party secretary decides to help the peasant. He thinks it will improve the Party's image. The peasant gets the money through the post in a special Party envelope. Inside

are five hundred crowns. He writes again: 'Dear God, thank: the money. Next time don't send it through the Party. Th bastards kept half.'

This joke, which has Jewish origins, is also told in Ireland, where the Orange Lodge takes the role of the Party.

The second type of discrimination joke is that dealing with discrimination by majorities against minorities. This type of discrimination is not peculiar to the Soviet Union, and many Soviet minority peoples, especially the small and remote ones, are relatively well treated and even get benefits not available to the Russians. Even so 'racial' arrogance is deeply ingrained on the Russian mentality and has been played on by Party demagogues ever since Stalin revived strains of Great Russian chauvinism and anti-Semitism in the mid-1930s.

What's the difference between Moses and Stalin?
Moses led the Jews out of Egypt. Stalin led them out of the Central Committee.

Stalin and his successors never explicitly abandoned Bolshevik policies outlawing racial discrimination, but they have repeatedly trampled on the rights of Tatars, Georgians, Armenians, Uzbeks, Jews and other ethnic and national groups. This discrimination is reflected in countless jokes, many of which can be traced back directly to Jewish sources. Here is one rather complex example of such a borrowing:

During the Great Patriotic War the Germans set up a loudspeaker on the Eastern front and call on the Red soldiers to surrender: *'Russ sdaysia, Russ sdaysia!'* (Russian, surrender). A voice with a heavily Central Asian accent floats back from the Soviet side: 'You no use for us Uzbeks?'

This joke has its origins in the Russian Jewish pacifist joke of the late nineteenth century. The pacifist tradition was strongly rooted in the Jewish ghetto. Jews press-ganged into the Tsar's army were doubly offended: they were forced not only to fight, but to fight for a regime that oppressed them. And so the Jewish pacifist joke was born, with its delicious melancholy irony.

A regiment of Talmudic scholars conscripted by the Tsar. They prove to be excellent marksmen, with a sure eye and a steady hand. They get the target every time. They are sent immediately to the front. As the enemy advances towards their line, the scholars are ordered to fire. Nothing happens. The order is repeated. Again, nothing. The regiment's commander grabs the scholar nearest him, and screams: 'Why the hell don't you shoot!' The scholar turns round in shocked amazement: 'But those are men out there!'

Still, many ordinary Russians have no time for pacifism, which they see as a form of cowardice. And so the Russian joke about the Uzbek (above) is not a pacifist joke in this tradition, though it borrows its plot and punchline from Jewish sources. Instead it is an assertion of Russian superiority over the despicable Asiatic, and is matched by similar jokes about Mongols, Tatars, Buryats and other non-European peoples of the Soviet Union. The 'no use' punchline also occurs in Jewish jokes:

A Jew and a Cossack are up in court. The Jew has accused the Cossack of stealing his horse. The Cossack: 'I didn't steal it, I found it'. The Jew: 'Liar! I was on the horse at the time! You forced me off with your whip!' The judge: 'Cossack, was the Jew on his horse?' The Cossack, after a moment's hesitation: 'Well, I found both of them, but I had no use for the Jew.'

To be sure the laugh is on the Jew, but he keeps his dignity and our sympathy; and even the brutal Cossack is made to look at least semi-human. Here the 'no use for' punchline is an expression of self-irony; in the Uzbek joke it is aggressive mockery.

The third form of discrimination joke is that which deals with strong nations' persecution of weak ones. This is by far the biggest category of Eastern European jokes, and before the Sino–Soviet split it was a main joke-theme in China too. These jokes have much in common with Jewish anti-Russian or anti-German jokes, on which many are directly based. (During the Hungarian uprising of 1956 a riddle went the rounds: 'What's the difference between Nazis and Russians? For Russians, everyone's a Jew.')

Yet most Eastern European jokes on this theme are crude by comparison with the Jewish ones. In the best Jewish jokes anti-Semitism reels under bruising blows, but between the rounds, noises of sadness and regret creep in. Hatred for the anti-Semite is tempered

by piercing psychological observation, so extreme dehumanisatic
avoided. For the ghetto Jew, as Leo Rosten observed, 'insi
became a substitute for weapons: one way to block the bully's wrath
is to know him better than he knows himself'.

Most Eastern European and Chinese versions of this humour lack
these nuances and restraints. They show the Russian without human
features: an army, a train vanishing eastwards laden with grain or
steel, a hot-line telephone (with an earphone but no mouthpiece), or
a Comecon plan. The reason for this difference is not hard to find.
Czechs, Poles, and Hungarians, unlike nineteenth-century ghetto
Jews, do not live cheek by jowl with their oppressors. They have no
need or wish to 'know him better than he knows himself'. In general
they want only one thing: That he get the hell out and go back to his
own country. That said, there are still some extremely funny anti-
Soviet jokes. Here are two examples that might (and in one case did)
come straight from the ghetto:

A Pole walking home one evening is robbed and beaten by a
drunken Russian soldier. As the Russian lurches off down the
street, the Pole runs after him shouting: 'At least leave me ten
zloty! I still haven't paid my subscription to the Polish–Russian
Friendship Society!'

An advert in a Bucharest newspaper: 'Swap high level of
ideological training for geographically favourable location.' (The
original Jewish joke was: 'Swap several centuries of history for a
little geography.' More recently the East Germans have taken it
over: 'Swap comfortable four-room flat for small hole in the wall.')

Critics of Marxism wanting to dismiss it as a revived strain of
millenarianism have argued that its theories are founded in the
doctrines and beliefs of Judaism. On the whole such comparisons are
shallow and unconvincing. But it is undeniable that there are
analogies between the two traditions: both are socially committed,
i.e. centrally concerned with this-worldly destinies of human beings;
and both are ultimately optimistic, in that both look forward to a
paradise on earth, a new age of social harmony and peace in which
peoples will be reconciled and states will disappear. Jewish prophets
in the diaspora influenced by the solidarity and egalitarianism of the
ghettos preached radical doctrines of freedom, equality and justice.
Jews nurtured on this radical messianism found outlets for their

passions in the revolutionary movements of the nineteenth and early twentieth centuries. When the Soviet state was founded in 1917, many Jews saw it for a time as a haven of social progress and racial harmony, a beacon of internationalism, and a Blakean-style embodiment of the idea of a Holy Land of Promise.

But for the European Jew there was an important other side to the Promised Land idea. With emancipation came scepticism. Many dropped the belief that one day Jews would be reunited and that an age of justice would dawn. Some who had done well in business or the professions had built their own small Canaans in their countries of adoption and had milk and honey enough. Hence the Promised Land joke:

> 'Dear God!' says a Jew who is forced to flee his homeland and go to Jerusalem, 'two thousand years we pray in vain to return, and now it has to happen to me!'

Poorer Jews also grew cynical about the old vision when they saw the ghetto community gradually come apart and give way to a rapacious modern class system. Some still looked forward to the security of a national home, but many became disillusioned in the idea. This disillusion naturally found an outlet in humour. And it also spiritually prepared Jews for the failure of Promised Lands everywhere. Had they not always expected the worst? Best to keep Lands of Promise at the promise stage. Political jokers excavating the rich layers of Jewish humour inevitably spotted and used this analogy. Promised Land jokes carried over effortlessly into the Soviet age.

> 'Is it possible to build socialism in one country, like Stalin says?'
> 'It is, but then it's best to live in another country.'

> 'Have we already reached 100 per cent communism, or will it get worse?'

After Palestine and the Soviet Union, America was the third great Promised Land of the Jews. In the 1880s, pogroms and growing legal restrictions and military obligations led more and more Russian and Eastern European Jews to look to America as a refuge from their trials and sorrows; but would-be emigrants met obstacles at every turn. During those years the figure of the Jew who stubbornly dreams of joining friends and relatives in the *goldeneh medina* entered the

joke world. This brand of joke is also widely met throughout present-day Eastern Europe and the Soviet Union, where many still dream of a passage to America. A variant of it has even been reported from Guangdong in South China, where it takes on the local colour of one of the criticism and self-criticism sessions so common during the Cultural Revolution, and where Hong Kong takes the place of America as the land with golden pavements:

Xiao Wang is carrying out criticism and self-criticism at a production brigade meeting. 'Two years ago,' he intones, 'my father, my mother, my two brothers, my sister, my nephews, and my paternal grandmother deserted the motherland and went to live in Hong Kong. They are traitors to Chairman Mao and the Party. That was the criticism. Now for the self-criticism: I was stupid enough to stay here.'

Talmudic reasoning is another theme of traditional Jewish humour that has strong echoes in the political joke. Debating and interpreting the Talmud, that vast encyclopaedia of Rabbinical wisdom, was the main scholarly activity of Jewish communities before the late nineteenth century, and the Talmudic spirit saturated the whole of Jewish intellectual life. Talmudic reasoning is renowned for its ability to shift ground effortlessly and to reconcile conflicting views and judgements by establishing plausible links between them. These same qualities are at the heart of humour and it is not surprising that the Jewish joke is drenched in Talmudic style. Modern emancipated intellectual Jews scorned the Talmudic method as sheer casuistry and parodied it mercilessly in jokes, but many of these jokes were in themselves brilliant exercises in dialectic virtuosity, and were no doubt enjoyed as much for their own sake as for their satire. Emancipated Jews also joked venomously about the strait-laced rabbis and the temple board, whose authority they found irksome and oppressive.

The Soviet state is no theocracy. It has no priest caste and no sacred books. But Party officials in many of their roles strikingly resemble the ghetto rabbis. They wield tremendous power over society and legitimise this power by appealing to a fossilised ideology pieced together from the writings of Marx, Engels and Lenin. The central proposition of this ideology is the law of the dialectic. Everything is in ceaseless change and the direction of this change is only knowable to those in possession of 'correct consciousness'

gained through the study of dialectical materialism. The 150 or so volumes of the revolutionary 'classics' – like the 63 books of the Talmud and the 100-odd books of Midrashim – are a limitless source of quotations which, with some dialectical bending and trimming, can be used to justify any change of course. A special class of theorists is employed to do this work of exegesis, but Party-rabbis all down the line must have at least enough grounding in it to know how to phrase their reports and speeches in a suitable 'dialectical' way.

The Soviet dialectic joke parodies this arbitrary style of reasoning and borrows heavily from the Talmud joke to do so. The following joke is a good example of this genre. (To compare it with the original on which it is based, or with other similar jokes, consult the entries under *talmid chachem* and Talmud in Leo Rosten's *The Joys of Yiddish*.)

A Soviet adviser is lecturing to a class of Chinese Red Army men on dialectics.

'Two guerrillas enter a village. One is clean, the other is dirty. Which one has a bath?'

'The dirty one', answers a Chinese.

'No, comrades. You have not yet grasped the essence of the dialectic. The dirty guerrilla looks at the clean one and thinks that he is clean himself. The clean guerrilla looks at the dirty one and thinks that he himself is also dirty. So the clean guerrilla has a bath.'

The Chinese listen in silence. 'Or', says the adviser, warming to his theme, 'they both have a bath.' The Chinese look puzzled.

'The clean guerrilla advises the dirty one to have a bath, and then, for the sake of comradeship, joins him in it. Or maybe neither has a bath.'

'?'

'The first guerrilla is already clean, so he doesn't need a bath. The second guerrilla never has baths, which is why he is so dirty. Or, perhaps you were right in the first place, and the dirty guerrilla has a bath.'

'??'

'Because he is by nature a clean person, and doesn't like to be dirty.'

'You've lost me, comrade,' says one Chinese. 'It seems to me that the dialectic can mean anything you want it to.'

The adviser's eyes light up. '*Now* you've understood the dialectic!'

Resentment against Party officials also finds its outlet in jokes which borrow typically Jewish forms. Leo Rosten tells the following story about a young rabbi and a board member of the local synagogue:

> Young Rabbi Shulman finally summoned up enough courage to say to Mr Berenson, one of the *balbatim* of the community, 'I trust you won't mind my mentioning it, but I can't help noticing that . . . you always fall asleep when I'm preaching.' 'Why not?' replied Berenson. 'Would I fall asleep if I didn't trust you?'

This joke is repeated almost word for word in the Soviet Union, except that the board member is a Party chairman, the young rabbi is an inexperienced Party secretary, and the sermon is the secretary's report.

I have pointed out some styles and themes that the modern political joke has borrowed from the old Jewish tradition. But political jokes are anything but static. They mirror life in all its change, and they too are constantly changing, evolving new forms to cope with new moods and issues. One example of a recent form is the Radio Erivan joke.

Radio Erivan jokes were at one time very popular in the Soviet Union and the craze for them spread to Eastern Europe. They parody a Soviet radio programme in which a Party hack answers listeners' questions about politics:

> Q. Is it true that our glorious armed forces were called in by the Czechs to defeat fascist reaction? A. In principle, yes. The request was made in 1939, but for technical reasons could not be met until 1968. Q. What is alcoholism? A. Alcoholism is a transitional stage between capitalism and communism.

These jokes are so widely known that when the director of the real Radio Erivan rose to speak at a conference of Soviet radio officials in 1975, it was several minutes before the laughter died down. In Radio Erivan jokes the questions are put in a mock Jewish accent (and the answers given in an Armenian one). But there is little else to connect this rapid wise-cracking with the more leisurely style of older political jokes. Radio Erivan jokes are a typical form of humour for the big city, where people throw punchlines over their shoulders as they rush through doorways.

Political jokes, as we have seen, thrive best under systems that try to stifle opposition and dissent and to mould society according to some dogmatic vision. Looking around the world, it seems likely that the immediate future of the genre is secure, that the tide of misery and the gale of laughter will rise together in the coming years and that ever greater numbers of people cut adrift by crises will carry new strains of humour between countries and continents.

But the political joke will change nothing. It is the relentless enemy of greed, injustice, cruelty and oppression – but it could never do without them. It is not a form of active resistance. It reflects no political programme. It will mobilise no one. Like the Jewish joke in its time, it is important for keeping society sane and stable. It cushions the blows of cruel governments and creates sweet illusions of revenge. It has the virtue of momentarily freeing the lives of millions from tensions and frustrations to which even the best organised political opposition can promise only long-term solutions; but its impact is as fleeting as the laughter it produces.

REFERENCES

Benton, Gregor, and Graham Loomes, *The Big Red Joke Book* (London: Pluto, 1976).

Drozdzynski, Alexander, *Jiddische Witze und Schmonzes* (Düsseldorf: Droste Verlag, 1976).

Drozdzynski, Alexander, *Der politische Witz im Ostblok* (Munich: Deutscher Taschenbuch Verlag, 1977).

Freud, Sigmund, *Der Witz und Seine Beziehung Zum Unbewussten*, (Lipzig and Vienna: Dritte Auflage, 1921). For present English translation by James Stracey, see also *Jokes and Their Relation to the Unconscious. Vol. 6 The Pelican Freud Library*, (Harmondsworth: Penguin Books, 1976).

Gamm, Hans Jochen, *Der Flüsterwitz im Dritten Reich* (Munich, 1964).

Kao, George, (ed.,) *Chinese Wit and Humour* (New York: Sterling, 1974).

Koestler, Arthur, *The Art of Creation* (London: Pan Books, 1969).

Landau, Paul, 'Gesellschaft-Kultur', in Siegmund Kaznelson (ed.) *Juden im Deutschen Kulturbereich* (Berlin: Judischer Verlag, 1959).

Landmann, Salcia, *Der jüdische Witz: Sociologie und Sammlung* (Breisgau: Olten and Freiburg, 1960).

Levy, Howard S., *Chinese Sex Jokes in Traditional Times Translated and Described* (Washington, DC: The Warm-Soft Village Press, 1973).

Meyer, Antoine and Philippe, *Le communisme est-il soluble dans l'alcool?* (Paris: Editions du Seuil, 1978).

Orwell, George, 'Funny But Not Vulgar', in Sonia Orwell and Ian Angus

(eds) *The Collected Essays, Journalism and Letters of George Orwell, Vol. 3 As I Please, 1943–1945* (New York: Harcourt Brace Jovanovitch, 1968).

Orwell, George, 'Politics and the English Language', in *Shooting an Elephant and Other Essays* (New York: Harcourt, Brace and World, 1950).

Rosten, Leo, *The Joys of Yiddish* (Harmondsworth: Penguin Books, 1971).

Steinberg, Israel and Salcia Landmann, *Jüdische Weisheit aus Drei Jahrtausenden* (Munich: Deutscher Taschenbuch Verlag, 1968).

3 Auschwitz Jokes
Alan Dundes and Thomas Hauschild

Nothing is so sacred, so taboo, or so disgusting that it cannot be the subject of humour. Quite the contrary – it is precisely those topics culturally defined as sacred, taboo or disgusting which more often than not provide the principal grist for humorous mills. In a history of world atrocities which unfortunately includes far too many instances, it would be hard to think of any one example more gruesome than the methodical murder of millions of Jews in Nazi Germany. The sordid, unspeakably cruel and vicious details of the extermination of Jews in such concentration camps as Dachau, Buchenwald and Auschwitz has been amply documented many times over, e.g., by Terrence Des Pres in *The Survivor: An Anatomy of Life in the Death Camps* (New York, 1977). In reading the moving accounts written by survivors, it is hard to imagine that any humour could possibly arise from the mass gassing of thousands of individuals.

It is known that there is such a phenomenon as what has been termed 'gallows humour'.[1] But gallows humour generally refers to jokes made about and by the *victims* of oppression. They are jokes told by those supposedly about to be hanged, not by the hangmen. In situations involving great anxiety, it is not uncommon for participants in such situations to crack jokes to relieve the tension. So in wartime, for example, some individuals facing death are able to joke about it. These jokes may be a form of bravado, a kind of necessary defence mechanism, designed to articulate genuine fears and at the same time partly allay these fears through humour.

The aggressive tendency in jokes has been obvious at least since Freud's pioneering study *Wit and Humor in the Unconscious* appeared in 1905. So jokes told about the members of one particular ethnic, national or religious group may offer a socially sanctioned outlet for the expression of aggression towards that group. When members of the group in question tell jokes about their own group, it may still be a matter of aggression. The concept of self-hate may explain why Catholics tell anti-clerical jokes and why Jews tell anti-Semitic jokes.[2]

But there are some anti-Semitic jokes which would rarely if ever be told by Jews. It is one thing for a Jew to poke fun at the alleged

56

proclivities of Jewish women (either the Jewish mother or the Jewish wife), e.g., How do you keep a Jewish girl from fucking? Marry her. What's Jewish foreplay? Twenty minutes of begging. It would be quite another for a Jew to tell jokes about Second World War concentration camps. But such jokes do exist, though they are not ordinarily told by Jews. Strange as it may seem, there are traditional jokes about the plight and fate of Jews in the Second World War, jokes which are current in the 1980s in West Germany. This type of sick humour, which many will no doubt find to be in extremely bad taste, might be said to constitute a form of 'executioner's humour' rather than 'gallows humour'. Whether one finds Auschwitz jokes funny or not is not an issue. The jokes exist and they obviously must fill some psychic need for those individuals who tell them and those who listen to them. They demonstrate that anti-Semitism is not dead in Germany – if documentation were needed to prove that point.

In fairness, it should be noted that anti-Semitism is not confined to West Germany. One can find anti-Semitism throughout Europe, North and South America and elsewhere. Several of the jokes reported from West Germany, for example, have also been collected in England, Sweden and the United States. So the implication is clearly that, to the extent that anti-Semitism is international, the jokes expressing such prejudice are equally international. But we do not believe that there are parallels for all the Auschwitz jokes found in modern West Germany.

Here is a joke collected from an informant from Mainz in 1982:[3]

Wie viele Juden passen in einen Volkswagen?
How many Jews will fit in a Volkswagen?

506, sechs auf die Sitze und 500 in die Aschenbecher...
506, six in the seats and 500 in the ashtrays...

This joke is quite similar to the following text collected in Berkeley, California, in 1980:

How many Jews can you fit in a Volkswagen?
Fourteen.'Two in the front, two in the back, ten in the ashtray.

The Jew–ashes equation turns out to be an all-too-common theme in Auschwitz jokes.

*Wussten Sie schon, dass an der Olympiade 1936 in Berlin 50 000
Juden teilgenommen haben?*
Did you know that 50 000 Jews took part in the 1936 Olympic
games at Berlin?

Nein...
No...

Ja, doch, auf der Aschenbahn! *[als Asche]*
But yes, on the cinder track [as ashes]

Although historically inaccurate, the implication is that Jewish ashes
made the red-coloured (blood?) track. The joke alludes to Hitler's
attempts to keep Jewish athletes from participating in the Olympics.
The Nazis were embarrassed when a half-Jewish fencer won a gold
medal (for Germany) and when Jesse Owen, the celebrated Black
track star won his medals for the United States.

*Zum Abschluss der Olympiade in München hält Hitler folgende
Rede: Ich danke dem deutschen Volk, das die herrlichen Bauten
errichtete, welche diese Olympiade ermöglichten. Und ich danke
dem jüdischen Volk für die Erfindung der Aschenbahn.*

At the conclusion of the Olympic Games, Hitler spoke in Munich
as follows: I thank the German people who made possible the
Olympic Games by providing these wonderful buildings and I
thank the Jewish people for the invention of the cinder track.

The joke refers to the post-war pro-Semitic argument that the
German people received so many inventions and intellectual contributions from the Jewish minority, e,g., quantum physics,
psychoanalysis, etc. Hitler's 'respect' for these inventions is rendered
metaphorically as 'Jews are only good for burning'. In a shorter
variant collected from a 14-year-old informant in Tubingen, there is a
clearer reference to burning:[4]

Wozu hat man die Juden 1936 bei der Olympiade gebraucht?
What were the Jews used for in connection with the 1936
Olympics?

Für die Aschenbahn and fürs olympische Feuer.
For the cindertrack and for the Olympic flame.

Burning as a theme in these jokes is just as common as ashes. It is, after all essentially the same theme!

Kennst du die jüdische Hitparade?
Do you know the Jewish Hit Parade?

Nein.
No.

Die geht so: Platz l 'Hey Jude'; Platz 2 'In the Ghetto'; Platz 3 'I'm on fire'.
It is 'Hey Jude' [Hey Jew], 'In the Ghetto' and 'I'm on fire'.

This joke is obviously of modern vintage inasmuch as the record titles refer to recordings made by the Beatles, Elvis Presley, etc. A variant of this joke was circulating in Sweden in the early 1970s: Which tune is Number 1 on the German hit parade? 'Hey Jude' with the Gas Chamber Choir.[5]

Was ist der Unterschied zwischen einer Tonne Koks und 1000 Juden?
What is the difference between a ton of coal and a thousand Jews?

Die Juden brennen länger.
Jews burn longer.

Warum fahren die Juden nicht mehr so gerne nach Italien in Urlaub?
Why don't Jews like to go to Italy any more for their holidays?

Weil sie dann über den Brenner müssen.
Because they have to go through the Brenner [Pass].

Brenner is the German word for burner as in gas burner.

Other elements of the Holocaust are to be found in Auschwitz jokes.

Ein Kind spielt mit einem Stück Kernseife. Da sagt die Oma: Willst du wohl die Finger von Anne Frank lassen?!
A child plays with a cake of soap [*Kernseife* is a type of soap that is raw and unscented]. Granny says, 'Stop playing with Anne Frank's finger.'

The Germans did experiment with transforming Jewish corpses into soap, a metaphorical *reductio ad absurdum* to convert 'dirty' Jews into an agent of cleanliness (as in attempting to make Germany '*Judenrein*', clean of Jews which has been linked with a German anal–erotic national character).[6] The poignant *Diary of Anne Frank* had a dramatic effect on many contemporary Germans who refused to believe right-wing assertions that the diary was a fake. The joke seems to suggest that the child should not play with Anne Frank. In other words, the dead should be allowed to rest in peace. Perhaps there is also an implication that the younger generation should not play with the products of Nazi Germany – even though the joke cycle itself does represent a form of play with such products.

> Two [Jewish] children are sitting on top of a roof near a chimney. A passerby asks, 'What are you doing up there?' 'We are waiting for our parents.'[7]

> A Jew is walking down the street carrying a gas container, with a pipe connecting it to his mouth. A passerby asks, 'What are you doing?' 'I'm addicted.'

> Why did so many Jews go to Auschwitz?
> The fare was free.

> *Was ist der Traum eines Juden?*
> What is a Jew's dream?

> *Ein Fensterplatz im Hochofen.*
> A window-seat in a high oven.[8]

A new scapegoat has been added to the German repertoire: the Turk. The influx of Turkish migrant workers in Germany and elsewhere in Europe has inspired a strong cycle of anti-Turkish jokes. One might think that the Turk could replace the Jew as the butt of jokes, but texts reveal the Jew remains. In the present context, it is important to notice how Jews and Turks are treated in the same joke.

> *Ein Türke und ein Jude springen vom Haus, wer ist schneller unten?*
> A Turk and a Jew fall from a house. Who falls down faster?

*Der Türke ist aus Scheisse, der Jude aus Asche, also ist der Türke
schneller.*
The Turk is shit, the Jew is ashes, so the Turk lands first.

In this parody of Galileo's experiment at the Tower of Pisa, the Turk
is ahead of the Jew because the Jew has already been destroyed. The
implication is that the Turk is yet to be exterminated. The Turks, like
so many immigrants to a country before them, are invariably asked
to do the most menial or *dirty* work. However, the German's
depiction of an undesirable in terms of faeces reflects a more general
scatological tendency. We find a similar anti-Turkish sentiment in
the following text:

*Ein Deutscher, ein Türke und ein Jude stehen vor der Entbindung-
station des Krankenhauses und warten darauf, ihre neugeborenen
Kinder sehen zu können. Da kommt die Krankenschwester heraus
und gesteht, dass sie die drei Kinder verwechselt hat und nicht mehr
weiss, welches Baby zu welchem Vater gehört. Der Deutsche sagt:
'Lassen Sie mich mal fünf Minuten allein mit denen.' Er geht rein
und kommt nach ein paar Minuten wieder heraus und verteilt mit
grosser Bestimmtheit die Kinder, 'Das ist Deins, das gehört mir . . .
usw.' Die Krankenschwester will unbedingt wissen, wie er das ge-
macht hat. Erst sagt der Deutsche: 'Das kann ich nicht sagen', aber sie
drängt immer weiter und so erzählt er schliesslich: 'Ich bin
reingegangen, habe den Arm gehoben und "Heil Hitler" gerufen.
Meiner ist sofort stramm gestanden und hat wieder-gegrüsst. Der
Jude hat sich in die Windeln geschissen und der Türke hat es
weggeputzt.'*

A German, a Jew and a Turk are waiting in the clinic to see their
new-born babies. A nurse comes and tells them that their children
have been mixed up and they do not know which baby belongs to
which father. The German says, 'Let me be in there undisturbed
for five minutes.' He goes in and comes back a couple of minutes
later and with great certainty says, 'This is your child, this is
mine. . . etc.' The nurse wants to know how he has done this. At
first the German says, 'That I cannot say.' But she presses him
further and finally he tells, 'I went in, raised my arm and shouted
"Heil Hitler." Immediately, my son lifted his arm and returned the
same greeting. The Jew shit in his swaddling clothes and the Turk
cleaned it up.'

The mixing up of the children may reflect the German's continuing concern with racial purity. No good German would want to have a child with tainted blood, e.g., Jewish or Turkish blood. The German's reluctance to tell the nurse how he succeeded in identifying the racial stock of each baby suggests that he realises that racist ideology is unpopular. Still, he does in the end admit that he uses the Hitler salute to distinguish the true German from the inferior races. The joke implies that the Jewish baby is so frightened by seeing the dreaded Nazi salute that he shits in his pants, a common metaphor in German folklore. The modern twist is that the Turk, a low man in terms of social status, is identified by his cleaning up after the dirty Jew.

In KZ Dachau spielen die Türken gegen die Juden Fussball. Wer gewinnt?
In the Dachau concentration camp, the Turks and the Jews play soccer. Who wins?

Die Juden – Sie haben Heimvorteil.
The Jews – They have the home field advantage.

It is surely of significance that the German hatred of Turkish migrant workers is expressed in jokes which also include Jews. It is as if to say that when the Germans want to hate any group, they tend to do so in comparison with the longstanding hatred of the Jews. This is certainly explicit in the following joke.

Was unterscheidet die Türken von den Juden?
What is the difference between Turks and Jews?

Die Juden haben es schon hinter sich, die Türken haben es noch vor sich.
The Jews have behind them what the Turks have now before them [mass murder].

The implication from all these jokes is that German anti-Semitism is alive and well. There seems to be little evidence of remorse in these texts. Only the reference to leaving Anne Frank's finger alone hints at any compassion for all the millions of victims of Nazi death camps. The unchanging consistency of anti-Semitism is manifested in a final joke which finds Hitler in hell:

Hitler hat Jahrzehntelang in der Hölle geschmort, zur Busse für seine Taten. Schliesslich ist er gereinigt und kommt in den Himmel. Gott fragt ihn: 'Nun, Adolf, was würdest du tun, wenn du jetzt wieder auf die Erde zurück könntest?' Hitler darauf: 'Na, Juden vergasen!' Verärgert schickt Gott ihn für weitere drei Jahre in die Hölle – Als er zurückkommt, stellt Got ihm wieder dieselbe Frage: 'Was würdest Du tun?' 'Juden vergasen.' Wieder geht es für drei Jahre in die Hölle. Als er zurückkommt fragt Gott das dritte Mal: 'Was würdest Du jetzt tun, wenn du auf die Erde zurückkönntest, Adolf?' Hitler hat sich die ganze Sache überlegt und sagt: 'Ich würde schöne Autobahnen bauen.' Da fragt Gott zurück: 'Und wohin würdest du die Bahnen bauen?' Hitler: 'Vor allem ein, von Prag direkt nach Auschwitz.'

Hitler has been burning in hell for dozens of years for all his sins. Finally he is cleansed and he enters heaven. God asks him, 'What would you do if you could return to earth, Adolf?' Hitler answers, 'I would gas Jews!' Angrily, God sends him back to hell for three more years. When Hitler returns to heaven, God asks him again the same question, 'What would you do?' However, Hitler says, 'Gas the Jews.' Again Hitler is sent back to hell for three years. When he comes back, God asks him a third time, 'What would you do if you could return to earth?' Hitler has thought over the whole thing and says, 'I would build some beautiful highways.' God asks then, 'To what places would you build these highways?' Answers Hitler, 'Directly from Prague to Auschwitz.'

This joke was heard in Bavaria from a bus-driver who told it to amuse tourists on his bus. The joke contains a common argument, namely, that Hitler was right in some of the things he did, e.g., he built good highways (something of importance to a professional bus-driver surely!). The highways were in fact built largely to facilitate the transportation of German war machinery. But the joke also shows that the strength of anti-Semitism in Hitler (and perhaps in Germany as well) is such that not even the horrors of hell could change it. For the Holocaust was a hell and apparently that hell has not wiped out all traces of anti-Semitism in contemporary Germany. The premise in the initial portion of the joke that Hitler had suffered enough in hell to cleanse himself so as to be allowed possible entrance into heaven is itself worthy of notice. The question is whether there is enough penance in the world to allow a Hitler to go to heaven. Of

course, the joke clearly states that Hitler was not at all affected by his
stay in hell – he remains the vicious anti-Semite he was in life. That
may be a good sign for modern Germany, that is, the recognition of
the evils of anti-Semitism. On the other hand, the very existence of
the Auschwitz joke cycle may not be much of a harbinger of
healthier attitudes. It is somewhat alarming to realise that an idiom
such as 'bis zur Vergasung' (to be gassed, to be at the point of
gasification) is in common use in contemporary Germany referring to
someone carrying out an action to the point of extinction or utter
futility.[9]

Jews were treated in an inhumane way. They were not treated as
humans, but as a dirty problem to be solved or eliminated. Jokes also
dehumanise and may make light of a serious problem. It is too easy
to make light of Auschwitz and the travesty of human decency that
occurred there. But at least the Auschwitz joke cycle indicates that
Germans, or at any rate some Germans are admitting that the tragic
events of Auschwitz did happen. For many years during and after the
war, countless 'good' Germans claimed either that they knew
nothing of the atrocities of the death-camps or that they never
happened at all, being the fabrications of allied propaganda
campaigns. In this context, the Auschwitz jokes would at least seem
to be an admission that the horrors of the death camps are a reality
that has to be faced. But the reality is so ghastly, so terrible, so
frightful that it is difficult to face. This is no doubt one reason why
these jokes exist. They allow the joke-teller and his audience to
admit that Auschwitz is a part of German history – ironic that the
name Auschwitz includes 'Au' ('ow' as in pain) 'schwitz' (sweat) and
'witz' (joke). But while it could conceivably be a healthy sign for
Germans to admit the historical reality of Auschwitz, it is at the same
time disturbing to think that the recognition of the grim reality has
not ended centuries-old anti-Semitic sentiments in Germany.

It is difficult to ascertain just how old and how widespread these
Auschwitz jokes are in Germany. We can testify that they are not
easy to collect and, to date, German folklorists have not reported
them. Still, a revealing couplet from a poem entitled 'Auschwitz' by
Ulrich Otto Berger published in 1966[10] suggests that these jokes have
been around for some years:

Der Volksmund weiss heute zu erzählen
mehr als einen Witz über Auschwitz.

The folk speech of today knows how to tell
more than one joke about Auschwitz.

As long as such jokes are told, the evil of Auschwitz will remain in the
consciousness of Germans. They may seem a sorry and inadequate
memorial for all the poor, wretched souls who perished at Auschwitz,
but when one realises that comedy and tragedy are two sides of the
same coin, we can perhaps understand why some contemporary
Germans might need to resort to the mechanism of humour, albeit
sick humour, to try to come to terms with the unimaginable and
unthinkable horrors that did occur at Auschwitz.

NOTES

1. See Antonin J. Obrdlik, ' "Gallows Humour" – A Sociological
   Phenomenon', *American Journal of Sociology*, vol. 47 (1942) pp. 709–
   16; and Elfriede Moser-Rath, 'Galgenhumor wortlich genommen',
   Schweizerisches Archiv für Volkskunde, vol. 68/69 (1972/1973) pp.
   423–32.
2. For an early discussion of self-hate, see Kurt Lewin, 'Self Hatred
   Among Jews', *Contemporary Jewish Record*, vol. 4 (1941) pp. 219–32.
3. Unless otherwise indicated all texts were collected by Thomas
   Hauschild in West Berlin during the summer of 1982 from informants
   ranging in age from 26 to 60 years.
4. We thank folklorist Utz Jeggle in Tubingen for sending us this text.
5. We are grateful to folklorist Bengt af Klintberg in Stockholm for
   providing all the Swedish texts cited in this essay. He indicated that
   such 'judevitsar' (jokes about Jews) were popular among teenagers in
   the early 1970s.
6. See Alan Dundes, 'Life is Like a Chicken Coop Ladder: A Study of
   German National Character Through Folklore', *Journal of
   Psychoanalytic Anthropology*, vol. 4 (1981) pp. 265–364.
7. This and the following two texts were collected directly in English
   translation from Dr Vera Bendt in Berlin in April 1982. We are
   indebted to Dr Bendt for calling our attention to the Auschwitz joke
   cycle in the first place.
8. This text was also sent to us by Utz Jeggle from Tubingen. Oven jokes
   are also found in the United States and Sweden. A text collected from
   a Jewish young man from Los Angeles in 1981: What's the difference
   between a Jew and a pizza? A pizza doesn't scream when it is put in
   the oven. The Swedish version: What is the difference between a Jew
   and a bun? The Jew screams when he is pushed into the oven.
   Another Swedish text asks: What was Hitler's worst shock? When he
   got the gas bill. In an English text collected in Leeds in 1973: How do

you get a Jew in a telephone [booth]? Throw a ha'penny in. How do you get him out? Shout gas. See Sandra McCosh, *Children's Humour* (London, 1976) p. 227,# 723.

9.   We are indebted to anthropologist Ulrike Linke for reminding us of the prevalence of this metaphor. See Peter Schutt, '*Der Mohr hat seine Schuldigkeit getan. . .' Gibt es Rassismus in der Bundesrepublik? Eine Streitschrift.* (Dortmund, 1981) p. 25. See also Alphonse Silbermann, *Sind wir Antisemiten?* (Köln, 1982) for a more general discussion of anti-Semitism in modern Germany.

10.   See Peter Hamm (ed.) *Aussichten* (München, 1966) p. 263. We thank Professor Wolfgang Mieder of the University of Vermont for callng our attention to this poetic allusion to Auschwitz jokes.

An expanded and updated version of this chapter under the same title can be found in the journal *Western Folklore*, vol. 42 (1983) pp. 249–60.

4 Is the Pope Catholic? A Content Analysis of American Jokelore about the Catholic Clergy

John L. Oldani

A frequently used example to explain the folklore genre of a pointed rhetorical question[1] is the expression, 'Is the Pope Catholic?' Such a text is often sarcastically applied when the listener feels that the questioner has asked an obvious or foolish question, one where the answer is or should be known. The texture of this 'question' is an obvious concrete reference to the leader of the Roman Catholic Church; there is no conspicuous slur intended, no apparent threat, no inferiority/superiority relationship. This rhetorical question appears to be, simply, an example of a joke of 'transcendent nature'.[2]

There are dozens of similar pointed rhetorical questions throughout American folklore which serve similar purposes: Is a pig's ass pork? Does a bear shit in the woods? Is Nixon a Republican? Does a chicken have lips? The sarcasm is obvious, but a real invective is not present. One accepts such a reply with the teasing function it serves.

In the early seventies, however, the pointed rhetorical question seemed to have taken on a more direct meaning while still retaining its original function. Several informants supplied the following text: Does a Pope shit in the woods? (actually used by Lily Tomlin in the movie, *The Late Show*, Warner Bros, 1977). Is a Pope's ass pork? This example of metafolklore[3] had not been given to this collector previously and the sudden appearance, from many different informants, could not be dismissed as a mere question. Why the changes in this particular folk text? The other forms had remained relatively constant, but the one rhetorical question directly relating to the Pope had changed into an absurdity which superficially did not even function as a pointed rhetorical question – and yet it did!

At about the same time in the lore of the American folk, the nun joke fad began to appear: A few examples will suffice:

What is black and white and red all over? A wounded nun.

What is black and white and transparent? A nun in a baggie.

What is black and white and black and white and black and white? A nun rolling down a hill.

What is a nun with one leg? Hop-a-long chastity.

The sudden appearance of both types of texts cannot be explained away as meaningless. Two important symbols within the ritual of the Catholic Church were now part of the overt oral tradition of the American people. If the task of the folklorist is to make the unconscious conscious, and to discover what exactly the lore does for the folk, then these new forms must be studied for meaning in context.

A second aspect of these concrete expressions involves the presence of a 'religion' as part of the texture and genre. For whatever reasons, this cultural universal has been for the most part curiously neglected by folklorists.[4] Specifically, the lore surrounding the Catholic Church in America has a very meagre research corpus.[5] The historian, the anthropologist, the sociologist, even the novelist, have all applied their disciplines to the presence of the Catholic in American society.[6] If a total perspective is to be achieved on the character of the American it is necessary for the student of folklore to add his analysis to religion as an important thread in the American tapestry.

This chapter is a partial attempt to fill this large gap in folklore studies of religion. Specifically, it will examine the jokelore surrounding the American Catholic. (The joke 'genre' is the most frequently used text in descriptions of the Catholic, his ritual, and his dealings with other denominations.) By using versions of the texts, rather than variants, and by considering texture and context of the jokelore, this study will be directive rather than exhaustive.

THE ESOTERIC–EXOTERIC FACTOR

In 1959, William Jansen published a landmark position paper highlighting the place of the folk as a group *vis-à-vis* another group within a pluralistic society. Jansen coined the expression, 'the esoteric–exoteric factor in folklore'. The esoteric applies to what one

group thinks of itself and what it supposes others think of it. The exoteric is what one group thinks of another and what it thinks that other group thinks it thinks.[7] Two groups could effect many different, but interrelated, stereotypes but both factors operate from the group's sense of belonging. The esoteric factor can benefit by a strengthening of that sense, and the exoteric can be exhibited in the same sense but may result from a fear of, mystification about, or resentment of the group to which one does not belong.[8] Jansen further delimits factors which may make a group liable to the esoteric–exoteric factor: (a) isolation, whether by age, region, language, lack of education, or religion; (b) possession of a special knowledge by a group; (c) consideration of one group by others as being particularly admirable, particularly favoured or particularly awesome.[9]

The theoretical premises of the esoteric–exoteric factor are many, varied and intricate.[10] Usually, stereotypes are effected and often stereotypes of stereotypes result. Such folk expressions of a people's character are constant, often unfair, perhaps inaccurate but, nevertheless, they exist, already recorded in oral tradition and free from investigative bias.[11] What is of primary interest is 'determining precisely the trait or set of traits the folk has singled out for emphasis'.[12]

The esoteric–exoteric theory seems ideally suited to a consideration of the position of the Catholic in American society as seen through jokelore. To be sure, Catholics are 'isolated' through costume, dialect, observance of holidays; they are often viewed as possessing a 'training' which seems peculiar; they are sometimes perceived as 'particularly awesome' or different, with the seat of their religion in a foreign country.[13] Indeed, the lore of Catholics, as the largest single denomination in America by sheer numbers, is ideally suited to the whole esoteric–exoteric concept.

Because of the many facets of the Catholic religion and the relationship of the jokelore, in each facet, discussion will be limited to one major aspect: the role of the clergy.[14] Most of the jokes were collected during fieldwork and were deposited in the Southern Illinois University at Edwardsville Folklore Archive, with appropriate annotations. The fieldwork was conducted in various settings. Priests were interviewed in rectories; nuns were contacted in convents. Former priests and nuns were used as informants in their new roles. Participant observation was used at various church functions – picnics, pot-luck suppers, bazaars – both Catholic and Protestant.

The collector never denied his religion, Catholicism, to any informant. In some cases, the information was volunteered; in all cases it made no difference in the telling of the joke. Some variants were found in the Folklore Archive at the University of California, Berkeley. Versions chosen for this chapter were those which had more complete textural and contextural annotations and existed in the most examples. The esoteric–exoteric concept is primarily applied to the informant and his analysis. Generally, a Catholic tells the jokes esoterically with various levels of meaning and a Protestant relates a joke exoterically as a member of the out-group.

THE CLERGY

In many ways, the priest is the central figure in the Catholic religion. The Pope is a priest, as are the cardinals, archbishops, bishops, and monsignors. Priests, alone, are allowed to celebrate the Holy Sacrifice of the Mass in which the consecration of the Body and Blood of Christ is central. Priests administer the sacraments to the faithful, including the rite of Reconciliation, Penance, or as it is popularly known, Confession. Among other things, a priest counsels engaged couples before marriage, instructs grade-school children in the faith, administers to the sick, preaches the Gospel, and serves the parish as a patriarch. Indeed, he is called, 'Father', by his flock and is, simply stated, believed to be Christ's disciple on earth and to have received an inspiration from the Holy Spirit, called a vocation, to dedicate his life to the service of the Church. It is important to note that only males may receive this vocational inspiration and that priests may never marry.

Moreover, priests wear a distinctive garb, a folk costume, both in their daily activities and while they are celebrating Mass. The vestments in the latter are highly symbolic, in the position they are worn on the person of the priest, how they are put on, and in the significance of the colours. Indeed, the esoteric factor is quite strong in this ritual because only Catholics are continually exposed to the vestments during Mass and even among Catholics, not many can explain what each article of clothing means.

Before the Second Vatican Council, the Mass was celebrated in Latin throughout the world. After Vatican II, each country was given permission to rewrite the ritual in the vernacular, ostensibly to make the celebration more meaningful.

In this brief description, one can isolate several elements surrounding the priest, alone, which are congruent with the esoteric–exoteric factor. Indeed, in all the above descriptions and areas, American jokes are legion. Consider the following:

The First Sermon

The new priest at his first Mass was so afraid he could hardly speak. Before his second week at the pulpit, he asked the pastor how he could relax. The pastor replied, 'Next week it may help if you put Martini mix in the water pitcher. After a few sips, everything should go smoothly.' The next week, the young priest put the pastor's suggestion into practice and really loosened up by talking up a storm. After his sermon, he asked the pastor how he liked the sermon. The pastor replied, 'There are a few things you should learn before addressing the congregation again:

1. Next time, sip instead of gulping the Martinis.
2. There are 12 disciples, not 10.
3. There are 10 commandments, not 12.
4. David slew Goliath. He didn't kick the shit out of him.
5. We do not refer to our Saviour Jesus Christ and His disciples as J. C. and the boys.
6. We do not refer to the cross as the 'Big T.'
7. The Father, Son, and Holy Ghost are not referred to as 'Big Daddy, Junior, and the Spook'.
8. It is Virgin Mary – not Mary with the cherry.
9. And last but not least, next week, there is a taffy-pulling contest at St Peter's – not a peter-pulling contest at St Taffy's. [15]

The Power of the Press

A priest wanted to raise money for his parish church, and being told that there was a fortune in horse racing, decided to purchase one and enter him in the races. However, at the local auction, the going price for horses was so steep that he ended up buying a donkey instead. He figured that since he had it, he might as well go ahead and enter it in the races, and to his surprise the donkey came in third. The next day the racing sheets carried this headline: PRIEST'S ASS SHOWS.

The priest was so pleased with the donkey that he entered it in the races again, and this time it won. The paper said: PRIEST'S ASS OUT IN FRONT.

The Bishop was so upset with this kind of publicity that he

ordered the priest not to enter the donkey in another race. The newspaper printed this headline: BISHOP SCRATCHES PRIEST'S ASS.

This was just too much for the Bishop and he ordered the priest to get rid of the animal. The priest decided to give it to a nun in a nearby convent. The headlines the next day read: NUN HAS BEST ASS IN TOWN.

The Bishop fainted. He informed the nun that she would have to dispose of the donkey and she finally found a farmer who was willing to buy it for $10.00. The paper stated: NUN PEDDLES ASS FOR TEN BUCKS.

They buried the Bishop the next day.[16]

There are several interesting items in 'The First Sermon', relating both esoterically and exoterically. The joke was initially collected from a Catholic woman who had been reared in the Catholic Church through her high-school years. She is still a practising Catholic and tells this joke 'every chance she gets'. To her it represents the fallibility of the priest – the representative of Christ on earth yet human in his qualities. The theme relates to folk expressions which are informally used among anti-establishment types. This latter group may be the underlying reason for viewing the joke as funny since the Catholic Church is often viewed as the 'establishment Church' among churches with its rigid organisation and hierarchical structure.[17] Further discussions with the informant revealed her distaste for the 'impersonal quality of the Church as a big business'. The joke, indeed, reveals a 'hip' language which is absurd, and hence funny, in a formal situation like the Mass celebration. There is a further implication that the alcohol 'loosens' up the priest so that he can speak freely; fear of reprisal kept him from speaking such when he was sober. Esoterically, the rebel in the priest is shown, as part of the younger generation of clergy.[18]

Note, too, he consults his pastor, presumably a wiser and older man, who suggests the use of the Martini in place of the water. The implication may be that the pastor, himself, 'a father-figure' to the young priest, has done the same thing many times in the past. Perhaps his reasoning was different and certainly his results were!

Esoterically, there is the comment that 'there are a few things you should learn' before preaching again. Here, the pastor, speaking symbolically as a Catholic parishioner, is echoing the belief of many modern Catholics that priests are not being properly trained, the changes in Vatican II have hindered the celebration of the Mass, and

that perhaps anyone can be a priest.[19] There are currently national Catholic programmes to 'ordain' married men as deacons to do the preaching, distribute Communion, and visit the sick because there are not enough priests to meet the needs of the Catholics. These facts are known by the Catholics as an in-group, and perhaps, unconsciously enunciated in this form of oral tradition. To be sure, the joke has been collected many times, but always from a Catholic. There may be an element of the safety-valve theory[20] here for Catholics who are sometimes esoterically and exoterically seen as 'oppressed' and express the exoteric stereotype only because of what they think Protestants represent. Also, as an esoteric component, Catholics are aware of the consecration in the celebration of the Mass where water and wine become the blood of Christ and may be so habitually involved with the celebration that they can fantasise about changes, however absurd. Again, esoterically, the joke may be viewed as a concrete example of what some non-Catholics have long believed about Catholics. The priests are, indeed, human, do imbibe, can and do get drunk, and are aware of the vernacular. And, too, there is the element of invention in the joke in that the 'Martini' or the use of the water was done before the homily. In the Catholic service of the Mass this simply does not happen as ritual. The homily always occurs early on in the celebration, after the reading of the Gospel, and then the consecration begins in which the use of the water and wine become important. The 'in-group' would recognise this inaccuracy but the humour in the joke obscures such details.

Lastly, it may not be too far-fetched to suggest that Number 8 in the joke relates to current discussions surrounding the Mother of Jesus and her virginity. Some noted theologians have risked censure recently with statements questioning the validity of this dogma. Universities are now offering courses on the 'Cult of the Virgin', and folklorists have suggested some 'fancy' in the depiction of the Mother of a Hero (Jesus) to be a virgin and only perceived by Christians.[21] Again, there is an element of the esoteric here.[22]

The second joke was collected both in fieldwork as an oral tradition and as part of xerox lore, the paperwork empire, or office lore. It was mailed to the writer as an example of some modern folklore, anonymously 'created' but still existing among the folk in such different variants.

The motif of this second joke simply revolves around the need for a parish priest to make money to support his church. Again, this theme is viewed both by the in-group and the out-group in a similar

fashion. Priests are 'always' preaching money from the pulpit and, in their love for gambling (witness the stereotype of bingo games in Catholic churches throughout America), they are not adverse to experimenting with other forms of the sport. The humour results from what Koestler has called the 'simultaneous presence in the reader's mind of the social reality with which he is familiar and of its reflection in the distorting picture of the joke'.[23] The play on the word 'ass' – at least three meanings – represents this distortion. And a nun, who vows chastity, 'peddles her ass' for a 'cheap' ten bucks smacks of an exoteric stereotype of nuns as craving sexual gratification because 'they are human'.

Note, too, the actions of the bishop in the joke. He is a superior of a diocese who formulates policies for the entire diocese and is, in effect, the 'boss' of the priest. The priest does as he is ordered, but the bishop gets 'upset', 'faints', and finally 'dies'. The implication here, esoterically, may be clear. The leader of a diocese simply cannot cope with such a trivial matter as the headlines in a newspaper. How can he cope with the really urgent problems of a diocese within the everyday, mundane, societal context?[24] Exoterically, there is a stereotype of priests loving priests in a sexual way.[25] When the headlines state that the 'Bishop Scratches the Priest's Ass', the reaction is much milder than those related to the other headlines. When all Catholic informants were asked about the why of this headline, most of them interpreted it as a fear of homosexuality on the part of the bishop. But, more importantly, non-Catholics noted he was only *mildly* upset because the homosexuality was, perhaps, actually a reality and the protest was mild for fear of further investigation. Since it appears in a relatively fixed form of xerox lore, this second joke may perpetuate stereotypes, exoterically. In this sense, then, nativism is still extant.

The jokelore related to the celibacy of priests is perhaps the largest of any sub-genre within the jokelore of Catholics. Sometimes the jokes are related to puns with sexual connotations; sometimes they relate to the desires of the priest for sexual gratification only to have him repress himself in absurd ways; sometimes they relate to the Catholic layperson's fear of the priest's 'human' desires and become a form of protest humour; and sometimes the jokes about celibacy even concern a preservation of ego-identity as in the parody of the self. The following jokes will aid in the explanation of these occasions.

Why do priests wear underwear when they take a shower?
Because it is a sin to look down on the unemployed.[26]

This joke was collected numerous times, both from Catholics and
non-Catholics, but first identified by a Catholic priest! In the original
version, the priest was mocking himself *à la* one of our earlier
structures. This seems to be a Catholic's conception of a Protestant's
conception of a Catholic *vis-à-vis* a Protestant. A sub-motif is the
social concern of the Catholic Church for the downtrodden (unemployed) members of the society. Often this is viewed hypocritically by
Catholics and non-Catholics alike in the 'gushing' outspoken concerns of the former; in actuality, it is often just that, words and not
actions. In context, Catholics have expressed this rationale for the
humour in the joke. The priest, of course, was referring to the sight
of his penis. It, too, should be 'unemployed' but the sight of it may
cause arousal, which in itself is another sin. The sins of hypocrisy, of
impure thoughts, of masturbation, and of neglecting a neighbour, are
all illustrated in this joke. Here, too, there is the popular stereotype
of the Church as oppressive, guilt-inducing, and superior. Perhaps
the 'bisociation'[27] of Koestler explains the superficial humour in this
joke: the esoteric–exoteric factor adds levels of meaning which effect
greater understanding. There may even be an element of what
Simmons has termed 'ego-identity' applied to ethnic jokes.[28]

Pat and Mike were working on the street in front of a house of ill
repute. After a while a Baptist minister came walking by the house.
He walked on past and then turned around and came back to the
door, looked up and down the street, and went inside. 'Did you see
that?' asked Pat. 'Yeah,' said Mike, 'but you know how the
Baptists are.' They went back to their work and pretty soon a
Rabbi came walking down the street. He strolled up to the door of
the house, looked up and down the street, and went inside. 'Did
you see that?' asked Pat. 'Yeah,' said Mike, 'but you know how
Jews are.' They went back to work and a few minutes later a priest
came walking up the street, came to the house, and walked right in.
'Did you see that?' asked Pat. 'Yeah,' said Mike, 'there must be
some girl in there deathly sick.'[29]

Here the construction workers are obviously Irish, and thus,
stereotypically, Catholic. In such a picture, the priest is holy,
superior, a 'father' figure, and celibate. He can do no wrong, commit

no sin, or so Catholics are supposed to be taught. And above all, the priest is celibate! Fears of all Catholics are expressed in this joke. It is a flaw they suspect the priest has, but it must be denied perhaps for the esoteric sense of belonging or for the 'safety-valve'. Note, too, within the joke are stereotypes of other groups held by one out-group or minority, and the eventual rationalisation on the part of the Catholic workers. Indeed, one of the jobs of the priest is to visit the sick – surely that is what he is doing at the brothel! Here wish-fulfilment is psychologically important. Not only is it hoped that the priest was visiting a sick person, but he was administering the Sacrament of the Sick (Extreme Unction) and thereby converting another person to Catholicism – 'the one true religion'. The implication is that the priest was converting a Mary Magdalene through a final confession where all former sins would be absolved.

The Priest and the Rabbi

This rabbi and this Catholic priest were once flying together in a plane, and they are not talking to each other, so the Catholic priest decides to open the conversation and he says, 'Look here, Rabbi. We are all by ourselves, so just between you and me, have you ever eaten ham?' And the rabbi looks all around and he says, 'Yeah, Yeah, I have tasted ham.' So they fly along in silence a little bit farther, and the rabbi says to the priest: 'Tell me something, Father. Have you ever had a piece of ass?' So the priest looks all around, and the rabbi says, 'Oh, c'mon, Father, I have been honest with you; I won't tell anybody.' So the priest says, 'Well, yeah, I have.' And the rabbi says, 'It's a hell of a lot better than ham, isn't it?'[30]

This *blason populaire*, pitting the rabbi against the priest, highlights the celibacy of the priest. The motif clearly implies that the priest, as every priest, has had a sexual encounter and is not totally virginal, as the esoteric stereotype projects. There is also a superiority/inferiority relationship involved in the joke. The priest, in his initially superior way, pokes fun at the rabbi by hitting his 'taboo' or stereotype, but suggesting that one cannot avoid something as delicious as ham. In a superb one-upmanship, the rabbi counters with the taboo of the priest and tells him that, indeed, he (the rabbi) would rather abstain from ham! Note the folk expression which the rabbi uses for sexual intercourse. The rabbi can marry, become more 'human' and, therefore, use the slang. There is a food usage here

and, importantly, the priest understands it and can identify with it. Note, also, the joke takes the form of the confessional whereby the priest is doing the confessing to a member of a different religion. Presumably, he cannot even tell his sins to another priest in the anonymity of the confessional – a fear, distrust, which is esoterically held by many Catholics, is applied to the priest whose profession involves the absolution of sins through the Sacrament of Penance.[31]

The following two jokes are somewhat alike and yet somewhat different in their approaches to the sanctity of the priest. The first admits of some falling-out by the priests who were 'not too holy', and the second underscores this belief with the vernacular which the priest uses.

Three priests went into an airport to purchase three tickets to Pittsburgh. One of the priests was very holy and he was going to Pittsburgh to visit the Pope. The other priests weren't very holy and were only going along to keep the other company. When the three came to the ticket window, there stood a bra-less ticket salesgirl in a see-through blouse. The two priests who were going along for the ride went crazy at the sight. The very holy priest was quite embarrassed and appointed one of the other priests to go forth and purchase three airline tickets. The first priest walked up to the salesgirl and said, 'I would like three tickets to Tittsburgh.' He threw his hand over his mouth because he was so embarrassed at what he had just said. The other not-so-holy priest said, 'Don't worry, Father. God will forgive you for your sin, I'm sure. I shall go purchase the tickets so that we may be on our way.' So, he walked up to the salesgirl and said, 'I want three Titts to Pittsburgh.' Immediately, he ran back to the other two priests hiding his face in his hands. The priest who was very holy looked at the two and said, 'I'm ashamed of both of you. If you're not careful, one of these days St Finger is going to come down here and shake his peter at you.'[32]

A Catholic family was having problems with their kid, Patrick. So they went to the school and took Patrick to the teacher, and then to the counsellor, but Patrick wouldn't cooperate. He was eight years old and bratty. They tried psychiatrists and psychologists, but Patrick wouldn't cooperate. The parents were at a complete loss. Finally, they took him to the priest. They leave him alone with the priest, who says: 'What seems to be the trouble young man?'

Patrick says: 'Fuck you.' The priest says: 'Fuck me? Do you know who you're talking to? I am the priest of this parish. And maybe someday I'll be the bishop of this diocese. And after that, maybe archbishop of the archdiocese, and after that, maybe a cardinal and who knows, maybe even Pope! Fuck me? – No. Fuck you, kid!'[33]

In the first joke, note the suspension of belief one must hold. They were going to see the Pope *in Pittsburgh*! They were going there so that the stuttering and misapplication of tits could take place with the prefix to burgh! The joke is made up to fit the situation, and yet it is important to show the human quality of the priests who experience sexual arousal by looking at a buxom young woman. Note, too, the one priest who was 'holier', as if there are degrees of holiness among priests – another esoteric concept – also falls prey to the flesh. He is so shaken by the appearance of the young woman that his thoughts fall below his belt and the expression he uses is the folk derivative. It is absurdity applied to the priesthood which accounts for part of the humour in the joke, but more importantly, there is, it is believed, the conflict between the young and the old priests so often held, stereotypically, following Vatican II.

Much of the turmoil in the Catholic Church in the seventies, if we are to believe some of the recent accounts,[34] has resulted from the liberality of the young priests who are preaching for birth control, recognition of homosexuals within the Church and more liberal divorce laws, among others, in opposition to the conservative, presumably older priests, who desire to remain within the standards of the same Church. The admonition by the 'holiest' priest at the end of the joke can be applied seriously to 'aberrant' priests who have advocated the above liberality. This is a pure esoteric joke explication which seems to encapsulate the whole controversy with the Catholic Church. Ostensibly, there is the celibacy question of the priest, but the level of the joke is much deeper than the exoteric quality reveals.

The second joke allows for the priest to speak as if 'one of the gang'. As a priest he may even be Pope someday (akin to the American Dream for priests) and he will have absolute control, even infallibility. This latter doctrine speaks to the point that the Pope is infallible in matters of faith and morals; he speaks Church doctrine and he is not to be questioned by the Catholics who are members of his Church. The absurdity of this final command to the incorrigible youth is appropriate in the language of the folk, but given as a

command. Here, too, is the esoteric concept which implies that whatever the Pope says, the 'sheep-like' Catholics do. In this case, the expletive can only be achieved symbolically!

It is interesting to note also that, in this second joke, the psychiatrists and psychologists could not handle the hyperactive child – they could not handle or do their jobs, so they bring the boy to the priest. Here is the role of the priest as omnipotent. This seems to be the Catholics' conception of the Protestant conception of the Catholic in contrast to the Protestant. The stereotype within the stereotype functions for both groups: for one, it seems to preserve an identity; for the other, it reinforces a prejudice and may serve as another safety-valve both for a priest to reaffirm his powers and position and, esoterically, for Catholics to dispel any fears they may have on changes in the role of the priest within the Church.

The view of the role of the priest within the changing Church can also be seen in the jokes surrounding the ministering of the sacraments. Indeed, the priest still retains the primary responsibility for performing the sacraments; such a role is acknowledged both esoterically and exoterically. In both groups, however, the 'mystery' behind the celebration of the sacrament, whatever it might be, lends itself to a rendering through jokelore. In this way, also, one function of a folklore, that of explaining the world to ourselves in personally acceptable terms, operates efficaciously. And no jokes about the sacraments are more popular than those surrounding the Confession. Consider the following:

A reporter decides that he wants to do a story on a day in the life of a priest. He gets a priest to agree. When the priest was to give absolution and penances in the confessional, he asked the reporter to sit behind the confessional out of view. The first man comes up to the confessional and says, 'Father, I have sinned. I have had an illicit affair with three women this week.' The priest answered, 'Your penance is to donate $5 and you will be absolved.' A second man comes up to the booth and says, 'Father, I have sinned. I have had an illicit affair with three women this week.' The priest answered, 'Your penance is to donate $5 and you will be absolved.' Just then, the priest had to go to the bathroom so he asked the reporter if he could handle the confessional for a couple of minutes. He said he could. While in the booth, a man comes up and says, 'Father I have sinned. I have had an illicit affair with two women this week.' The reporter lowered his voice to a confidential

whisper and said, 'Listen we have a special this week. It's three illicit affairs for $5. Go out and have another one and come back.'[35]

Here the Sacrament of Reconciliation is reduced to a bargain basement sale. It appears to conform to a popular stereotype that an absolution can be bought, that a man cannot forgive another's 'sins', and if a man could forgive another then anyone could do it, *à la* reporter. Moreover, there is a hint that the sinner is not really repentant and that he will probably commit the same sins again – why not 'joke' about them? Note, too, the human quality of the priest who 'goes to the bathroom' during the middle of a confessional sitting. This serves to underscore the exoteric concept of the role of the priest in administering the sacraments. Yet the subject is a reporter who evidently thinks the life of a priest is newsworthy or perhaps worthy of investigation. There may be a mystery in the secular as well as the spiritual sense. It is not clear from the content of the joke if the reporter deliberately misinterpreted the significance of confession or it was his own joke. Such duality allows for the full play of the joke and can be interpreted successfully on several levels within the in-group and the out-group perspectives.

Lastly, there are jokes about the clergy related in a strictly and totally esoteric manner. These are jokes told among the various orders of priests within the Catholic Church as indices of 'friendly/familiar' rivalry. One of the most popular is the following:

Three members of different orders, Franciscan, Dominican and Jesuit were arguing which order was the best or which order God favoured the most. They argued half the night and finally decided to take it to the 'Man'. So they wrote the question down, asking which order God favoured the most, and put the slip of paper on the altar, expecting the answer the next morning. The next day they returned, looked at the paper and found the following answer: I favour none of the orders of priests. God does not play favourites; all are equally good.' (Signed) God, SJ[36]

The signature with the SJ appended refers to the Society of Jesus, popularly known as the Jesuits. The obvious reference is that God, Himself, in this joke, is a Jesuit. Again, the joke is known primarily in an esoteric way since each order within the Catholic Church usually appends initials after a signature. In the above joke, if OFM

had been used after God's signature, it would have indicated that God was a Franciscan or the Order of Friars Minor. If an OP had been used after the signature, it would show that God was a Franciscan, or Order of Preachers. Depending on the context, the signature could be different, making for several variants of the joke. Catholics, as the in-group, would recognise the punchline of the joke and derive particular humour from it; an exoteric quality would seem to be lacking in this particular area of jokelore surrounding the Catholic clergy.

Furthermore, the content of the joke suggests the continuous arguments within the Church among various religious orders concerning the 'need' for so many different groups – an esoterically-viewed implication. Historically, of course, the Jesuits have been the object of much controversy, including antagonism within their own Church from other Catholic orders of priests.

There is, too, within the joke, the notion of direct Divine intervention in the settlement of disputes as representative of one antiquated notion within the Church which is resurrected by a 'hip' reference to God as the 'Man'. Such coupling of the old and the new suggests the 'tendency wit' of Freud.[37] There is a real need for this joke among the Catholic priests, but the 'need' must be kept 'in the family'.

In these versions of Catholic humour related to the priest, several aspects of the functions of the folk and the folklore were shown to be operating. Whether functioning as actual mirrors of the state of things, as safety-valves, or as unmasking factors, they are types drawn in the oral tradition of the folk and cannot be frozen or stopped. They are quite revealing on several levels of study and may be the most revealing source for consideration of the place of the Catholic in American society. To be sure, the pointed rhetorical question, 'Does the Pope shit in the woods?' places the leader of the Catholic Church in a human, or absurd or incongruous context in the combination of two former pointed rhetorical questions. Here, in this one new text, the whole esoteric–exoteric theory seems to be operating fully. The out-group can ask the question because of their long-held belief that the Catholics have an irrational bond to the absolute pronouncements of a man, who is a human, or 'only a human'. Esoterically, the Catholics believe this is what the out-group thinks they (Catholics) believe and do, but in reality, may not. The Catholics can use the same question for a different reason. For the esoteric quality of the text can function to suggest that, indeed, the

Pope is *not* infallible in all matters. Is this not an acceptable form of aggression, a proper safety-valve, a permitting what is not permissible? Indeed, is the Pope Catholic?

NOTES

1. Alan Dundes, 'Some Minor Genres of American Folklore', *Southern Folklore Quarterly*, vol. XXX (1966) p. 29.

2. Jeffrey H. Goldstein, 'Theoretical Notes on Humor', *Journal of Communication*, vol. XXVI, no. 3, (Summer 1976) p. 110. Goldstein uses the term to explain jokes which are on a different level from ethnic jokes. Laughter at the joke by the involved group is neither a mechanism of denial or of differentiation. The example Goldstein uses for this type of joke is the following: Schwartz and Goldberg were in a cafeteria drinking tea. Schwartz studied his cup and said with a sigh, 'Ah, my friend, life is like a cup of tea.' Goldberg considered this for a moment and then said, 'But *why* is life like a cup of tea?' And Schwartz replied, 'How should I know? Am I a philosopher?'

3. Alan Dundes, 'Metafolklore and Oral Literary Criticism', in Alan Dundes, *Essays in Folkloristics* (New Delhi, India: Ved Prakash Vatuk, Folklore Institute, 1978) p. 42. Dundes uses the term metafolklore to apply to the 'folklore about folklore'. For example, as he points out, everyone knows the formula for a Knock-Knock Joke Fad, but there are examples within this folklore that are metafolklore – Knock, knock. Who's there? Opportunity. The meaning is obvious and an aberrant form of the Knock-Knock joke cycle.

4. Conrad M. Hyers (ed.) *Holy Laughter, Essays on Religion in the Comic Perspective* (New York; Seabury Press, 1969) is an attempt to link religion and humour or laughter. Often, however, the essays use literary sources and equate the humour in religion with 'divinity', variously defined. No folklorists are represented in the book. Also Stanley Brandes, *Metaphors of Masculinity, Sex and Status in Andalusian Folklore*, (Philadelphia: University of Pennsylvania Press, 1980) cogently discusses the image of the clergy through jokes in Andalusian society in Chapter 10.

5. Gershon Legman, *Rationale of the Dirty Joke, An Analysis of Sexual Humor*, First Series (New York: Grove Press, 1968) states that 'the very few jokes still to be encountered accusing the ministry (priests) of immorality, indicated by their small number ... the very great decay into which religion has fallen in the last half century' (p. 417). If one accepts such a premise, then the large number of jokes circulating specifically about the Catholic clergy today must indicate a *very* healthy Church! None of the jokes in the present discussion was considered by Legman.

6. John Tracy Ellis, *American Catholicism* (Chicago: University of

Chicago Press, 1956) and Thomas T. McAvoy, *History of the Catholic Church in America* (Notre Dame, IN: University of Notre Dame Press, 1969), are the classic works by historians. James T. Trent, *Catholics in College: Religious Commitment and the Intellectual Life*, (Chicago: University of Chicago Press, 1967) uses sociological/ anthropological perspectives. Andrew Greeley, *The American Catholic, A Social Portrait*, (New York: Basic Books, 1977) covers most traditional methodological bases. This would be the best book, at least the most provocative, to read about the Catholic in modern America. And John Powers, *Do Black Patent Leather Shoes Reflect Up?* (Chicago: Contemporary Books, 1976) is a novel by a Catholic about growing up in a strictly Catholic, Chicago neighbourhood. The title, itself, is a bit of esoteric folklore, recognised by Catholics.

7. William Hugh Jansen, 'The Esoteric–Exoteric Factor in Folklore', *Fabula: Journal of Folktale Studies*, vol. II (1959) p. 206.
8. Ibid., p. 207.
9. Ibid., p. 210.
10. See Alan Dundes, 'A Study of Ethnic Slurs: The Jew and the Polack in the U.S.', *Journal of American Folklore*, vol. LXXXIC, no. 332 (April–June, 1971) pp. 186–203, for a superb elaboration of the possible structures of the esoteric–exoteric factor.
11. Ibid., p. 186.
12. Ibid., p. 190.
13. Many tracts, works of fiction and sermons were written and/or spoken in the nineteenth century about the nature of the Catholic, especially his supposed attempt to take over the US and make everyone Catholic. Books on the subject of this anti-Catholic thought are legion. Two historians, John Higham, *Strangers in the Land* (New York: Atheneum Press, 1963) and Ray Allen Billington, *The Protestant Crusade* (New York: Rinehart, 1952), have stated that Catholics have been the object of the most continuous and pervasive prejudice in American history. Andrew Greeley, *An Ugly Little Secret, Anti-Catholicism in North America* (Kansas City: Sheed Andres and McMell, 1977) has recently continued the theme with his impressive statistical data from the National Opinion Research Center.
14. Specifically, 305 jokes were collected for this research. They were grouped into six categories and there was doubt about the limits of such a small grouping. What is represented in this discussion is the most pervasive of the jokelore related to the Catholic, i.e. the clergy.
15. Seems to be related to Type 1824, The Parody Sermon, in A. A. Aarne, *The Types of the Folktale*, 2nd revision (trans. and enl. by Stith Thompson) (1961).
16. Both jokes are located in the Folklore Archive, Southern Illinois University at Edwardsville. Informant for 'The First Sermon' was a woman, 39, Catholic, housewife, mother of four children, 'American' as her description of her nationality stated. There was mention of its circulation around Anheuser-Busch Brewery and Monsanto Chemical Company among office workers. The writer collected it a number of times in fieldwork, with slight variations and little annotation.

17. Comments often made by informants during fieldwork.
18. Arthur Koestler, *The Act of Creation, A Study of the Conscious and Unconscious in Science and Art* (New York: Dell, 1964) refers to this form of laughter when he discusses incongruity as occurring from 'two mutually incompatible codes or associative contexts which explodes the tension'. (p. 35).
19. Gary Wills, *Bare Ruined Choirs: Doubt, Prophecy and Radical Religion* (Garden City, New York: Doubleday, 1975) considers such topics. Stanley Brandes, 'The Priest as Agent of Secularization in Rural Spain', in Edwards C. Hansen, Joseph B. Aceves, and Gloria Levitas (eds) *Economic Transformation and Steady-State Values: Essays in the Ethnography of Spain*, (New York: Queens College Press, 1976) through his fieldwork in Spain shows the ways in which the priest has affected the 'Little Tradition' of the Spaniards and their Catholicism.
20. Walter Zenner, 'Joking and Ethnic Stereotyping', *Anthropological Quarterly*, vol. XLIII (1970) pp. 93–113, considers the ethnic joke as a strengthening factor which often acts as a catharsis and safety-valve.
21. Alan Dundes, 'The Hero Pattern and the Life of Jesus', in Dundes, *Essays in Folkloristics*, pp. 223–62, considers this but does not directly state such a notion.
22. Carol A. Mitchell, 'The Sexual Perspective in the Appreciation and Interpretation of Jokes', *Western Folklore*, vol. XXXVI, no. 4 (October 1977) pp. 303–30, discusses a variant of the same joke but applies it to the perspective of appreciation by both or either sex. Her interpretation is not applied to Catholics' appreciation of it as a religious joke.
23. Koestler, p. 72.
24. Greeley, *The American Catholic*, discusses his theory of the incompetency of the American hierarchy throughout his work.
25. Billington, *The Protestant Crusade*, discusses this aspect of prejudice in his consideration of nineteenth-century literature, especially in his accounts of the work of Maria Monk, who was, supposedly, a nun, duped by priests, sexually abused by priests and who herself observed priests in sexual encounters with each other. The book was a fake but very successful in flaming the fires of anti-Catholicism. Jokes about the clergy and nuns in similar poses exist to this day.
26. Collected from a Roman Catholic priest, aged 37, during a conversation, 1975.
27. Koestler, p. 64.
28. Donald C. Simmons, 'Protest Humor: Folkloristic Reaction to Prejudice', *American Journal of Psychiatry*, vol. CXX (1963) p. 567. Simmons believes that some ethnic groups have created situations and/or jokes purposely to preserve ego-identity. Having collected this specific joke from a priest, the writer might apply this theory specifically.
29. Collected from a man, aged 28, non-Catholic, construction worker, East Alton, IL, 1977.
30. Collected from a man, aged 21, non-Catholic, salesman, Bethalto, IL, 1976.

31.   It is worthy to note, psychoanalytically, that the joke takes place in an airplane. Almost every variant collected has the same setting – different dialogue, but the identical setting – flying in an airplane! Such an act of flying has been interpreted as a symbol of sexual intercourse. If this premise is accepted, the priest has, at least in this joke, whose setting seldom varies, vicarious sexual gratification. Martha Wolfenstein, *Children's Humor, A Psychological Analysis* (Bloomington: University of Indiana Press, 1954), uses this idea of flying in relation to moron jokes. She credits Freud with the original conception and discusses his work with dreams of flying. Note, too, the best-selling novel by Erica Jong, *Fear of Flying* (New York: Holt, 1973) which is a direct symbol of the act of sexual intercourse.

32.   Collected from male, aged 26, non-Catholic, computer operator, Alton, IL, 1974.

33.   Collected from female, aged 22, Catholic, student, Belleville, IL, 1978.

34.   Greeley, *The American Catholic*, summarises many of these accounts and lists others in a bibliography. The young, conservative, Catholic writers advocate a stricter adherence to Catholic doctrine and often decry the presence of 'novelty' in the manner of the 'folk' Mass.

35.   Collected from a non-Catholic who thought the joke was in the proper but not popular perspective ('For a certain price, you do a certain amount of sinning'), aged 21, Berkeley, CA.

36.   Collected from a Catholic priest, aged 40, a member of the Paulist order, Berkeley, CA, 1981.

37.   Sigmund Freud, *Jokes and Their Relation to the Unconscious*, James Strachey (translator and ed.) (New York: W. W. Norton, 1960) uses this term to refer to the joke as being both funny and purposeful – a serious intent, that is, in addition to the humour.

5 A Phenomenological Analysis of Humour in Society

Chris Powell

If it is indeed the case that sociologists have paid less attention than is warranted to the topic of humour, we need to attempt to suggest some possible channels for exploration of its social import. One of the more interesting points to be made is that many sociologists have made quite suggestive and indeed often telling comments on humour *en passant*. The most obvious examples are writings on 'minority' or 'subordinated' groups which allude to the use of humour as an irritating, albeit comparatively benign, element of more heavy-handed control apparatuses. Examples would include Henley[1] (discussing women) and Plummer[2] (gays) as well as others referred to in this volume. So a few authors have clearly thought humour worthy of at least an aside comment on the way to dealing with more 'serious' matters. To redress the imbalance accorded to the serious discussion of humour, this chapter will challenge the question of low priorities (which, of course, in a sense merely reflects the marginalised status of the subject) initially by reference to the famous 'Lodger Experiment' of Harold Garfinkel.[3]

To briefly remind the reader, one of Garfinkel's concerns was to establish the strategies by which people constitute 'sense' and 'meaning' in their everyday lives. One 'aid to the sluggish imagination', as he puts it, is to ask people to behave 'inappropriately' in any given social context or situation. With the 'Lodger Experiment', Garfinkel requested that his students should adopt the role of 'boarder' in their parental homes and to perceive and record their families reactions. In general terms, Garfinkel attempts to illustrate the relative ease with which 'social disruption' can be established and thereby (on one level at least) suggests that 'normal social relations' are rather tenuously balanced. The experiments imply that behaviour which is, on the surface, fundamentally unthreatening (indeed in context is quite the reverse) is, because of role and context

86

'inappropriateness', experienced by social actors as problematic, even deeply disturbing.

Garfinkel's students received sufficient clues and cues from their subject relations to declare that their behaviour had clearly been interpreted as being untoward, out of place, inappropriate, abnormal or wrong. Their cues were communicated by expressions of astonishment, bewilderment, shock, anxiety, embarrassment and anger. So behaviour incurred an initial reaction which was clearly related to the definition the subject placed upon it. Garfinkel stresses that such reactions represent attempts to 'normalise' the 'problem', which can range from the 'tentative' to the 'definitive'. It is axiomatic for Garfinkel, of course, that no behaviour is irretrievable – we always make sense of everything – even if we have to work harder at it some times than at others.

So, clearly, Garfinkel's subjects perceived in Lemert's term 'primary deviation'[4] which necessarily linked with varying degrees of negative reaction. In turn negative reactions gave rise to the attempt to obtain confirmation from the 'deviant' as to the 'correct' definition. These rapidly produced, but logically organised, accounts were made discernible mainly by verbal queries or statements. By such mechanisms the 'initiating deviant' is given grounds to recognise the 'nature' of his or her behaviour. Garfinkel's 'pseudo-lodgers' were harangued in the pursuit of explanations which, of course, are never required when communication is defined as 'on the level'. People demanded: 'What's the matter? What's gotten into you? Are you sick? Why are you mad?' etc. Student failure to accept these accounts, expressed by querying the very assumption of 'untowardness' the accounts were generated by, served to exacerbate the relatives' sense of perplexity, in itself generating increasingly negative and desperate accounts formulated to re-establish if not 'order' then at least 'meaning'. Indeed Garfinkel gives us the distinct impression that 'meaning' in one important sense should be equated with 'order'.

What is especially interesting about all this is the form of interpretation and account Garfinkel recounts, and the discernible order of stages in which different accounts are presented. How in fact 'retrieval' takes place. Garfinkel places most emphasis on what could be termed 'formal' negative definitions and members' pursuit of 'explanation' couched in such terms. However, (and this is significant for our discussion of humour) he refers to two 'unsuccessful' cases (Garfinkel's quotes) where 'the family treated it as a joke from the beginning and refused to change'. Of presumably 'successful' cases

Garfinkel later states: 'Occasionally family members *would first* [emphasis added] treat the student's action as a cue for a joint comedy routine which was soon replaced by irritation and exasperated anger at the student for not knowing when enough was enough'. I assume that 'enough' refers to a combination of both behaviour and time. I want to suggest then, that an anomalous, strange or untoward event, idea or cultural expression is often initially defined as 'funny'. The converse of this is that a 'humour response' is likely when a social role of some kind is perceived as having been infracted. The point here is that in *general terms* we can speak of a kind of progression or graduation in terms of the way *individuals* attempt to make sense of the ostensibly 'senseless' or 'nonsense'.

The present research has concentrated exclusively on the 'micro situation'. At this level the typology shown in Table 5.1 is offered as a basis for analysis and for further discussion later in this chapter. It must be stressed however, that the general trend of the process and reaction described is not limited to this level but can, and should, be regarded as applicable at all levels of analysis.

To take Table 5.1 a stage further the typology shown in Table 5.2 is offered which extends Table 5.1 in the direction of the society or state.

Now Garfinkel's objective was to emphasis how the audience of an 'expression event' makes sense and order of it. Two further aspects

Table 5.1   Rule Breaking and Individual Reaction

Perceived 'primary deviance'		Interpretation or account	Reaction
A	Yes	Not seen as threatening; the 'meaning' not considered	Ignore
B	Yes	No direct threat; 'meaning' considered; evaluation 'not serious'	Humour
C	Yes	Greater threat; 'meaning' considered; evaluation 'serious and unintentional'	Crazy
D	Yes	Greater threat; 'meaning' considered; evaluation 'serious and intentional'	Evil

can be presented. Firstly, the commonplace recognition that one person's 'order' equals another person's 'control': 'order' indeed *is* control. Besides reconstituting control in terms of one's own consciousness about the way things really are, there is inevitably a significant dialectical and interpersonal aspect. In other words, any given response represents an interpretation of someone else's expression which effectively constitutes a social control. This is perhaps a rather wide-ranging definition of 'control' but is nevertheless one considered quite justifiable.

We can examine Table 5.2 to elucidate these questions of 'perceived rule breaking', 'societal reaction' and 'control'. Initially, it is quite clear that different social groups are differentially equipped in respect of their ability to promote or to resist different strategies and definitions in concrete social situations. If we assume 'perceived primary deviance' let us explore the options open in terms of reaction and control. Superficially, it seems clear that one option is always to ignore the 'expression event'. Commonsensically as well as sociologically it seems reasonable to say that this option is invariably adopted when the 'broken rule' appears of negligible significance and the reactor is relatively unthreatened. In social terms the communications implication is that X's expression (or indeed X her/himself) is undeserving of a more elaborated response. The art of ignoring then constitutes a mild and informal (though invariably unpleasant for the recipient) form of control, whereby X and any wider social audience are made aware of Y's disapproval. Implicitly X is invited to take account of Y's negative assessment, to reflect or re-evaluate his/her expression, or at least to self-censor in future encounters. Any wider audience is invited to share Y's definition and to reject X's expression or X.

The option to ignore is theoretically open to reactors of both super and subordinate statuses. However, various people have identified this as a viable strategy for the powerless. 'Dumb insolence' has been read correctly as a resistance device, for instance, amongst pupils in schools, inmates in prison, etc. It is persuasive to read in this micro-power light, as well as in the more pragmatic one, police interrogator attempts to deny suspects the formal 'right of silence'. It is, however, important to point out that such resistance strategies on behalf of the powerless is not without its dangers. The suspect's silence may well incur, for example, physical violence. An even more everyday example might be the case of the irritating boss who demands a response to his sexist or racist comment, and who can apply a wide

Table 5.2 Rule Breaking and Social Reaction

Social actor or group (X's) ideas, behaviour or cultural expressions perceived as anomalous	Social actor or group (Y's) interpretation of X's ideas, behaviour or cultural expressions	Y's categorisation of reaction to X's ideas, behaviour or cultural expressions (= reaction to X)	Sociological implications of event and reaction	Power variables in the viability of options	The social organisation of control
A Yes	No significant perception of social threat. The meaning of X's expression is not addressed	Ignores	Control: mild and informal (Y communicates to X and possibly, a wider social audience the 'nature' of X's expression)	Super and subordinates	(a) Interpersonal group (b) State ISA
B Yes	No significant perception of personal or social threat. X's meaning is defined as (a) not serious or (b) impervious to change	Humour	Control: mild, informal/formal (If formal focussed symbolically)	Super and subordinates	(a) Interpersonal group (b) State ISA
C Yes	A perception of personal or social threat. X's meaning is addressed: defined as 'unintentional'. A temporary problem?	Drunk/drugged	Control: variable, informal/formal (Y may engage state intervention)	Super and subordinates. (super monopoly of the formal)	(a) Interpersonal group (b) State ISA
D Yes	A perception of personal or social threat. X's meaning is addressed: defined as 'unintentional'. A long-term problem?	Ill: physical/mental	Control: variable/harsher informal/formal. (Y may engage state intervention)	Super and subordinates (super monopoly of the formal)	(a) Interpersonal group (b) State ISA RSA
E Yes	A perception of personal or social threat. X's meaning addressed: defined as 'intentional'.	Evil	Control: harsher informal/formal. (Y may engage state intervention)	Super and subordinates. (super monopoly of the formal)	(a) Interpersonal group (b) State RSA ISA

Key: ISA = Ideological State Apparatus   RSA = Repressive State Apparatus

variety of sanctions (including 'humour') when none is forthcoming. The point is that communication, even in the guise of non-communication, overwhelmingly takes place on the terms of the powerful. It is they who can in practice monopolise speech or withhold it; they who can demand speech or silence from subordinates. The act of ignoring is a viable control option for all sectors of society, but more so for the powerful.

Two, perhaps connected, social descriptions commonly utilised in order to make sense of untoward actions or expressions are those of 'drunk' and 'drugged'. These are invoked where Y feels threatened and also when X is perceived as not really in control of him or herself. 'Evidence' in the form of 'past history' or specific pieces of apparatus clearly reinforces the viability of these definitions. The 'problem' is hopefully temporary and will dissipate in time. The rupture with 'normal' behaviour and ideas does not require further investigation – it has been both depoliticised and diminished. An informal response to the 'problem' is to isolate the 'deviant', if possible, until he or she is 'back to normal'. This can be achieved in serious cases by the intervention of a state agency in the shape of a police officer and a night in the cells. In 'extreme' cases the successful application of the 'alcoholic' or 'addict' label may result in removal of the individual concerned into a 'drying out' centre or clinic, under the care of medical staff. Although the use of the categorisations is open to all sections of society, the most powerful groups are better located to formalise them and to institute proceedings on such bases. A fairly obvious example would be the response in the Soviet Union, where alcoholism is recognised as perhaps the primary social problem. Certainly alcohol abuse has been indicted as the major cause of property violations. Apparently no sober person could engage in theft in a socialist society as the theft would really be from oneself! Nor is such ideological mystification and manipulation restricted to the Soviet Union. The Social Democratic Scandinavian states maintain startlingly similar perspectives. In Finland, for instance, the Alcohol Research Institute was actually established before the Criminology Institute, and even today is far better funded. Increasingly (most notably in Denmark) drug abuse provides the explanation for unacceptable social performance.

A further resource available in the reservoir of meaning for dealing with untoward communications or expressions would be categories such as 'crazy', 'mad' or 'insane'. These definitions are usually applied in situations in which X's 'provoking act' is experienced by the reactor Y as in some way threatening. The threat can contain a variety of nuances. It can be a direct, personal physical

threat. It can also be a communication breakdown in which Y experiences the feeling that X is behaving in a way that seems to locate him or her outside what is assumed to be a commonsense social universe. Such might constitute a threat to Y's own consciousness in that one's own ability to function 'rationally' in the 'real world' is temporarily placed in jeopardy. It is also likely that Y may see X as constituting a danger to him or herself – in other words that X's own ability to function in the world becomes questionable or doubtful. X's action is interpreted as being unintentional, beyond his or her control. The implication of this, of course, is that again X is not responsible for his or her action and thus is ineligible for formal sanctioning or punishing. Logically and morally one can only countenance punishing 'the guilty'. Once more, the application of the 'crazy' label, in formal terms at least, depoliticises the event by denying it a meaningful status. Associated with this logic is the belief that X's problem (which is also, perhaps more so, benign Y's!) is probably not something that will just go away on its own, but which may require, or at least 'benefit from', some kind of outside professional intervention. However, defining an individual's or social group's activities as 'crazy' is one thing, 'doing something about it' is quite another. The key variable once more in terms of the definition of the situation and the implementation of a 'solution' is that of social power.

R. D. Laing,[5] amongst others, has illustrated that the relatively powerless in any given social situation are those most vulnerable to the 'insane' categorisation. Many feminist[6] writers observe that women seem especially eligible for this treatment. Conversely, attempts by the relatively powerless person or group to define a 'superior's' activities as 'insane' are less likely to bear fruit than to cast doubt on that body's own personal or collective mental stability. Often those who wish to politicise issues not conventionally acknowledged as 'political' use 'insane' labels and definitions. In so doing they imply that the powerful are not really in control, although they believe often that their control is all too real. Examples might include the 'insane' counterproductive character of the penal system, the 'insanity' of nuclear proliferation or of 'wine lakes' and 'butter mountains'. The powerful then attempt to re-establish a clear non-political definition by reference to the obvious insanity of those questioning the 'normal' and the 'inevitable'. At the micro, as contrasted with the macro level, in the final analysis state agencies can intervene with or without the acquiescence of X, to do something about him or her. This control debate is conducted in terms of medical and psychiatric discourse or rhetoric. The culminating

location of the actual control is the mental institution and its practitioners – doctors and psychiatrists. This combination can be conceptualised (see Table 5.2) as an ideological state apparatus (ISA) and (where treatment is enforced) probably as a repressive state apparatus (RSA). The same holds true for the drink and drug combinations.

Perhaps the most obvious (and certainly most openly acknowledged) definition in terms of accepting the notion of 'control' is that of 'evil'. 'Evil' is used to describe the 'seriously threatening' and the 'intentional'. Evil is usually temporarily stabilised in public consciousness in terms of those practices which are seen to infringe criminal law, although it is now relatively uncontentious to assert the negotiated (if not the enforced) character of such law. Clearly again, some groups and individuals are much more capable of (a) institutionalising their definitions of evil as criminal; and (b) of mobilising formal agencies of social control (the army, police, the judiciary and prison staff) to act against the perpetrators of such evil. Such agencies and the locations they inhabit (barracks, police stations, courts and prisons) can be seen as repressive state apparatuses which also function with a powerful ideological element.

Finally, to turn to 'humour'. A humour response is often resorted to where there is no significant perception of personal or social threat. The object or agent instigating humour is defined as either being 'not serious' or as 'impervious to change'. Thus sociologically the communication of a humorous reaction serves as a mild control which can be exercised either informally (in response to specific concrete contemporary people and their behaviour) or formally (in response to symbolic representations of people and behaviours). The first is invoked totally informally in the interpersonal situation where no one is constituted as, or takes on board, the status of 'a comic turn'. The latter refers to activity taking place in a defined humorous context whether it be a joke-telling session amongst friends, a stand-up comic in a working men's club or a TV situation comedy. At the informal levels, and those activities which can be regarded as orientated towards and experienced by a limited and fairly specific audience, humour can either be conceptualised as elucidating group norms or negotiating and maintaining group, i.e. shared, notions of reality. At the more macro and formalised mass media level, humour is more to do with some ideas concerning over-all social values and 'normal views' of reality. Mass media humour is orientated towards an idea of a lowest common denominator of core social values and what are perceived as challenges to such values. Humour can be utilised (as by definition a benign response) against symbolic enemies

whose concrete form requires a rather harsher response. A radical trade union leader thus can inspire vituperation and calls for legal sanctions in popular press editorials and ridicule in the cartoons, but clearly both are attempts at control, both of the individual and perhaps rather more importantly, of public opinion.

It should be apparent that the above typology is merely that. Many instances of perceived rule breaking can be defined differently by different social audiences, or differently by the 'same' audience at different times. Although there may be some implication of a limited kind of gradation in relating the various definitions to perceptions of 'seriousness' (and ultimately perhaps 'intentionality' is a factor in allocating seriousness), the primary point here is that the definitions can merge, and other definitions be resorted to or reverted to. In other words, definitions are constantly in the process of negotiation. Nothing is static except perhaps the over-all strategy of social control. The tactics, though, are almost infinitely variable, at least theoretically. In practice, of course, the 'goodies' available in the control bag are most effectively consumed by those with most hands!

These points are perhaps strengthened by further consideration of the examples used above. Thus Plummer[7] has argued that most of these resources for denying valid meaning to homosexual activities and relationships have been used. Feminist[8] demands are similarly invalidated through all these devices, as indeed are most emerging political demands. Often, of course, the control strategies are contradictory. One illustration of this may be found in courtroom situations where there is no disagreement as to the defendant having perpetrated the act of which he or she has been accused, nor indeed of the act being unacceptable. The argument simply takes place in terms of the defendant's responsibility and the event's 'seriousness'. The prosecution invariably aims to procure via negotiation a definition of responsibility and seriousness; the defence the opposite. The latter argues perhaps, that the offence is so innocuous that it should be overlooked or virtually ignored. This, of course, has always possibly been an option for a police officer at an earlier stage. The defendant and his representatives may argue in terms of what Matza[9] calls 'techniques of neutralisation'. Responsibility may be denied or diminished in terms of the undue influence of drugs or drink, or by the accused's mental incompetence. In the contemporary court scene, humour is generally restricted to a means of accomplishing another definition by counsels. This is a phenomenon, generated in and through conflict, regularly recognised by TV

situation comedy writers.[10] Once more humour is always a possible option of conclusive management for a police officer on the streets. So different social audiences can elect different definitions at the same time. Some historical examples also suggest that strategies of control can sometimes merge, the stocks and the *charivari* being instances of where humour in its ridicule guise can be seen as part of a quasi-formal punishment.

For evidence of how the 'same' social audience can apply different definitions at different times to ostensibly the 'same' phenomenon, it is pertinent to consider the ways in which the mass media in Britain dealt with the rule of Idi Amin in Uganda. It is important to point out that Idi Amin's coup in 1971 initially received a favourable response from the overwhelming majority of Western commentators. Milton Obote's plans for nationalisation did not accord with Western politico–economic interests and Amin was portrayed as a 'genial giant'[11] with no political ambitions. It is in fact quite clear that abundant evidence already existed to strongly question this image. Amin had been involved in a massacre in the Congo five years previously and his background was rife with stories of violence and brutality. Over-all, his period in power is best read in terms of a relative continuum of violence rather than an especially steady amplification. In the immediate aftermath of the coup, East African sources were recounting stories of atrocities especially in respect of the Langi and Acholi tribes. The British press ignored these events.

Generally the encouragement or the promotion of ignorance is always an option to controllers at all social levels. At the state level one can cite recent efforts to suppress publicity concerning 'riots' in black townships in South Africa or, at the organisational level, Merseyside Police attempts to do a similar thing in Toxteth. One month after the coup in Uganda the *Daily Telegraph*[12] proclaimed:

> From Africa one commonsense voice has come through loud and clear. It is that of General (now President) Amin. He ... advised other African leaders rather to solve their own domestic problems than to concentrate their attention on South Africa.

By July 1971, after six well-documented months of Amin atrocity, the Ugandan leader visited Britain. The *Daily Mirror*[13] described him as 'a thoroughly nice man', 'as gentle as a lamb'. As Britain was implicated in Amin's accession to power,[14] such reactions are perhaps not entirely surprising. Indeed, the British government was

the first to recognise the new president. The decision to ignore in this context is thus less to do with the isolation and marginalisation of Amin (i.e. the control of him) as with the control of wider public awareness as to what the West generally was condoning.

Gradually, however, it became impossible to ignore negative events in Uganda, although which events were really negative from the point of view of the British media and state definers is questionable. What is clear is that Amin's rule became 'problematic' and his activities demanded explanation. It was over a year after his visit that such became the case. An initial effort was made to define Amin away in terms of his being an eccentric or a bit of a joke. Racist stereotypes were used denoting him as an egocentric black clown.[15] Whilst constituting a real threat only to his fellow countrymen, he was initially only an embarrassment to Western governments, governments which after all have not always been fastidious in defence of human rights in Third World nations, especially where the profitability of Western companies might be placed in some jeopardy. Whilst Amin had assumed power and received British military supplies, Western states were supporting the heavily repressive Shah's regime in Iran. The Shah never found himself defined negatively in the Western press. During the same period the United States, particularly, was heavily implicated in the coup replacing the elected Allende government in Chile by Pinochet's dictatorship, and other examples are too numerous to mention.

Amin's somewhat blatant, rather too 'over the top', behaviour was a mild embarrassment, then, but not in the earlier period a threat. It can be argued that the clown 'Big Daddy' definition of Amin required some renegotiation when Western interests became threatened. Amin's posturing was underpinned by his Africanisation policies which led to the flight of Asian refugees, mainly to Britain and Canada. This policy was unpopular with many underprivileged white working-class people but not quite so to the leader-writer of the *Daily Telegraph*[16] who felt the immigrants 'might be useful to the British economy'. Woodrow Wyatt in the *Daily Mirror*[17] commented that the Asians would help to give 'moderate and sensible leadership to the existing Indian and Pakistani communities'. Amin can be considered (as perhaps can most black people in the British media) as less than fully adult. The *Daily Telegraph*,[18] regretting a government decision to keep open an interest-free loan to Uganda, declared for example that 'Britain should take a tougher line until he behaves himself'. A general tension and ambivalence over Uganda was

articulated by slightly more negative definitions in which Amin was declared 'crazily unpredictable',[19] and causes of his craziness were sought. The following week the *Daily Mirror* offered: 'Suggestions that President Amin is going mad may be a little harsh – but he may be suffering from punch-drunkenness'.[20] The article went on to refer to Amin's not-too-successful amateur boxing career.

'Craziness' became a fully established definition of Amin when it became clear that his Africanisation policies were going to directly affect Western interests, with suggestions that 85 per cent of British-owned businesses were to be taken over. The professionally qualified Harold Wilson, for example, is quoted in the *Daily Telegraph* as calling Amin a 'mentally unbalanced paranoiac'.[21] Amin is variously described as having 'an addled mind', being 'an hysteric', 'being in a dream world'. By mid-September 1972 the *Daily Telegraph* felt the need to renegotiate again: Amin 'could be dismissed as a comic opera figure were it not that . . .'. The *Daily Telegraph* shared the view of its ideological ally Julius Nyerere of Tanzania (who they had earlier condemned for his meddling in South African affairs) in calling Amin 'irrational and dangerous', although of course Nyerere had been asserting just that for almost two years. Furthermore the International Commission of Jurists had provided clear evidence for 80 000 murders having taken place in this period.

By late 1972, the Western media consistently reported atrocity cases from Uganda accompanied by increasingly negative definitions of Amin. All the control mechanisms discussed above were used. The *Daily Mirror* declared: 'Amin is not just the dangerous joker he has been considered'. He was recast as 'the power mad, ruthless dictator of Uganda, an irresponsible thug and barbaric despot'. The *Daily Mail* fell into line: 'Idi Amin is not Africa's Harry Secombe'. The *Mirror* once more: 'Not long ago Idi Amin was regarded to as a genial fat giant. Amin has turned out to be a barbaric despot.' From then until his overthrow, general 'joke' and 'crazy' accounts of Amin were boosted at specific periods by an outright simple assessment of him as the personification of evil. The obvious instances of the unequivocal condemnation are the murder of Dora Block, the imprisonment of Dennis Hills, the murder of Archbishop Lunum and the student massacre at Makerere University. Thus 'valuable victims' pushed the media over into the use of terms and phrases such as 'thug', 'an outrage to standards of human decency', 'Black Hitler', 'brutal dictator', 'tyrant'. Cartoons (especially a series in the *Daily Mail*) equated Amin with Hitler. 'Insane' definitions included:

'General Amin is a madman', 'perverted mind', 'in the unstable mind of a man like Amin there can be no way of knowing where peasant propaganda ends and paranoid obsession takes over', 'this deranged megalomaniac', 'egocentric hysteric'. In 1975 the *Daily Telegraph* laid it on the line: 'his entertainment value has worn thin, his comments are piffle, really not funny'. But still the cartoons kept coming.

What had caused the problem? Take your pick. Amin was under 'physical and mental strain'. It was suggested that he was a victim of hereditary venereal disease. It was claimed that drugs used to mitigate the symptoms of the disease were affecting his mind. Some of his worst excesses were put down to excessively heavy drinking bouts. Psychiatrists better qualified than Harold Wilson were sought who would state confidently that Amin was mentally ill and suffering from (again according to which psychiatrist you listened to) paranoia, schizophrenia or manic depression. Simple old evil though, reinforced by 'big black devil' mythology, was never eliminated from the accounts.

The case of Idi Amin is an excellent example of the development and career of negative definitions and their ability to perform control functions side by side. Humour was exceptionally important in establishing a basis for the utilisation of harsher definitions framed in terms of the archetype of the clown and continued to perform a very important role. Finally, the case demonstrates that reactions are not so much in terms of enormity of social offence as rather more mundane sectional interests which can latch morally on to the loftier banner, humour being employed as a social control device in the service of what is believed to be a universally shared and superior social morality.

The title of this book is *Humour in Society: Resistance and Control*. Logically it should seem necessary to clearly define these terms. First, it is clearly suggested here that all human communication can be read as control moves. Stedman-Jones's[22] observation that such a wide-ranging definition of 'control' renders it analytically useless is noted, but not accepted, for it can in fact sharpen and clarify social analysis. Radicals are too easily lulled into the belief that 'control' refers exclusively to the practices of 'the powerful'. 'Control' in this usage seems overly deterministic, hierarchial, totalistic and pessimistic. All social activities in all social institutions, all aspects of public and 'private' life pull and suck successful subordinates materially and ideologically further into the clutches of

their oppressors. Conversely 'resistance' refers to the practices of the powerless struggling to release themselves from the yoke of control. Radicals of different traditions tend to stress 'control' or 'resistance' as the para-explanation of social existence. In one sense the distinction between the two exists in radical circles, at least, so that an audience can easily differentiate the virtuous practices from the pernicious. 'Control' is a bad thing; 'resistance' good. Conservative thinkers, of course, reverse the value positions. The overt agencies of 'social control' (which includes a far narrower range of institutions) are to be approved of; 'resistance movements' (again a narrow range of social groupings) are to be repressed.

Sociologically, in phenomenological terms, it might make sense to dissolve 'control' and 'resistance' together – to recognise that irrespective of social location life consists of organising experience in such a way that our sense of it makes us feel comfortable in balancing these two social forces. This is a helpful collapse because it perhaps enables us to deal more adequately with interactions and encounters not only between sub- and superordinated groups, but also within them. The ultimate control is, in fact, the view we hold of social reality and our understanding of our own and other people's place within it, including our resistance to the actions and beliefs of others we dislike and repudiate. Life consists essentially of constantly negotiating our understandings with other people, establishing and maintaining by social controls and resistances our own virtue and those of our kind (although in their case not quite as much!) and the immorality and irrationality of others.

It can be suggested that humour plays a fundamental role in these negotiations. As such it can be seen as the baseline of social control, an initial defining mechanism which clarifies and differentiates for the users the 'normal' from the 'abnormal' or socially deviant. In some important senses humour can be equated with intelligence tests. To get the joke and to respond appropriately demonstrates one's social competence, one's grip over and understanding of the way things are. Not to get it threatens shared meanings and jeopardises one's social position. The point, of course, is that as with formal intelligence tests, what is really in the process of assessment is congruence with highly context-bound social assumptions, rather than with any absolute intelligence or sense of humour. Commonly many people feel so socially pressurised that they respond to 'the joke' even when they do not actually get it – and this is especially so in the case of subordinates in respect of superordinates' jokes.

Furthermore, differentials of power may impel subordinates to go along with the joke even when they understand but disagree with its direction, especially when directed at themselves! Invariably what is reinforced through this form of humour, and rarely challenged, is a dominant ideological position. One could go further and assert that, in any given society, humour is a control resource operating both in formal and informal contexts to the advantage of powerful groups and role-players.

It is not too problematic to claim that formal institutionalised mass-media humour is usually 'conservative'. It would indeed be unfathomable if this were not the case. Orwell's[23] optimistic observation that 'every joke is a tiny revolution' seems hopelessly naive. Formalised humour will generally fulfil an ideological function in supporting and maintaining existing social relations and dominant ways of perceiving social reality. Its great danger lies in its everyday, neutral 'non-serious' apparent character. Most situation comedies are based on events which 'everyone knows' are infractions of some code; the same is true of comedy routines. There is always a target be it actual or symbolic. Clearly by orientating humour against a specific target a general boundary maintenance function is also being performed. In other words, control is being operationalised upon the ideas, the actions or, importantly, the incipient ideas and actions of a wider social audience. A specific object of a joke can be equated or allied with a specific target of the criminal law. Not only this object is being controlled, but also those who would be or do as he or she appears to be or do. In simple terms, humour operates to set apart and invalidate the behaviour and ideas of those 'not like us' by creating and sustaining stereotypes and often projecting the practices of others to a presumed 'logical' but of course 'absurd' conclusion. What is achieved is a simultaneous bisociation of social integration and division.

This dialectical process also occurs in a so-called democratic structure in which hierarchical divisions are not formally recognised or which have theoretically been set aside. This is most apparent where, perhaps temporarily, group aims are similar but their wider ideologies are different. An example can be drawn from a period in the mid- to late-1970s of an anti-racist 'umbrella' organisation. The particular group observed was reasonably representative of others in operation at that time. The people came together (at least ostensibly) for a common purpose – the elimination of racism, or at least the more glaring expressions of racist activity. As such they had

to relate to and with each other and formulate agreed policies. However, the membership was by definition comprised of people with quite distinctive world views, in this case ranging very widely across the political spectrum and including people with an extensive variety of religious beliefs. Whilst the 'cause' had to be advanced, so too did sectarian purity, simply because this was crucial to people's identity. Humour was the standard mechanism of tension management whereby a sub-section's view of itself and the world could be marked and lauded in an apparently playful manner which did not too severely threaten the wider group. A less systematic observation of CND meetings leads to the conclusion that here, too, such practices are in operation. In such situations humour functions as a 'fish gum' rather than a 'super glue'.

What of humour as a 'tiny revolution', as a subordinate's control strategy or resistance? In respect of formal institutionalised humour, this author generally supports the view Trevor Griffiths[24] takes in his excellent play *Comedians*. To survive and prosper as a comedian or as a comedy writer within the structures of institutionalised humour seems to require an ideologically 'neutral' (that is for all practical purposes 'conservative') stance. Such is clearly not to deny that formal humour, especially in the form of satire, can be mildly subversive or be perceived as subversive. Colin Seymour-Ure's[25] article on *Private Eye* is an interesting discussion of the former. Equating the *Eye* with earlier court jesters, he argues that both can be identified as 'licensed fools'. As such both are, in the final analysis, functional for their respective 'establishments' in that their very continued existence proclaims the openness and the liberality of those establishments. *Private Eye* restricts its 'critique' to an exposure of the foibles or corruption of individual members of the social elites rather than the corruption of the elite *per se*. The same possibly holds true of all satire shows ever to have been shown on British television. The function can be compared with that of a liberal commentator who bemoans the 'one rotten apple' in any given profession or institution and thereby sanitizes the profession or institution as a whole. At its most challenging it merely renders the over-all institution's 'ideal' representation of itself as problematic, suggesting that it is comprised of individuals as fallibly human as exist in society as a whole. The 'reduction' is thus from 'idealisation' to 'normalisation' – when 'normal' equals the 'inevitable' rather than the 'conventional'. In the final analysis this is comforting rather than disturbing to the wider social audience.

Having said this, it is nevertheless clear that on several occasions humour has been recognised by members of the elite as threatening key social values or institutions. The obvious example is the BBC's removal of *That Was The Week That Was*. Any establishment's liberalness in respect of cultural expression slips in periods of wider political, economic or ideological crisis, and sensitivities are more rigorously defended. As Lukacs[26] points out, it is at such points that conspiracy theories may make some sense. The establishment in question has to come together and assert its integrity in the face of a wider threat. What is really going on in such 'censorship' situations is that the humour definition is quite simply no longer acceptable to the 'censoring powers'. The phenomenon in question is 'serious' to them – too 'sacred' to be 'profaned' in humour! The clown's custard pies are experienced as bricks. The phenomenon in fact is negotiated in and out of different statuses, from comic to crazy to evil and back again until it eventually (but always really temporarily) settles and a world view is rearticulated.

Such a process takes place in both formal and informal contexts.[27] Despite the appropriate 'cueing', the attempts made to 'frame' the piece of communication as 'humour' by a particular actor have seemingly failed. Most of the time these cues (which may take linguistic, paralinguistic or musical form) are successful. This is especially so for those sectors of society with 'credibility', that is those having formal power or those recognised as 'comics'. The humour cues insist that we switch from or suspend our engagement in everyday life; what happens next is not to be taken too seriously. As such the cues are exercises in mystification. Problems emerge when some audiences or sections of an audience refuse to accept such a suspension. In such cases the ultimate defence (and it is a very strong one) of the humorist is simply to assert incredulously 'I wasn't serious' or 'It's only a joke'. This indicts the disbeliever or critic with the lack of a sense of humour implying that he or she is 'over-sensitive' and therefore not quite a normal human being. If successful this strategy, however, can doubly legitimise the original joke. Such defences are concerned with the mitigation of social hostility or tension via the re-establishment of a joke framework. Idi Amin, it could be said, tried quite hard to foster his image as an essentially amiable buffoon.

Clearly different sections of society are differentially equipped with sociolinguistic skills for carrying off such negotiations and renegotiations. People telling sexist or racist jokes in a sexist or racist society

are highly likely to be able to defend their definitions. On the other hand school children telling jokes at the expense of their teachers are quite susceptible to having their joke redefined and established as 'insolence'. Thus, for the powerless, humour, as with everything else, constitutes generally hostile terrain, Coser[28] demonstrating that most 'successful' joking is directed downwards. The problem for the powerless is that all too often it is the only terrain in everyday life on which they can compete with or resist the social controls of the powerful, as raising the stakes is highly likely to culminate in a worse situation. Sexual harassment, for example, for most women is simply usually more safely handled in a joke framework than by resorting to physical retaliation. As is so often the case in other spheres of existence, the temporary, and very rational, expedient inhibits the likelihood of real social change. In terms of such 'resistance' perhaps it could be argued that humour might have 'consciousness raising' potential in terms of social integration and division, but perhaps ultimately it is a 'resigned' expression and 'cheerful' demonstration of the subordinate's very weakness.

The implication of this kind of presentation is, of course, that it totally rejects the possibility (some might say sidesteps the necessity) of providing anything other than a fairly primitive and operational definition of what 'humour' is. There is cause for suspicion of absolutist positions which purport to provide definitive accounts that 'A' equals humour and the joke is 'X'. The connections made in the typology earlier demonstrate a close affinity with the stalwarts of 'labelling approaches' to the study of deviance, Becker,[29] Lemert[30] and Erikson.[31] It would be possible to paraphrase and slightly corrupt any of these authors' well-known observations on deviance and use them to represent the views on humour expressed in this chapter. Thus *à la* Becker: 'The humorous is that to which the label has successfully been applied; humorous behaviour (or communication) is behaviour that people so label.' Or: 'It is the audience which eventually determines whether or not an episode of behaviour or class of episodes is labelled humorous.' Just as 'deviance' can be divided into sub-categories (murder, homosexuality, etc.) which are also in the final analysis beyond essentialist definition, so too is the case with 'humorous' sub-categories of jokes, slapstick, satire, etc. The collapsing of these things has a logic.

This stress on and assumptions concerning the autonomy of the 'social definition' corresponds to the 'uses and gratifications' media theory. People may or may not accept any given joke definition or

joking framework. They may accept a joke definition and respond 'appropriately', but the meaning of the joke to communicator and receiver need not correspond. We 'read' different targets and different rules according to our own values and world view. Is Chaplin's 'Modern Times' a comment on 'incompetent labour', 'soulless automation', or something else entirely? The classic writers on humour, Hobbes,[32] Bergson[33] and Freud,[34] all provide valuable insights but all seem far too absolutist. Nevertheless, there is some value in trying to somehow align the 'uses and gratifications' model with a hegemonic model appropriate to the sociological study of humour, whether employed in social control or resistance. It seems quite reasonable to accept that, to use Stuart Hall's[35] term, there are probably 'preferred meanings'. Such constitute ideologically prescribed patterns into which most of us most of the time, and all of us in our unguarded moments, fit new experiences and communications, not least humorous ones.

This chapter represents a personal eclectic approach to sociology and humour for which no apologies are necessary. Despite the theoretical problems there has been an attempt to demonstrate that it is important to both delineate phenomenology's concern with the negotiation of social reality and to link this to the structuralist concern with the social contexts and structures within which these interpersonal practices – in our case humour as both resistance and control – take place.

NOTES

1.   N. Henley, *Body Politics* (Englewood Cliffs, NJ: Prentice-Hall, 1977).
2.   K. Plummer, *Sexual Stigma* (London: Routledge and Kegan Paul, 1975).
3.   H. Garfinkel, *Studies in Ethnomethodology* (Englewood Cliffs, NJ: Prentice-Hall, 1967).
4.   E. Lemert, *Human Deviance, Social Problems and Social Control* (Englewood Cliffs, NJ: Prentice-Hall, 1967).
5.   R. D. Laing, *The Divided Self* (Harmondsworth: Penguin, 1960).
6.   See, for example, C. Smart, *Women, Crime and Criminology: A Feminist Critique* (London: Routledge and Kegan Paul, 1977).
7.   Plummer, *Sexual Stigma*.
8.   See, for example, D. Spender, *Women of Ideas* (London: Routledge and Kegan Paul, 1983).

9. D. Matza, *Delinquency and Drift* (New York: John Wiley, 1964).
10. See, for example, 'Brothers in Law' and 'Rumpole of the Bailey' which were popular sitcoms on British Television (both BBC) in the early 1960s and late 1970s/early 1980s, respectively.
11. *Daily Mirror*, 26 January 1971.
12. *Daily Telegraph*, 24 February 1971.
13. *Daily Mirror*, 15 July 1971.
14. M. Mamdani, 'Class Struggles in Uganda', *Review of African Political Economy*, vol. 4 (1975) pp. 26–61.
15. *Daily Mail*, 20 August 1972.
16. *Daily Telegraph*, 16 August 1972.
17. *Daily Mirror*, 25 August 1972.
18. *Daily Telegraph*, 29 August 1972.
19. *Daily Mirror*, 30 August 1972.
20. *Daily Mirror*, 4 September 1972.
21. *Daily Telegraph*, 7 September 1972.
22. G. Stedman-Jones, *Languages of Class: Studies in English Working Class History 1832–1982* (Cambridge: Cambridge University Press, 1983).
23. G. Orwell, *The Collected Essays, Journalism and Letters of George Orwell. Vol. 3 As I Please*, edited by S. Orwell and I. Angus (London: Secker and Warburg, 1968).
24. T. Griffiths, *Comedians* (London: Faber, 1976).
25. C. Seymour-Ure, *The Political Impact of the Mass Media* (London: Constable, 1974).
26. G. Lukacs, *History and Class Consciousness* (London: Merlin Press, 1971).
27. M. Douglas, 'The Social Control of Cognition: Some Factors in Joke Perception', *Man*, vol. 3 (1968) pp. 361–76.
28. R. Coser, 'Laughter among Colleagues', *Psychiatry*, vol. 23 (1960) pp. 81–95.
29. H. Becker, *Outsiders* (New York: Free Press, 1963).
30. Lemert, *Human Deviance*.
31. K. Erikson, *Wayward Puritans* (New York: John Wiley, 1966).
32. T. Hobbes, *Leviathan* (London: Fontana, 1962).
33. H. Bergson, *Laughter: An Essay on the Meaning of the Comic* (New York: Macmillan, 1911).
34. S. Freud, 'Wit and its Relation to the Unconscious', in *The Standard Edition of the Complete Psychological Works of Sigmund Freud*, vol. 8 (London: Hogarth Press, 1960).
35. S. Hall, 'Culture, the Media and the Ideological Effect', in J. Curran *et al.* (eds) *Mass Communication and Society* (London: Edward Arnold, 1977).

6 Blue Jokes: Humour in Police Work

Simon Holdaway

The description and analysis of the occupational world of the lower ranks has become a major theme of sociological research on the police (Chatterton, 1979; Holdaway, 1983; Manning, 1977; Policy Studies Institute 1983). Researchers have now begun to chart an ethnographic map of routine police work, mostly of patrol duties in the inner city, paying particular attention to officers' perceptions of the area where they work, of the task of policing and of the population they serve. Some scholars have gone beyond a description and analysis of perceptions to document police actions – the strategies and tactics that officers routinely employ. This complex contouring of beliefs, values and attitudes and their associated actions, which officers regard as 'commonsense', is conceptualised as 'the occupational culture' of the lower police ranks.

Importantly, many studies of the occupational culture stress how the public imagery of the British police, with its formal appearance of rationality, bureaucratic rigour and professionalism, shields a rather different reality (Manning, 1977; Cain, 1973). The lower-ranked officers, particularly constables and sergeants, adapt formal policy and law to reinforce their understanding of effective police work; to reinforce the 'commonsense', which may be rather different from the perspective of their senior officers, from people working in related institutions like the courts and social work, and from large sections of the public. It is therefore argued that police work is not what the law, formal policy or some other set of directives says it should be: policing *is* essentially what the lower ranks do in their day-to-day work on the streets and in police stations. To understand police work it is necessary to probe beneath the public imagery gleaned from formal and from popular accounts to observe and participate in policing-in-action.

In urban Britain, the lower ranks continue to place emphasis on work which pulsates with action, offers an appealing and continuing hedonism, and which is principally concerned with crime. Officers certainly use the law but in so doing they act with discretion, which

106

involves the use of rules lodged in their knowledge of the occupational culture. These occupational rules are often in tension with statutes and/or the disciplinary regulations of the service. For the lower ranks, policing therefore involves the preservation of a sure measure of secrecy, of interdependency between and of teamwork amongst colleagues.

This 'practical policing' of the lower ranks is clearly in conflict with the highly disciplined and formal models of police work which are readily presented for public consumption (Holdaway, 1977). The tensions arising from the conflict between what the lower ranks are supposed to, and on occasion say they do, and what they actually do requires the creation and sustenance of a protective structure to strengthen their culture. This structure shields them from police managers, lawyers, social workers and other people who, at certain times, have a legal right and duty to monitor police practices. Maurice Punch (1979a, p. 28) in his study of an urban force, describes one of the central problems facing research into the police:

> The core explanation has to be focussed on how the norms and practices of the police organisation, the police occupational culture, and police work create a powerful, informal system, protected by solidarity, secrecy, and astute accounting procedures, that deviates considerably from the rational administrative model and from the public image of unity, respectability, and responsibility presented to the outside world.

A related issue refers us not so much to how the rank-and-file protect themselves from scrutiny but to their affirmation and sustenance of the occupational culture itself. The lower ranks' commonsense world of action and hedonism, of crime work and of impending disorder is partial. Other researched evidence confirms that police work is quiet, spasmodic, and largely concerned with incidents that are not directly related to crime; policing involves a vast diversity of tasks carried out in a setting of comparative calm (Morris and Heal (1981) summarise this work). Police perceptions of their work and the social environment within which they perform it are highly selective; yet the occupational culture remains the primary resource for a working knowledge of how to deal with the pot-pourri of incidents which require a police presence. The traditions of policing 'live' within the occupational culture, as partial a view of police work as that culture happens to present.

This chapter takes its departure from the view that policing is socially constructed, which is to accept that the occupational culture of the lower ranks departs so dramatically from the actual conditions of police work that a wide range of supportive devices are needed to maintain it. The question for the researcher is therefore to ask *how* the world of policing is routinely sustained from day to day. Attention will be given to just one aspect of an answer to this question – to story-telling which is often humorous in content and style, and to joking. The concern here is with just one of a range of controls and techniques of management employed by the lower ranks to sustain a semblance of what they regard as normal policing. The narratives which form the basis of the analysis cluster around a number of the central themes of the police occupational culture. These are the teamwork character of police work; the designation of distinct roles adopted by members of the police team; and the creation of policing as an exciting, fast-moving activity.

The illustrative data used are taken from a covert, participant–observer study of policing on a British urban police sub-division, named Hilton (Holdaway, 1983). This study, which involved two years' research during the course of the author's work as a police sergeant, was an attempt to detail and analyse the occupational culture of the lower ranks. One aspect of this broadly based project was a consideration of the role joking and story-telling plays in the traditions of policing.

STORY-TELLING AND HUMOUR: THE USE OF NARRATIVE

When studying the police, researchers have tended to neglect the function of narratives and joke-telling within the occupational culture. In some studies the frequency of these forms of communication is mentioned but no analysis of particular narratives can be found (see, for example, Policy Studies Institute, 1983). Of course, sociologists researching other settings have concerned themselves with story-telling and jokes, arguing that these phenomena perform a number of social functions. The release of tension within and between groups, self-aggrandisement, easing the process of socialisation for a newcomer to a group, the creation of consensus and the relief of boredom are cited by researchers (Coser, 1959, 1960; Roy, 1960; Zijderveld, 1968). A considerable amount of academic work

into the social functions of humour therefore suggests the pertinence of relating the use of narrative to the tensions and contradictions experienced by the members of work and other organisations.

Most helpfully, Mary Douglas (1975, pp. 90–114) suggests that jokes, with no less application to other forms of verbal communication like narratives, contain two elements. First, a control on human behaviour is juxtaposed with that which is controlled. Secondly, the juxtaposition is such that the behaviour which is potentially controlled triumphs. In relation to the police, humour is therefore a device which mediates between different levels of organisational structure. Humour and narrative expose the underlying reality of the occupational culture which, as we have noted, differs sharply from the public image of police work. Narrative expresses the adaptations by the rank-and-file to formal and potentially constraining structures; adaptations to force policy, to the law and so on. Further, Mary Douglas argues that humour confirms the importance and dominance, indeed, the supremacy of the adaptation over and against the constraints of the formal structure. She writes, 'Whatever the joke, however remote its subject, the telling of it is potentially subversive. Since its form consists of a victorious telling of uncontrol against control, it is an image of the levelling of hierarchy, the triumph of intimacy over formality, of unofficial values over official ones.' (p. 98).

From this perspective, it is clear that the extensive use of humorous narrative and jokes, so common to the police, may be related to conflicts between the values, beliefs and attitudes found in the occupational culture and to those of the formal police organisation as they are framed by senior officers, by the law and by other possible sources of constraint. When police officers tell stories to each other they are engaged in maintaining their definition of policing as *the* practical, commonsense way of performing the task of police work. This so-called practical definition is compared with and triumphs over other definitions from police policy, the law, the courts and people who can legally constrain the practices of the rank-and-file.

To an 'outsider' who is not familiar with the nuances of meaning which pervade police action, many of the humorous narratives and jokes re-told in this chapter will not seem funny. Once a researcher, however, has cracked the veneer of the occupational culture and is able to place them within their social context they will be appreciated and open to analysis. As the various themes of narrative and of the

jokes to be discussed are classified, it should be noted that exaggeration, dramatic inflection, a lack of factual accuracy and very probably untruth enters into them. The immediate context of story-telling is usually lighthearted. However, the scenes observed and documented are not settings where sociability takes place for its own sake; narratives and jokes sustain the occupational culture in an intense fashion. In these contexts, the lower ranks share their apprehensions about others' views about policing which can and, in part, do threaten their manner of work. These gatherings are crucial to the work group because, as the anthropologist Ulf Hannertz (1969, p. 111) points out with reference to 'mythmaking' in urban America:

> definitions and evaluations of self, others and the external world are developed, maintained and displayed with greater intensity than in other interactions ... An individual's vision of reality is often a precarious thing: we can find comfort in the knowledge that it is shared by others, thus acquiring social anchoring in an objective truth.

TEAMWORK

Officers employed together on a shift form a working team. Of course, some police work requires the coordination of various tasks for its satisfactory completion, which is but one aspect of policing as teamwork. A firmer emphasis, however, should be placed on the social relationships between officers which mould them into an interdependent team. (Goffman, 1968; Manning, 1977). Teamwork in this sense requires a disciplined and loyal membership; the unity of officers has to be assured and retained. Commitment to a team is not secured easily; teams of police officers are invariably tenuous groups whose structure is always likely to fragment. The fact of team membership, the social relationships that bind members together into an interdependent group which includes supervisory and rank-and-file staff, and the risks of breaching team discipline are all the subject of humorous narratives.

First, some humorous narratives that concern the fact of team membership and the initiation of recruits into membership are presented. With his audience gathered for the regular night duty tea break at 4.30 a.m., a constable related this narrative about a PC who

had recently arrived at Hilton and was required to manoeuvre a bicycle around an obstacle course set out in the station yard.

We told him it was a test to see if he could ride a cycle in the force. We awarded him a certificate, 'Cyclists Union of National Transport' and down the side of the certificate were letters, C,U,N,T, in Gothic lettering. He showed it to his father, who was an ex-Chief Superintendent who realised it and didn't think it was so funny.

Drawing much laughter and satisfaction from colleagues, this nugget set the scene for further narratives, including one about a constable who was required to complete a rather different bicycle test. He had to ride up a ramp towards a window and negotiate various obstacles. 'Bicycle stories' provided an entrée for further description of how this same officer was told that some suspects were in a park, on an island in the middle of a lake. He went to the park and the lake, being told to run through the water to the island – which he did! Several other narratives followed and the sequence ended with one about a wayward PC who was told to check the Belisha beacons in the road outside the station, ensuring that they were flashing in the proper sequence. If out of sequence, the offending lamps were to be identified and their serial number, printed on the underside of the bulb, was to be recorded. This meant that the officer tried to clamber up the pole of the beacon, watched from the station by the rest of the shift.

These narratives, drawing delight from the officers listening to them, are entertaining in their own right; they also stress that the recruit is the member of a team. The bizarre 'tests' officers planned for recruits are a reminder of the power of colleagues, their interdependence with each other that follows from such a source of power and, therefore, their team membership. Laughter and appreciation is invoked by these narratives, as the centrality of the rank-and-file work group within the police organisation is affirmed.

The interdependency of the work team extends across the various ranks. Mutual support is expected as when a sergeant risked disciplinary proceedings for inadequate supervision of a constable guarding a suspect in a hospital, the constable being similarly prone to discipline. The prisoner had apparently asked to go to the toilet and then escaped from the officer guarding him by climbing out of a toilet window and then down a drainpipe. When reported, the

escape was explained by the constable and corroborated by his sergeant in rather different terms. They suggested that the constable gave chase but slipped on a wet floor, which had been recently cleaned. This incident was recounted by an officer when the PC and sergeant involved were listening, together with an inspector and two other constables. One of the PCs commented:

> 'He let him go, he lost him. We told a lot of lies about that, didn't we, Sarge? I mean, to get you off. I was supervising traffic points at the time.' All the officers laughed or smiled.

Here, the interdependency of the ranks is emphasised. 'I was supervising traffic points at the time' means 'I was doing other necessary work at the time', and the obligation of secrecy, necessary to protect the officers concerned, triumphs over the acknowledged but secondary obligation to honour discipline regulations in this case.

Team discipline was also invoked when some aspect of the occupational culture might become apparent to a member of the public.

> Several police cars arrived at the scene of a call to a suspected break-in. The informant who lived near to the relevant premises was present. Several cars, including the inspector's vehicle, were at the scene and the incident was investigated. After a time, Hilton's R/T car arrived and one of the officers present shouted in a jocular manner, 'Last again, last again'. Laughter followed but the inspector quickly interjected, 'Keep quiet, keep quiet'.

Laughter prompted by the officer's comment points to the occupational features of hedonism and action. However, by exposing these values of their culture to public view, the officers breach team-rules and the inspector intervenes to prevent trouble.

THE RELIEF: ROLES AND RANK

Although teamwork, interdependency and secrecy are maintained by the lower ranks and deemed central to their culture, tensions which are sometimes expressed openly and sometimes left latent are found amongst any group of officers who work together regularly (Reed *et al.*, 1977). For example, some of Hilton's staff are not firmly

committed to the ploys used by a number of their colleagues when suspects are interviewed. Other constables are not so much dissenters as likely to extend the limits of acceptable behaviour set by the work group. The excesses and dissent of colleagues is one regular subject of humour and narrative. Broad themes of these often-humorous narratives concern the existence and importance of a cohesive work group; the boundaries of tolerance set by that group; the centrality and supremacy of the core of the occupational culture within the organisational hierarchy; and its place in the continuing traditions of police work.

A probationer constable who did not use force when arresting prisoners, was generally rather restrained when dealing with people held in custody, and not tuned to the speed and hedonism so important to his colleagues, was the subject of comment when the shift met for a tea break:

PC: 'There's something wrong with _____ tonight, you know. There's definitely something wrong with him. He told somebody to "fuck off" today. Then we had this "suspect shout" and he's running along beside this bloke he knows, asking him when he's going out for a drink and there could have been this PC getting his head kicked in some way down the road. There's something wrong with _____.'

On another occasion and in the presence of colleagues, a sergeant commented on this constable's style of work:

'Have you been beating up prisoners, then?' Another officer said, 'Yes, he has. I wouldn't mind so long as he didn't leave them paralysed in the corner of the detention room. Do you know what he [the prisoner] did to _____ [officer]? He pulled his tie off. Just flicked it off when he went to speak to him.' Other sergeant: 'Didn't that annoy you ...?' PC: 'Not really, Sarge.' PS: 'Well, don't hit him then.'

The officers who comment here draw a humorous response from colleagues. Their affirmation of the occupational culture, particularly of interdependence between colleagues and the use of force on 'prisoners' is an attempt to integrate the young constable into the dominant culture.

Directed to an audience of police officers who work together, the

comments relate the individual actions of a constable to the collective experience and expectations of the team. The dominance of the occupational culture is being affirmed as particular incidents and a particular individual are related to more generally based expectations of work, which are shared and accepted amongst the group.

Humour is also used to attempt to control the behaviour of an extremely excitable officer who rushes to the scene of any incident and displays a flair for provoking aggressive encounters with members of the public. He has a habit of using his personal radio to 'speak-through' to colleagues, asking them to stop vehicles he has seen speeding in one direction or another and which he suspects are stolen. One excited request from him suggests that a suspected stolen car will have to be chased before it stops. Drawing laughter which is heard over the whole radio system, another PC interjects, 'Is this a real chase or a John chase?' Limits of acceptable behaviour are being charted by this humorous comment; the role of the officer in question is being defined – points further clarified in the following data.

The shift are gathered for a tea break, PCs, sergeants and the inspector are beginning to tell stories, when a constable directs his entrée to the inspector in charge of the shift:

> You weren't here when it happened but it's the funniest thing I've heard. Old _____ was sitting on the pan out there one night duty when he heard a chase coming down _____ [road in which station is situated]. So he hoists his trousers up and the next thing we see he's standing in the High Road with his truncheon in his hand holding his trousers with his other hand. The car hadn't come down _____, it had turned off somewhere. When we asked him, he said, 'Well, I thought they were going to come down here and I was going to throw my stick at the windscreen'. He had his shirt on, no epaulettes, his trousers weren't done up and his shirt tails were flapping and he had his stick in his hand. He was ready to throw the stick at the car.

This narrative clarifies the officer's role amongst his group of colleagues; others can compare their style of work and acceptance of the traditions of the occupational culture with his exuberance. Boundaries of tolerance are marked out, prescribing limits of acceptable behaviour. The traditions of the occupational culture are being stated and sustained.

Similar points of analysis can be made about humorous comment

directed towards other officers. A constable who is prone to the frequent, highly exaggerated telling of stories is 'sent up' with equal frequency because he is so immersed in the excesses of the occupational culture that he almost discredits it. Here, as he begins a story about a car chase, ready to lace his account with lavish drama of danger and speed, a colleague interjects: 'Tell us about it, Bill. Dangerous I bet. Great chase, eh?' Another officer who has a reputation for driving at very fast speeds whatever the nature of the incident he is heading for, is subject to similar remarks, which always draw laughter from colleagues. This PC has just returned from a call to premises where suspects might have been attempting to enter illegally. Inspector: 'No "Suspects On" then?' PC: 'No.' Other PC: 'Your imagination then?' Inspector: 'But he was there first.'

Graffiti is another medium used to circumscribe unacceptable behaviour and to make the traditions of the occupational culture public knowledge. A constable who has developed a reputation for using excessive violence on suspects becomes the subject of a cartoon drawn on a toilet door. The cartoon portrays the officer with a swastika on his forehead; his name and the words, 'Obturbanfurer _____ is a wanker. Ya Vohl' are printed above the picture. Other captions are added as time goes on. A gun is drawn in one of the PC's hands and a truncheon in the other. The caption, 'Did you say that kid stole some sweeties? Let me sort him out' is added.

In these various ways, officers are made the subject of humour and narrative; work roles are clarified, deviance is prescribed and the boundaries of tolerance etched into the working experience of Hilton's officers. Actions which are formally forbidden because they break discipline regulations and possibly the law are momentarily exposed within an acceptable form of communication and social context. The occupational culture is affirmed and sustained as a dominant and primary source of tradition.

Although the supervisory ranks are integral to the police team, some humour and stories also stress the hierarchy of rank, not least when misdemeanours committed by officers holding managerial rank are exposed. This was clear in the account of the prisoner who escaped from his hospital bed. By drawing attention to the behaviour of sergeants and inspectors, PCs are stating the importance of interdependency between ranks. If supervisors discipline or criticise them for their own shortcomings, they have some inside knowledge of their superiors' behaviour which can be used to embarrass them should the occasion arise. A constable asks an inspector, 'Would you

get me a [take-away] meal, sir?' Inspector: 'I see.' PC: 'I'm always getting them for you, sir.' When another constable uses the personal radio network to ask a sergeant to go to a particular address he replies that he was some distance from Hilton sub-division: 'No, I'm off at _____ [place name] at the moment. Get somebody else to do it.' The PC then asks a question on behalf of another constable who has heard the conversation: '_____ wants to know what you are doing at _____.' Sergeant: 'I want to know what _____ [PC] is doing in the station? He can go and check the premises.' When a new sergeant arrives at Hilton and is seen patrolling with another sergeant who has a reputation for 'verballing' (the 'adjustment' or creation of false statements of admission attributed to suspects), a constable asks this latter officer, 'Are you patrolling with the new sergeant? Teaching him to bend the evidence?' 'Sergeant _____ the swifter. Teaching him to give bent evidence.'

Of course, there are times when senior officers try to enforce discipline regulations and in the police there are regulations to control virtually any behaviour. Clear attempts by senior officers to discipline and therefore to challenge their subordinates can find their way into the corpus of tradition about the latent interdependency of all and, indeed, the particular power of the lower ranks. A Hilton officer often reminded his colleagues of a senior officer who had tried to discipline him for wearing a scarf under his uniform mackintosh, which regulations did not allow. His story stressed his refusal to stop wearing the scarf and that he obtained a doctor's note which stated clearly that he had to wear the scarf for medical reasons. The senior officer was defeated and a sense of triumph forms the central theme. As Mary Douglas has argued, in jokes, but here also in a less tightly structured formulation, humorous narratives express the control by subordinates of other potential sources of control.

A similar theme is found in the following story:

PC: 'Wouldn't it be nice to see him going over a red light just after he had retired?' Colleague: 'Or before he had retired.' PC: 'I was in a bank up _____ on one occasion and we had a Superintendent _____ here. He had left the job but he came into the bank and yours truly was standing at the counter. He told me that he hoped he wouldn't be here too long because he had his car outside on a yellow line. I said, "Look, guv'nor, your car is on a yellow line there and you'll get a ticket no bother." So he's straight out of the bank and moving it.'

During a quiet Sunday afternoon tour of duty, several officers share stories about the challenge lower ranks return to senior officers when attempts are made to control them. A constable draws on his experience of working at another station, telling a story about a sergeant who has retired from the force and refused to move out of his police house. Senior officers try to make him leave, but he continues to resist their requests, waiting for the local council to evict him. The story of this crafty challenge to senior officers not only stresses that the officer is eventually rehoused by the council but also that a senior officer's directive has been resisted to the benefit of the lower-ranking sergeant. This narrative is followed by another about an officer who has recently retired from the force and is suspected of an offence. Senior officers interview and ask him to go to the station with them. He refuses, arguing that if they want him at the station they will have to arrest him. Insufficient evidence is available to make an arrest on suspicion and the senior staff, tail between legs, have to abandon their enquiry.

The challenge lower-ranked officers make to their senior officers are clearly stated in these humorous narratives; in other data it is clear that peers who might taint the occupational tradition by their inappropriate behaviour of one kind or another are similarly subject to potential control. The central theme being played out in these comments and narratives is the dominance of the rank-and-file definition of police work. As stories are told, personal experience is often related to the corpus of collective tradition. The lower ranks' interdependent, team-like character of police work is exposed and juxtaposed to the formal organisational model of policing. As the lower ranks' definition triumphs so, day by day, the occupational culture is richly sustained.

ACTION, SPEED AND EXCITEMENT

Long periods of quiet, interspersed with incidents of various kinds, typifies the time-scale of routine police work. Around 40 to 50 per cent of all requests for assistance made to the police have no direct relevance to the investigation of crime or to the detection of criminal offenders (Punch, 1979a). Most police work is reactive, a response to a request for help from a member of the public (Bottomley and Coleman, 1981). This mundane reality is at odds with the idea of the

fast-moving, action-packed occupation which is central to the occupational tradition.

It is interesting that one of the favourite times for story-telling is the 4 a.m. tea break, when few requests for police assistance are likely to be made by the public. It is not uncommon for stories which emphasise action to be told at this quiet hour. These narratives generate an expectation of police work which pulsates with action, as a response to a challenge from a hostile world and as highly hedonistic. But remember that the researched evidence suggests that the speed and the sheer pleasure of action is rarely present in the 'real world of policing'; it has to be constructed and sustained within and by traditional, frequently humorous narratives.

Details of car chases are often shared and respect for the skill of 'bandit drivers' is expressed:

He was a pretty good driver and he had his wrist in plaster when he finished as well. He was pretty good. He didn't hit any cars on the way round and he didn't have any crashes at all. So he did pretty well.

'Bandit drivers' provide a sense of challenge to police action; chasing after a car that is thought to be stolen is a particularly attractive and potent experience. Indeed, a chase is of sufficient importance amongst the rank-and-file to take priority over official orders to desist from such activity. When force headquarters issue an order prohibiting all except advanced police drivers from pursuing a car, a chase takes place and forms the substance of a story.

PC: 'Oh yes, he put up a good fight.' SDH: 'Well, did he stop of his own accord?' PC: 'No, only because a couple of cars were put across the road and he didn't have much choice. Mind you, there were lots of cars there, all chasing him.' Other PC: 'Yes there were cars everywhere, Sarge. Pandas, R/T cars, everything'. PC: 'Yes, that police order really went down well.' (Laughter)

Once again, the officers' definition of policing is juxtaposed with the attempt to control made by senior officers. A humorous narrative is a format which makes the challenge explicit, as well as resolving the conflict in favour of the lower ranks. The traditions of the occupational culture are sustained.

Stories of chases are particularly ripe for embellishment; trivial

offences can be interpreted in more serious terms. For example, a few days after they arrest a number of juveniles for causing a slight disturbance in the street, which the inspector in charge of the shift regards as a serious matter but, in fact, ends without any offences being reported, officers reinterpret the trivial disturbance as an affray, which is a very serious offence. Other stories restate the tradition by stressing excitement and bravado which is typical of the past:

> Yes, you can think it's quiet but I can tell you if you were station officer on a Bank Holiday like _____ [officer] was, and you expect nothing to happen and you have eighteen prisoners by midnight, then that's how this station goes. It was an affray. _____ was the duty officer and _____ [prisoner] was in here and he'd already been pushed up against the wall by yours truly. Then Sergeant _____ walks in with a gun. It was a shotgun they'd fired into a pub. He went up to _____ and said, 'Who had the gun?' and smashed him straight round the face and the bloke went up the wall and up the ceiling. (Laughter)

After attending a potentially serious disturbance at a club which caters for black youths, officers return to Hilton and recount what has happened, stressing the danger of the situation and their bold manner of dealing with it. A dog-handler then comes into the main station office where most of the shift are gathered. His dog is carrying a large knitted hat in its mouth:

> The inspector asked, 'Is that the war trophy? Good boy.' PC: 'Yes, we brought it especially for you.' The inspector then launched into a hostile comment on how 'it is necessary to use dogs for the coloureds because they're so bloody violent and that's why you want them. I can tell you I was at _____ [scene of violent demonstration] when we had the horses and I can tell you we were really pleased to see them.' Other stories of similar incidents followed.

In this incident, which places officers in potential danger, a dramatic imagery of war is invoked. The particular account is soon transposed to more general themes of a world where a challenge to the police, speed, action and hedonism are dominant. Indeed, further data suggest that these aspects of tradition are sometimes wholly constructed by officers.

Having taken part in what a sergeant and inspector call a chase, one of them tells a story, emphasising what actually happened and includes the humorous line, 'It must have been the only chase where we slowed down to avoid overtaking.' On another occasion, two officers recall how they played a cat and mouse game, travelling back and forth along a road in pursuit of a car which they suspect is being driven by a drunken driver. One of the officers adds that his colleague simply sat in the passenger seat, enjoying the bizarre episode, making no attempt to get out of the car and stop the other vehicle. The officer who is criticised uses wry humour as he replies:

'If you're not careful, I'll tell the true story. I'll tell the truth.' I asked, 'What's this?' The police driver said, 'I'm not worried. It doesn't worry me.' His critic then ended the exchange.
'Yes, I'd watch it because I'll tell the truth.' (Laughter)

At times, humorous narrative mediates between the occupational culture and other aspects of the police organisation. In this example, the concern is a rather different one, where the particular perspective of the occupational culture – the chase and elements of excitement and action – are recognised as rather distant from the 'real events' being described. The tension between the police perception, action and the reality to which they point is exposed and healed by humour. Normal policing continues.

SUSTAINING THE REALITY OF POLICE WORK

Jokes and humorous stories are regular features of life at Hilton Police Station. Once situated within the tensions between the occupational culture, law and police policy their importance becomes clear. The tenuous character of the occupational culture, which is basically at odds with the 'real' working experience of Hilton's officers, as well as with all the potential constraints that can be placed upon their work, needs to be continually sustained and enriched. Within this social context of police work, the traditions of the occupational culture circumscribe the behaviour of errant officers, boundaries of tolerance for what is considered to be normal policing are affirmed, possible interventions into the world of the rank-and-file officer are identified and challenged. So the individual working

experience of an officer is placed within the collective tradition, being gathered up into the stock of knowledge which orients practical police work and retains for officers the semblance of commonsense. The shift of constables, sergeants and inspectors gathered together for a chat and a laugh are literally sustaining police work itself.

REFERENCES

Berger, P. L. and T. Luckman, *The Social Construction of Reality* (London: Allen Lane, Penguin Press, 1967).

Bottomley, A. K. and C. A. Coleman, *Understanding Crime Rates: Police and Public Roles in the Production of Official Statistics* (Farnborough: Gower, 1981).

Cain, M. E., *Society and the Policeman's Role* (London: Routledge and Kegan Paul, 1973).

Chatterton, M. R., 'The supervision of patrol work under the fixed points system', in S. Holdaway (ed.), *The British Police* (London: Edward Arnold, 1979) pp. 83–101.

Coser, R. L., 'Some social functions of laughter: a study of humor in a hospital setting', *Human Relations*, vol. 12 (1959) pp. 171–81.

Coser, R. L., 'Laughter among colleagues; a study of the social functions of humour among the staff of a mental hospital', *Psychiatry*, vol. 23 (1960) pp. 81–95.

Douglas, M., *Implicit Meanings; Essays in Anthropology* (London: Routledge and Kegan Paul, 1975).

Goffman, E., *Asylums: Essays on the Social Situation of Mental Patients and Other Inmates* (Harmondsworth: Penguin, 1968).

Hannertz, Ulf, *Soulside: Inquiries into Ghetto Culture and Community* (New York: Columbia, 1969).

Holdaway, S., 'Changes in urban policing', *British Journal of Sociology*, vol. 28, no. 2 (1977) pp. 119–37.

Holdaway, S., *Inside the British Police: A Force At Work* (Oxford and New York: Basil Blackwell, 1983).

Manning, P. K., *Police Work: The Social Organization of Policing* (Cambridge, Mass. and London: MIT Press, 1977).

Morris, P. and K. Heal, *Crime Control and the Police: A Review of Research*, Home Office Research Study No. 67 (London: HMSO, 1981).

Policy Studies Institute, *Police and People in London*, 4 vols (London: PSI, 1983).

Punch, M., *Policing the Inner City: A Study of Amsterdam's Warmoesstraat*, (London: Macmillan, 1979a).

Punch, M., 'The Secret Social Service', in Simon Holdaway (ed.) *The British Police* (London: Edward Arnold, 1979b).

Reed, Jr, M. S., Burnette, J. and Troiden, J. R., 'Wayward cops: the functions of deviance in groups reconsidered', *Social Problems*, vol. 24, no. 5 (1977) pp. 565–75.

Roy, D., 'Banana time: job satisfaction and informal interaction', *Human Organization*, vol. 18 (1960) pp. 156–68.

Zijderveld, A. C., 'Jokes and their relation to social reality', *Social Research*, vol. 35 (1968) pp. 286–311.

7 'Jokers Wild': Humour in Organisational Culture

Steve Linstead

Humour is a complex and paradoxical phenomenon which reflects many of the difficulties which are experienced by investigators in other areas of social life. Is it, for example, a device utilised by individuals for coping with uncertainty, exploring ambiguous situations, releasing tension or distancing unpleasantness? Or does it owe its genesis to social structures, and the contradictions and paradoxes within them? If so, does it subvert these social forms, support them or accommodate them? Does it depend on a social group for its definition *as* humour? These are some of the questions which will be addressed in the opening section of this chapter. This is followed by an analysis of two forms of humour which occurred in ELS Amalgamated Bakeries[1]: the standardised (or 'canned') joke and the situational (or 'spontaneous') joke. From this analysis it will be demonstrated that humour is complex and contradictory in its relationship to organisational cultures, but in the many functions it performs and symbolic alignments it makes possible, it is an essential and important part of organisational life.

There are special problems involved in investigating humour. We take it for granted as a natural part of social life, yet much of its effect is to question this sort of ossification in other forms of activity and life. It is quite easy to become solemn about humorous phenomena, and, in becoming self-conscious about something which is usually regarded as natural and spontaneous, to witness it evaporating before our eyes.

> Humour becomes such an integral part of the ongoing life process that recording its occurrence forces one to an unnatural degree of self-consciousness. The self-consciousness then operates to create a different mood, and humour has vanished. It is impossible to be simply spontaneous and simply thoughtful at the same time. These two states are mutually exclusive.[2]

Humour then demands the sort of 'playfulness' in the adoption of new perspectives that C. Wright Mills has argued is essential for the

wider investigation of social phenomena.[3] It also demands that the investigator, or 'reader', submit him/herself to the *jouissance*, the pleasure of the text, which Barthes recommends to us.[4] In its constant capacity to be ironic, reflexive and deconstructive of its own formative influences, humour as a style has many characteristics to be recommended to the researcher into social life. The work which exists on humour ranges across a number of disciplines including philosophy, psychology, anthropology and, more recently sociology, without any individual discipline as yet having developed a substantial corpus of research. In the summary which follows, points of convergence between individual writers and disciplines are emphasised, rather than presenting either a comprehensive survey or a coherent programme for the sociological study of humour. The following account is necessarily selective, but represents the major and most relevant themes traversing the study of humour.

HUMOUR AS A 'PLAY' FRAMEWORK

Bateson's study of otters established that 'real' action and 'playful' action, although behaviourally identical, were categorically distinct and required some metacommunicative indication to distinguish between them.[5] Goffman concentrates his attention on this 'key', or the sets of conventions which transform meaningful activity into something distinctly different and suppress its original meaning.[6] Fry identifies interrelationships between humour and play which carry the 'non-literal' capacity of the former into the latter.[7] These include the particular context of each which differentiates them from other 'forms of life' (e.g. business, grief, conflict); their sensitivity to shifts in the balance between spontaneity and thoughtfulness, which demands considerable skill in handling them; and the importance of interpersonal relationships in the context of the occurrence of humorous occasions, even where jokes are being told out of their original context. This can also be extended to a consideration of social structure.

Emerson supports Fry's view that humour presents a framework in which meanings can be offered which would not normally be offered in everyday life, and for which the individual need not be held responsible in subsequent interaction.[8] However, although the individual *activities* of play and humour are removed from their

normal, 'serious' context, humour and play as *classes of activity* still have 'serious' impact in the real world. They are of considerable importance in sustaining and establishing non-humorous or non-playing activity.

HUMOUR AS EXPLORATION

The capacity of humour to suspend the normal definitional criteria of everyday acts is most commonly exploited in testing out interpretations in uncertain or unfamiliar situations. Turner identifies uses of the 'joking mode' in the industrial sub-culture to 'test the atmosphere', to disarm accusations of failure or stupidity, and to deliver unpalatable or potentially unpalatable messages with a softened impact.[9] But as Emerson observes, the acceptability of the 'serious' content of the joke varies with each situation, and must consequently be repeatedly renegotiated.[10] Such negotiations depend on the conditions of interaction, usually beginning with a series of ambiguous gestures which test the possibility of the acceptance or rejection of a transition from humorous to serious content. This ambiguity also allows the possibility that acts may be retrospectively defined (e.g. 'I was only joking' is a typical response when a gesture has run into difficulties on a serious level). Although this ambiguous quality of humour can be exploited as a protective device until real-world ambiguity is resolved, in creating the possibility of redefinition it also involves risk. Thus any successes achieved in negotiating the status of an action may be subsequently overturned.

HUMOUR AS PERFORMING A BOUNDARY FUNCTION

Humour may not only exploit ambiguity, but may effectively remove it for all practical purposes. Davies observes that ethnic jokes clarify boundaries 'by making fun of peripheral and ambiguous groups'.[11] Such boundaries are both social and geographical (external) and moral (internal), the latter defining acceptable, characteristic and competent behaviour. Davies identifies typical characteristics of stupidity and stingy/craftiness which define categories of excluded groups for most societies. This opposition can be seen to work for other groups, as it corresponds to Gowler and Legge's

undifferentiated/differentiated axis on their model of categories of meaning.[12] *Stupid* acts are often naive, or unselfconscious, and fail to observe differentiations between both the self and the world, and meanings and contrasts which are clear to the average member of the group. *Crafty* or *stingy* acts take such differentiations to extremes, digitally defining a world without licence, ambiguity or 'lubrication' in meaning, and are extremely self-conscious in constructing social relations. A further comparison may be drawn with the work of Lacan, *stupid* behaviour arising from a failure to resolve the mirror-stage in the development of personality and to differentiate between self and other, *stingy/crafty* behaviour arising from excessive desire for the other, order and control.[13] Ethnic jokes reveal a fundamental social construction of oppositions which underpins humour itself.

HUMOUR AS A COPING DEVICE

Davies concludes his discussion of ethnic jokes by summarising their capacity to reduce anxiety over failure *vis-à-vis* large perplexing institutions, to provide moral guidance and reduce anomie, and to provide legitimation of an individual's situation in relation to others' failures or successes.[14] Turner sees humour as reducing discomfort and easing tension or frustration.[15] Fry cites authors who have identified humour functioning as a simple mitigation of failure; a redemption of unpleasant situations; a means of establishing harmony in the face of loss; and generally a means of coping with defeat.[16] It may also be a 'surrender' message which disarms an aggressor, or a reaction to a triumph over another which allows the vanquished to continue without suffering total annihilation. Fry points out that humour, particularly through smiles and laughter, can play many roles in 'peck order battles' but coping with adversity is one of the most common and significant. In a symbolic extension of this appreciation, Cohen and Taylor see humour as a means of distancing the unpleasant, predictable or boring parts of our lives from our 'real selves' by regarding them with less seriousness.[17] This capacity, however, serves also as a means of accommodating us to those parts of our lives, and of ensuring that we remain within their conventions and roles. The demystification of social interaction here is not a preliminary to social change, but a means of distancing individuals from their circumstances, allowing them to proceed with decreased commitment, emphasising other aspects of their selves.

HUMOUR AS A CHARACTERISTIC QUALITY OF SOCIAL STRUCTURE

Douglas relies on Bergson and Freud in arguing that jokes are an attack on control and organisation. For her, all jokes have a subversive effect on a dominant structure of ideas and represent a triumph of informality over the formal. In analysing humour, she suggests that we should look for 'the joke in the social structure'.[18]

Douglas further suggests that the re-ordering of the social structure produced by the joke need produce no real alternative, other than to simply suggest that any ordering of experience is arbitrary and subjective. Powell contends similarly that humour *contains* resistance as it *expresses* it,[19] and Golding notes humour working to 'rescue' myth from complete exposure.[20]

This does not reduce humour to the mere frivolity it may appear. The processes of abstraction and simplification which produce myth are *necessary* for the accomplishment of everyday life, and myth forms are so familiar and habitual that they require comparatively little work to sustain them. Conversely, to challenge them requires considerable insight, energy and creativity. Humour achieves this within its own symbolic framework of the 'non-real'. It is often the case, however, that the material relations underlying the social structure about which we symbolically joke make the potential cost of negotiating a *transposition* to the real too great to contemplate. This is not the same as saying that the challenge of humour is not 'real'; it is suggested that its framing is different.

JOKE FORMS

Douglas distinguishes between two forms of joke, the 'standardised' joke, set in a standard context which organises the whole joke within its verbal form, and the 'situational' joke which organises the situational context into joke form.[21] Fry adopts the terminology 'canned' and 'situation' or 'spontaneous', and introduces the third term of the 'practical' joke. It is the first two terms which are relevant to the examples and discussion which follow.

For Freud the essence of wit lay in the neat and economical spanning of gulfs between diffferent or alternative ideas. Fry sees the situation joke as completing a leap from one level of abstraction of

existence to another, producing a paradoxical situation where the 'portion of life which is the joke comments upon the joke which is the portion of life'. Although 'canned' jokes are often abstracted further from 'situation' jokes and are idealised and modified to reproduce a verbal format and perfect oppositions, they are never self-contained. They intervene and become part of the ongoing life process of the various situations in which they are told and re-told, and depend on this for their impact. It is in Douglas's sense, the often unconscious appreciation of the 'joke' in the social structure which makes it possible for jokes to be recognised as such. In many cases where standardised jokes do not appear in *content* to be relevant to the social interaction of which they are part, they will strike implicit chords, invoke shared experiences, and relate to underlying oppositions, contradictions and relationships which are part of wider structures informing the interaction.

At this point, it is useful to turn to two examples of the 'standardised' joke collected during participant-observation at ELS Amalgamated, a large manufacturing confectionery baker in the north of England. The author was well known to the bakery staff at the time of the research, having previously worked as a machine operator on a full-time basis before becoming a student, and had worked on all of the ten large, parallel production lines in various capacities. There were no problems in being accepted by the workforce; it was no secret that during working hours I would be mentally collecting material for a thesis but this did not affect normal interactions. I was attached to a group of machine operators in the Fruit Pie Department as one of three reserve operators trained to take over their duties, which consisted of the preparation and mixing of fruit, gel and dough for transmission from the mezzanine level to the fruit-pie machines which stood at the head of the production line on the floor below. The machine operators on the mezzanine were all male, whereas the production line was predominantly female; some were long-serving, and there was a general air of competence, confidence and cohesion about the group which was evident in its relationship with colleagues and supervisors. The examples given here were noted from memory at a convenient moment after they occurred, and are reconstructed to be as close to the form and impact of the original as possible.

The first 'joke' was originally brought to work by one of the students in a rag magazine, in the form of a cartoon, but it was subsequently retold in verbal form.

The original cartoon presented two workmen, one apparently a bricklayer laying a path, and the other his labourer. The bricklayer, kneeling beside his work, was gesturing with one arm to the labourer standing beside a pile of paving-stones.

Bricklayer: 'Slab!'

Labourer: 'Who do you think you are ... Wittgenstein?'[22]

The economy of this joke is such that any 'thoughtful' attempt at explanation might do violence to its richness. However, the joke seems to follow the pattern of a natural and common interchange between workmen. The first gives a command which is curt, impolite and offends the labourer, who may be seen as slacking or lazy, or simply waiting for instructions. The labourer responds by apparently reminding his colleague that he does not have the authority to address him in such a fashion, (possibly with the usual implication that no one does). But then the interchange turns and becomes a joke by bringing in a completely unexpected dimension in the response when the labourer says '...Wittgenstein'.

The joke exists on a number of levels. Firstly, its economy is such that it is effective though differing in one word only from the expected pattern of a normal interaction. Secondly, it is surprising that not only should the labourer be familiar with Wittgenstein but that he should imply this of his partner also. Thirdly, the implication of officiousness is made ironically by reference to a context of which officiousness was not part (i.e. the 'message' of the joke becomes, from this perspective, 'Surely you must be speaking as a linguistic philosopher playing a language game of ostensive reference, *unless* you wish to appear officious?'). This is, of course, offered reflexively, with recognition of its ambiguity. Fourth, this in turn makes possible the introduction of the dimensions of interaction and power into the original example given by Wittgenstein. Not only is the slightly unrealistic quality of the language game implied (as is also implied by Wittgenstein) but the importance of relationships of power and authority in establishing the language game in order to achieve practical accomplishments is suggested (an importance which is not emphasised by Wittgenstein). Where forms of linguistic interaction such as Wittgenstein depicts *do* occur, they tend to exist as a result of the practical demands of the job for speed, accuracy, delicacy or concentration. Thus they occur in some, but not all, instances in hospital operating theatres and garages dealing in mechanical repairs. They are, however, 'bracketed off' from normal interaction by virtue

of some comment, action or overture by the participants as being a
distinct and crucial 'phase' of operations. Another example, which
was related by a decorator, is about a group of painters and labourers
working with a limited number of tools. Not knowing to whom
exactly his request should be addressed, the painter desiring the
screwdriver would merely shout 'screwdriver' repeatedly until one
was brought or an excuse provided. That the painters were reflexively
aware of the bracketing of this procedure from normal interaction,
and its *abnormality* was illustrated by their occasional inclusion of
requests for the 'vegetable rack' or the 'bath brush'. A further layer
of irony was created on the rare occasions when the useless item was
produced.

Fifth, the richness of connotation available in the signifier, 'Slab', is
emphasised by the adoption, or offered adoption, of a most unlikely
reading; usual readings and usual forms are disrupted, and alternative formulation becomes possible. 'Slab' for both the joker and
Wittgenstein becomes ambiguous, is prised free from referential
meanings and dominant connotations. Sixth, the joke is multiply
incongruous. Jokes about philosophers are rare, as philosophy is a
serious matter. Philosophers who write about bricklaying are rare, as
is Wittgenstein's direct style of writing. That bricklaying and
philosophy are linked in the work of a philosopher, and then reversed
and linked in the work of a bricklayer constitutes the incongruity
which contributes to the joke.[23]

This analysis however takes no account of how the joke was
received and understood. Of the students who heard it, some were
able to respond in some part to some of the characteristics suggested
above, although often simply connecting the name of Wittgenstein
with the fact that they were hearing a joke produced a response. Few
knew much, if anything, about Wittgenstein's work. What cemented
the joke for them was its appositeness to *their situation*. The position
of the erudite labourer being curtly ordered around was comparable
in many ways to their own ironic position as highly intelligent, skilled
and educated people being forced to work at menial jobs and being
subject to orders from people who were less qualified and intelligent
than themselves (which is not to say that they found it unacceptable).
Many of the permanent operatives in the factory were graduates who
might otherwise have been unemployed, and they saw similar
parallels in their own situation. Even uneducated operatives, and
particularly machine operators, were able to identify with the social
situation of the joke as being apposite to their situation with what

they felt to be rude and incompetent supervision. Their conviction of their own superior competence made identification with the 'philosophical labourer' possible. Davies remarks in the context of Iron Curtain jokes about bureaucrats:

> In such circumstances the ever-present modern industrial anxiety about stupidity and failure is alleviated by projecting these qualities on to those who have obtained bureaucratic power and political success. The jokes undermine the legitimacy of the elite members' success by ascribing to them the quality of stupidity, the hall-mark of failure in a rational social order.[24]

We can detect a similar process here. As the joke became current and was told, retold and explained, officious supervisors and even other workers were referred to as 'fucking Wittgenstein' by people who had not, and would never have, the slightest idea of what Wittgenstein meant by a language game but were nevertheless able to respond to those aspects of the joke which represented the joke-in-the-social-situation, accomplished its reversal, and offered some temporary symbolic escape from orthodox control.

The second joke example is slightly more dramatic. The verbal form in which I first heard, and have since told the joke, has been altered slightly in order to translate it into its present prose format, but to preserve its impact.

> A small boy, seven or eight years old, was playing near a garage when he saw two mechanics begin welding a car. He watched and drew closer, fascinated by the blue and red sparks, the dark goggles and the huge cylinders of oxygen and acetylene. At length, the welders put down their equipment and broke for lunch. The boy watched them disappear into a nearby pub and crept inside the garage. He put on the large goggles and the industrial gloves and picked up the lance. Just as he approached the car he heard a voice.
> 'Hello there,' said the voice.
> He turned to see a man in a scruffy brown overcoat. He thought he might be in trouble but the man was smiling.
> 'Do you like sweeties?' said the man.
> 'Ye-es,' replied the boy, innocently.
> 'Do you like riding in big cars?'
> 'Ye-es.'
> 'Do you like ...,' there was a pause, '...playing with willies?'

'Oh,' said the boy, unsure. 'I don't know.'

'Well,' the man seemed breathless, 'do you like playing with bottoms?'

The boy was relieved as he realised the man's mistake.

'I'm not a *real* welder, you know,' he said.

This joke, when told verbally, is a superb example of the 'canned' joke affecting the interactional situation. It seems to walk a very thin line between the acceptable and the unacceptable, toying with ideas which threaten to transform it into an obscene or sick joke. The first of these 'threats' is that some disaster may befall the boy, leading to a sick joke; the second, at a number of levels, is that the joke may become an obscene one about masturbation, buggery, or the taboo topic of child molestation. The hearer or audience cannot see how the joke will turn out, and often are at the point of stopping the teller, anxious that the joke might embarrass them both. The only potential ending which they can see, and which they come to both expect and hope for, is that the joke will become a shaggy dog story.

In the end, they are wrong. The direction changes with wonderful economy: the joke is about welders, as has been evident all along and is the one perspective which the audience characteristically fails to adopt. The joke, interactionally is on them, and they are surprised and relieved to find it so. The joke did not overstep the limits of decency after all, and this adds to its power in that part of the joke is at the expense of the audience and they are happy for it to be so.

When the joke is told within the industrial sub-culture, (allowing that it can be identified), but especially as it was told at ELS Amalgamated, there is a social structural joke which makes it even more satisfying.

At ELS Amalgamated, as in many industrial organisations, welding was a sub-division of engineering. If it were felt to be necessary, connections could be traced back through the traditional disciplines of the smithy to establish an association between those who work with metal and magic; in this case the 'mystique' of welders and engineers could be accounted for by their material circumstances. They possessed better pay structures and rates; contractual overtime which could not easily be stopped; better facilities; better unions; visible transferable skills; often more spare time and more autonomy, and more prestige. There was also a feeling that 'fitters' had something the others had not: charisma, mystique, or simply luck, but the myth was that 'fitters get all the

crack'. If it was going, it went to the 'fitters', 'it' usually being one or more of the women who socialised with the factory workers in the pub next door. There was definitely substance to the myth, as was researched on numerous occasions.

The 'joke' consisted in the reversal of the social image of the 'fitters' as smooth he-men with enormous heterosexual charisma into that of the scruffy-coated pervert with his interest in masturbation, sodomy and small boys. That this ascription came from the mouth of an innocent, and effectively neutral, observer heightened the humour and economy of such a reversal. It was, for a moment, nice to 'get one back' over the 'fitters': for some time after the joke was current, references to 'welders' and 'welding' would raise a satisfied smile amongst the other workers.

The 'canned' or 'standardised' joke, then, owes much of its impact to its exploitation of the circumstances of interaction and social structure surrounding the context of its telling. The situational joke draws more directly upon this context, which is prominently part of the joke, as might be expected. At the deeper levels of structure, the oppositions and reversals which are the foundations for humour would seem to be similar for both types of joke.

The following example presents a situation about which humorous material was generated and jokes created. Some of the comments on the incident are not in themselves humorous, but are included as revealing interesting dimensions of the context of humorous creation.

Scenario: Fred's Finger

Fred D. was a seasoned operator of one of the large fruit-pie machines at ELS Amalgamated Bakery. Each machine requires three people to operate it, and the plant as a whole comprised two adjacent production lines making individual and family-size pies, each served by two machines making approximately 8000 and 4500 pies per hour respectively. The operator was expected to keep his machine running, liaise with the fruit and dough mixers upstairs, supervise the other two people who worked on the machine, and train any newcomers. Fred had been doing this with distinction for some years.

On one particular shift, one mixing of fruit was proving difficult for the fruit-depositing mechanism to handle. Instead of dropping measured portions of fruit into the moulded pie-bases before lidding,

it was clogging up and depositing unevenly, thus producing reject pies and extra work. In attempting to clear an obstruction, Fred, against all he knew to be good practice, inserted his hand into the unguarded mouth of the depositor and lost the tip of his middle finger. Fred collapsed, and it was a short time before anyone realised what had happened and the machine was stopped. Fred was treated, but no one could tell where his finger-end was and approximately 4000 pies, being suspected, were thrown away.

The incident stimulated much discussion and comment. Most of this was heard in a period from six weeks after the accident, when it was still a source of conversation or illustration, although it had lost some of its original currency. Informants were varied, but most of them began by saying things like:

(a)
'Don't let Fred hear this but. . .'
'Don't ever tell Fred anybody said this. . .'
'He's not here now but when he comes back don't let him find out or he would be upset.'

Another comment was:

(b)
'I can't remember 'em all now, but when it happened there were loads o'jokes about it. It sounds terrible, dun't it, but tha'd hear a new 'un every break. I wish I could remember 'em.'

Other comments included:

(c)
'God knows why he did it, it was stupid. He knew that as well as anybody. He knew that machine inside out. He knew it better than t'fitters.'
'I don't know why I did it. Just stupid I suppose.' (Fred himself).

(d)
'You don't put your hand into a machine to steal fruit. You do it to make the job run and get product out, which is what they're after. I know it wasn't safe, and he might have gone t'wrong way about it but why penalise a bloke for having t'firm's interests at heart and sacrificing his bloody finger for it?' 'They'll not give him a warning,

but he won't get any compensation unless he tries to prove negligence, like with the depositor being unguarded and that, although it doesn't really need one. But if he tries that, they'll fucking shit on him.'

(e)
'I was down by t'oven with my waste truck and there's Harry M. (Supervisor) throwing 4000 pies away 'cos they couldn't find Fred's finger and he didn't want to stop production. "Nay, Harry", I said, "there's no need to empty t'whole, oven and chuck all this lot. Have you looked for it?" "It'll do him fuck-all good now", he says, "they can't put it back on again".'

'Gerry H. (Supervisor) were great when he heard about Fred. "Fetch Quality", he says "and get me a deviation recipe for Meat and Apple".

'They were going to get some "finger hunter" stickers made and pack them 4000 pies.' [Promotion boxes usually bore a sticker marked 'Bargain Hunter'].

(f)
Operator 1: 'Fred's walking straight into a warning when he comes back.'
Operator 2: 'How's tha' mean?'
'Well, they found his finger tha' knows.'
'Did they?'
'Ay, but Health Inspector says his fingernail were dirty.' (Pause)
'Fuck off.' (Reluctant laughter). 'That's disgusting.' (More laughter).

(g)
Group of operators discussing one of their number, in his prescence, with some banter.
'He doesn't give a bugger. He doesn't care what fruit he mixes. One minute its like rock and t'next it's like piss. It was him did Fred, you know, if he hadn't stuck a load of porridge down t'hole Fred wouldn't have stuck his hand up depositor an' would still have his finger'.
(In this attempt at hyperbole the speaker has found himself saying something more than he intended. There is laughter but it is uneasy and dies quickly. It is rescued by the operator attacked).
'If I had my way, I'd chop you all to fucking bits!' (Chases others towards canteen).

It has been noted that the operators had a strong sense of identity and autonomy, and a sense of their own competence as against that of their supervisors. They felt that in a real sense they were responsible for running the plant smoothly, but that any privileges which they held depended on sticking together as a group and supporting each other where possible. 'It took us a long time to get where we are, and to learn how to work together,' was said by one operator, 'and we've had to fight for what we've got – that's why they respect us.' The operator group was accorded respect, but supervision and management had to be reminded of the strength of the group periodically, and posed a constant threat to their status and autonomy. The struggle for control was a real one in this area.

Machine operators worked on the floor below the *mixing operators* and were closer to the production process. They were dominated by the process to a greater extent and were more easily controlled, coerced or treated disrespectfully by supervisors. They were thus afforded slightly lower status than 'mixer-men', having slightly less freedom. The problem of autonomy was a key one on the plant and was emphasised by the aphorism: 'It's a long way up them stairs, but it's longer back down.' That is to say, it was difficult to become a mixer-man, but once demoted (through *incompetence*) it was even harder to regain status. Key ideas on the plant were *competence*, *solidarity*, *autonomy* and *untouchability*. This latter referred to the need for operators to cover all contingencies when exercising their autonomy, taking unauthorised breaks, etc., to make sure that the supervisors 'couldn't touch them'.

Dangers to the operator culture could be seen in displays of incompetence, lack of community, separation or isolation of individuals, or unwarranted increase in direction from outside. Operators constantly monitored these tendencies to forestall divisive interventions.

The disaster which befell Fred was potentially threatening in a substantive way as a demonstration of incompetence. However, it was also important symbolically to the operator culture.

Each culture has its own special risks and problems. To which particular body margins its beliefs attribute power depends on what situation the body is mirroring. . . . To understand body pollution we should try to argue back from the known dangers of society to the known selection of bodily themes and try to recognize what appositeness is there.[25]

The concept of 'untouchability' was isolated by Fred's action. Not only had the supervisors 'got something on him', but he had been physically and symbolically touched by the production process. There was little product-identification in the job itself, the operator having no investment of himself in his pies. The symbolic implication was that just as the *production* process would consume those who got too close to it, as Fred did, the *control* process would similarly consume the status and autonomy of those operators who failed to effectively resist it. In addition, the physical property which was a symbol of competence, the hand, had been mutilated, and Fred carried this symbolic reminder with him constantly.

A recurrent problem for the operators was boundary management, as we would expect from the work of Douglas and Davies. Not only were there the external problems of maintaining a clear idea of group membership, but there were moral problems of maintaining cohesion via correct action, making the group morally distinct from management. Fred's accident posed problems by transgressing the moral boundary of competence, but also by physically and symbolically crossing the boundary between self and production. Fred had failed to maintain his distance, his perspective and his individuality as a member of the operating group: in his zeal to boost production he had then physically become part of the process.

The first set of comments (a) came from a sensitivity to Fred's likely feelings should he hear the comments which were to follow, but also attempted to frame those comments as humorous, if unkind. However, they underline Fred's marginal status: they preface the humorous attempts to retrospectively account for Fred's action and to redeem it where possible. Fred is singled out from the community in humour in order to negotiate his reincorporation; the comments are necessary to prevent this singling out being transposed into reality and prejudicing his actual reincorporation. Not only is the concern to save Fred from being stigmatised, but it is also to lighten the threat from management, the seriousness of the accident, and to make it possible to go on.

In section (b) the proliferation of jokes suggests that the problem was important. Douglas defines the 'sick joke' as a sophisticated form of humour which 'plays with the reversal of the values of social life: the hearer is uncertain which is the man and which the machine, who is the good and who the bad, or where is the legitimate pattern of control'.[26]

Bergson would see the incorporation of Fred into the mechanical

process as providing a basis for humour anyway: the 'sick'-ness is produced partly by an insensitivity to Fred's feelings which is in part excused by the preambles offered by the jokers. The joke form in the social structure does, as Douglas again suggests, appear to call 'imperatively for an explicit joke to express it'.[27] We have already been left in confusion as to the physical boundary between man and machine; the sick joke exploits this ambiguity by resisting potential attempts to redefine those parallel moral boundaries, as the social power structure is such that they might be *morally* if not *physically* redefined by management to the workers' and operators' disadvantage. Fred is distanced from the main body of operators symbolically in humour to confine the area of moral negotiation and preserve the main structure of ideas: ambiguity is encouraged so that his status may be redefined at a more advantageous time.

In section (c) we have examples of how difficult it was for operators to explicitly account for the accident in 'real' conversation, even for Fred himself. All that were offered were clichés: that it was an isolated instance, a momentary aberration. It was as such no reflection on Fred's over-all competence, and did not call for any further unpleasant introspection. The cliché admirably fulfilled the *function* of providing an account, without that account contributing to understanding the *meaning* of the act.[28]

The quotes given in section (d) were frequent and attempted to anticipate the rationality of the situation through management eyes. The feared 'hard line' never came and the incident was not used as a lever by management. There was nevertheless a heightened sense of the ongoing paradox of the work situation – the demands of production often drove workers to work unsafely, but line management accepted no responsibility for this and was *always* potentially liable to penalise the worker formally. In some cases, workers could be verbally warned to work safely in future but the demands of production were not modified, and so compliance was impossible.

In section (e), the explicit humorous content is directed towards supervisors, whose incompetence is stressed in terms of their excessive stingy/craftiness, or over-differentiation. It might in other circumstances be interpreted as stupidity, but it is worth preserving here the separation of the concepts which Davies initiated. Not only does Harry M.'s over-differentiation lead to an over-simplified conception of the production process, but it also reveals an ideological assumption that workers do not talk in the interests of the

firm or the job, but from a narrow perspective of their own individual interests and those of their fellows.

Another observation made by Douglas could be relevant here.

> ...the Bemba have such good confidence in their technique of purification from adultery that ... though they believe adultery has lethal dangers they give reign to their short-term desires.

> Easy purification enables people to defy with impunity the hard realities of their social system.[29]

For Harry M. it did not matter that the pressures of production and its associated difficulties had caused or contributed to accident and injury; it was more important that by waste of *sacrificial proportions* he could exorcise the pollution, *keep production going*, and avoid facing up to any unpleasant reflections. In a similar way the jokes directed at Gerry H. underline the realities of purification and differentiation (stingy/craftiness) by humorous hyperbole, and favour the more 'sensible' and 'competent' perspective of the operator group.

Section (f) gives the most common of the 'sick jokes'. In addition to that which has already been observed on the preservation of moral ambiguity and the distancing of Fred until his marginal status could be reassessed, this joke plays further on the conflicting pressures of production, preferred standards of personal hygiene and competence, and the demands of bureaucracy. Sabotage is not to be treated lightly – the ironic reversal of the joke points up the 'real' fact that Fred's over-zealous pursuit of production goals has led to his committing the worst possible crime in infringement of them.

A further dimension which enriches the interpretation of the joke lies in the idea of the pie itself. Hair and fingernails have in many cultures had magical significance, being known to continue growing after death. They are both of the body and not of the body, often being felt to contain the essence or spirit of the owner when he/she is absent, and hence their incorporation in many magical charms and spells.[30] The presence of a finger in a product to be ingested by others carries a sinister implication which goes beyond the concerns simply of hygiene and humanitarianism. The idea of Jack Horner eagerly sticking in his thumb in anticipation of the delight of another plum and being sorely dismayed to find the pie was baked by Sweeney Todd is available for symbolic evocation by the joke, in

parallel to the pleasant surprise/unpleasant dismay pattern which is followed by its form.

In the final section (g) the transposition of humour into the serious happens without the transposer realising that he is doing it, and the situation is subsequently rescued by the target of the joke redefining it as humour.

The 'joking relationship', where one partner grossly insults the other is a common one.[31] In this case the divergence of the demands of job and of community is underlined by the joker in his unwitting illustration of divergent job-images.

The 'image' of Fred's job was of constant movement and flow. The machine should run when all was going well, adjustments should be small, the process should be controlled, contained and economical, expressible in units of product or numbers. He was a 'finger on the button' man when all was running well. His finger was an important symbol, indicating precision and control.

The mixer men's characteristic image was of bulk not units. When the hoppers were full, the job could run, the man was not needed. Production was in bulk, intermittently, and bulk and stasis were important images. Activity was infrequent but intense rather than constant but peripheral. These images of the total pattern of work were not always compatible and mixing operators in seeking to achieve bulk, which symbolised a job well done, might neglect to ensure that the consistency of their product was transferable to the small units and flowing production which symbolised a job well done for machine operators. The realisation that operators did often work against each other, released by the joke, left the participants in an uneasy frame of mind for some time after.

Another operator, Phil, commented on the attitude of many of the workforce to weaknesses exhibited by other members, especially the way in which lower-status members (who were more threatened by management than were operators) rounded upon its manifestation 'like vultures'. 'Never show weakness,' he said. 'I only hope nothing ever happens to me. If I lost a leg, they'd laugh for a week then follow me up t'canteen doing Long John Silver voices.'

One of the stimuli for Phil's comment was the sudden death of Harold, in his early 40s, who had operated the chocolate machine in a separate room at the back of the factory. One comment made in the canteen when it was heard that he had died of a stroke whilst on the toilet was: 'He died as he lived – boots on, trousers down.'

Phil saw the whole thing as being in ironic bad taste. He was also

able to allow that a sort of comforting familiarity with death and the trauma of it all both underlined and facilitated coping with the precariousness of one's own situation. This was even further remarked by the fact that only Harold knew how to operate the chocolate room, and it took management a very sticky month to discover how to do it, even with the aid of outside engineers, due to the variability of the process and the alterations and adjustments which had to be made in operation. This posthumous display of virtuous competence made Harold legendary, but by its remarkable and singular nature underlined the dispensability of everyone else, and their need to underscore their competence by establishing group cohesion. The joking in these circumstances was simultaneously an avoidance of the explicit realisation of this situation, and a response to it, attempting a humorous reversal to borrow or seal in some of Harold's strength and competence into the remaining community.

A number of oppositions also work in the case of Harold to add to the economy of the dualism 'boots on, trousers down'. Harold led a solitary working life and suffered a similarly solitary death. Where sex and enjoyment encroaches on the working day it tends to be snatched, postponed, or quick and functional, and hence inconsequential as an experience. Death in this pairing acquires some of this comforting inconsequentiality, with a touch of rough familiarity about its squalor. There is irony in the 'rest room' becoming the room of more a permanent rest, where even the most private of places was subject to the final intrusion. The parallel in colour and consistency between chocolate and ordure, and their associations with life and death, creativity and waste was suggested by Bob Grafton-Small, whose thoughts run on such things and who spends much of his time in a suitably similar environment. There is also the symbolic dimension of marginality, determining the status of the toilet and waste areas, where organisational control is weak and worker autonomy strong, which is further underlined by the ultimate cessation of control. Finally, as the defaecation of certain prophets is felt to be sacred by their followers, we are given the sense that Harold's simple act has produced something of far greater worth than its material composition.

SUMMARY

A number of points on the nature and importance of humour in

organisational culture have been made in the earlier discussion and illustrated by the above material.

(a) Humour is a part of the natural life process and as such it is *commonly taken for granted*, or not recognised as having serious import, especially by social investigators.

(b) This is heightened by the fact that humour is *a framework for 'non-real' or 'play' activity*, an aside from normal discourse. The fact that it need not be taken into account in subsequent 'serious' interaction does allow messages and formulations to be 'risked' within its framework which would not otherwise be acceptable or possible.

(c) Humour allows the *exploration of new ideas* in situations of uncertainty or unfamiliarity. Similarly allowed are the *negotiation of taboo topics, sensitive issues, and marginal serious content*. The possibility of the *retrospective definition of actions* as either 'serious' or 'non-serious', 'real' or 'joking' imparts an ambiguity and risk to such negotiations which can be exploited.

(d) Humour performs a *boundary function* on both internal and external lines, policing groups in terms of membership and acceptable and competence behaviour. Oppositions of extremes of deviance as either *stupid* (undifferentiated) or *stingy/crafty* (differentiated) behaviour are commonly used. The tendency is to affirm the ordinary or negotiate over the extreme or absolute, but the status of the ordinary is constantly undercut and is not established as an ideal.

(e) Humour can function as *a coping device* to release tension, allay fear, forestall threat, defuse aggression or distance the unpleasant.

(f) Humour can represent an implicit contradiction, paradox or *'joke in the social structure'* made explicit. The 'joke' constitutes a reversal within its boundaries of the patterns of control in the 'real' world. In changing this balance temporarily, it both expresses and contains resistance. It may momentarily demystify the social order, but against the forces of myth and cliché promoting unreflective inertia, sustained challenge requires enormous creativity and energy to be exerted.

(g) 'Canned' jokes and 'situational' jokes are not entirely separate. Canned jokes are not sealed from the situation in which they are told as they always affect it and incorporate interaction into their pattern; situation jokes always have some impact beyond their context. It can be seen how 'canned' jokes may be perceived as

opposite to a cultural situation and may be taken up and receive connotation and incorporation into the culture. They are used to symbolically reverse and attenuate the privileged positions of supervisors and engineers. Situational jokes have similarities with 'canned' jokes at their deep levels of structure, and the examples here demonstrate the impact of situational humour in boundary management; in moral negotiation; in resisting potential symbolic and actual redefinitions of status and control; in the exposure and realisation of paradox; in demonstrations of incompetence in others; and in achieving group solidarity. Ambiguity was seen to be used and created in order to resist the threat of loss of autonomy and control.

CONCLUSIONS

Finally, a few observations about the demystifying role of humour may be in order. As has been discussed, humour has been identified as simultaneously exposing the myths of dominant ideologies and accommodating resistance to them. Such exposure has been seen as partial or incomplete; to view humour as completely subversive fails to account for its apparent incapacity to change society, whilst to dismiss it as a mere frivolity underestimates its symbolic power.

It does seem possible, however, that the following formulation might represent an advance towards a more adequate conceptualisation of the significance of humour in culture.

(a) Humour and joking *does* expose myth completely but only within its own confining framework of the 'non-real', 'play', or the 'non-serious'.

(b) In order for a change in the social order to be achieved, the symbolic reversals of humour must be transposed to a 'real-life' framework, and actualised in a real situation.

(c) The negotiation of such transpositions is not accomplished from an equal *material* basis. Not only does habit and inertia favour the dominant *status quo*, but interests, power and capital also lend the advantage to the dominant/hegemonic code.[32] This does have considerable influence on what may be defined as humorous and serious, without being absolutely determining.

(d) Myth generally acts in favour of the dominant/hegemonic in its naturalising effect and its foreclosing of reflection and alternative formulations. But it does not do so exclusively – sub-groups and

sub-cultures can and do naturalise their own forms and possess their own myths.[33] Such oppositions can become stereotyped into formal oppositional codes. The force of humour is to disrupt and reverse the direction or deterioration of thought in such naturalisations whether dominant/hegemonic or oppositional and to produce a stimulus for them to be renegotiated in 'real-life' frames. The rules which prevent access to the derivation of myth may be safely broken within the frames of humour.[34]

(e) Such negotiation will depend on the material and interactional bases of social relations, and the extent to which the myth and its alternatives diverge. The practical accomplishment of everyday living must remain possible, as must sense-making and the symbolic ordering of its contexts. Ambiguity is important both in the sense of practical bargaining in the real-world and in the reordering of the symbolic in the non-real world. It is when ambiguity is lost and the limits and margins lose their potential as a ground for creative redefinition and negotiation that conflict occurs and resistance solidifies or evaporates.

(f) Finally, the power of humour to stimulate change should not be underestimated. The pens of Erasmus, Swift, Pope, Dickens and other great satirists and humorists bear testimony to this. The feeling that 'nothing I do is taken seriously' or 'they're all laughing at me' has proved enormously disabling for individuals and for whole governments on occasion. Books, pamphlets and TV programmes are not burned or banned for their serious content alone. Humour can have great impact in the world by having its content transposed and defined as serious, but also by transposing real-world content into the humorous frame, and defining it as humorous in an indelible and irreversible way. Its impact may be more effectively destructive in this way than through the more tortuous channels of negotiation and construction. In achieving this, and here a consideration of style would be relevant for future work in the field, it creates landmarks for other resistances and formulations which can offer potential for more substantial social change.[35]

NOTES

1. This chapter is a shortened form of part of the author's PhD thesis, 'Ambiguity in the Workplace: Some Aspects of the Negotiation and Structuration of Asymmetrical Relations', Council for National Academic Awards, Sheffield City Polytechnic, submitted in 1983. The thesis is based on participant research conducted at ELS Amalgamated Bakeries, a large manufacturer of prepared confectionary cakes and pies. I am grateful to John Gill, David Golding and Dan Gowler for helpful criticism, and most particularly to Bob Grafton-Small for a sustained critical dialogue over a period of protracted gestation.

2. William F. Fry, *Sweet Madness: A Study of Humour* (Palo Alto: Pacific Books, 1963) p. 5.

3. C. Wright Mills, *The Sociological Imagination* (London: Oxford University Press, 1959) pp. 211–12. 'The sociological imagination, I remind you, in considerable part consists of the capacity to shift from one perspective to another, and in the process to build up an adequate view of a total society and its components.'

4. Roland Barthes, *The Pleasure of the Text*, translated by Richard Miller (London: Cape, 1976). See also 'The Death of the Author' and 'From Work to Text' in *Image–Music–Text*, essays selected and translated by Stephen Heath (London: Fontana, 1977) pp. 142–8 and 155–64; and 'The Theory of the Text' in R. Young, *Untying the Text: A Post-Structuralist Reader* (London: RKP, 1981) pp. 31–47. In his introduction to the latter essay, Young notes: 'The closest word to "jouissance" in English would be enjoyment if the English word had a little more frisson. "Jouissance" means enjoyment in the sense of enjoyment of a right, of a pleasure, and, most of all, of sexual climax. "Jouissance" and "significance" invoke the sense of an ecstatic loss of the subject in a sexual or textual coming – a textasy.' (p. 32).

5. G. Bateson, 'The Message "This is Play"', in B. Schaffner (ed.) *Group Processes* (New York: Proceedings of the Josiah Macy Jr Foundation, 1955) pp. 145–242.

6. E. Goffman, *Frame Analysis* (London: Peregrine, 1975) p. 43.

7. Fry, p.8.

8. 'Normally a person is not held responsible for what he does in jest to the same degree that he would be for a serious gesture. Humour, as an aside from the main discourse, need not be taken into account in subsequent interaction. It need not become part of the history of the encounter, or be used for the continuous reassessment of the nature and worth of each participant, or be built into the meaning of subsequent acts. For the very reason that humor officially does not "count," persons are induced to risk messages that might be unacceptable if stated seriously.' (pp. 167–70). Joan Emerson, 'Negotiating the Serious Import of Humour', *Sociometry*, vol. XXXII (1969) pp. 169–181.

9. B. Turner, *Exploring the Industrial Subculture* (London: Macmillan, 1971) p. 43.

10. 'While it is understood that persons have some leeway in joking about

topics which they could not introduce in serious discourse, the line between the acceptable and unacceptable content is ambiguous. So it must be negotiated in each particular exchange.' Emerson, p. 170.

11. Christie Davies, 'Ethnic jokes, moral values and social boundaries', *British Journal of Sociology*, vol. 33, no. 3 (September 1982) pp. 383–403.

12. D. Gowler and K. Legge, 'Negation Synthesis and Abomination in Rhetoric', in C. Antarki (ed.) *The Psychology of Ordinary Explanations of Social Behaviour* (London: Academic Press, 1981) pp. 243–69.

13. See Rosalind Coward, 'Lacan and Signification: An Introduction', *Edinburgh 76 Magazine*, no. 1 (1976) pp. 6–20.

14. Davies, p. 396.

15. Turner, p. 43.

16. Fry, p. 106.

17. S. Cohen and L. Taylor, *Escape Attempts* (London: Penguin, 1976) p. 34.

18. M. Douglas 'Jokes', in *Implicit Meanings: Essays in Anthropology* (London, RKP, 1975) pp. 90–114. 'My hypothesis is that a joke is seen and allowed when it offers a symbolic pattern of a social pattern occurring at the same time. As I see it, all jokes are expressive of the social situations in which they occur. The one social condition necessary for a joke to be enjoyed is that the social group in which it is received should develop the formal characteristics of a 'told' joke: that is, a dominant pattern of relations is challenged by another. If there is no joke in the social structure, no other joking can appear.'

19. C. Powell, 'Humour, potential sociological directions', paper presented to the British Sociological Association, Sociology of Humour Study Group, University of Aston, April 1983.

20. D. Golding, 'Establishing "Blissful Clarity" in Organisational Life: Managers', *Sociological Review*, vol. 28, no. 4 (1980) pp. 736–82. On p. 776 is an example of the management of 'North Midlands District' who, in offering a transfer to Central District to Sheila, one of their staff, suggested that her husband might get a job in Central Town. 'In communicating this simplification the management domination myth is threatened with "exposure", because it contradicts an even more pervasive domination myth in "western" societies, that of the sovereignty of the husband as "primordial breadwinner" in the structure of the family. The seriousness of the suggestion that Sheila's husband should contemplate a job in Central Town and give up his present job to enable Sheila to move to Central Town is confirmed in the "taking seriously" of the engineers.

    The management domination myth was in fact subsequently rescued from complete "exposure" by the introduction of humour. The engineers enacted an "action replay" in which the roles played were exaggerated and the issue was diffused in hilarity. Nevertheless, the episode became part of folk-lore and remained as a potential threat, which illustrates the need for continual reinforcement of myth.'

21. Douglas (1975) pp. 96–7. Fry's terminology differs slightly: 'Canned

jokes are defined as those which are *presented* with little obvious relationship to the ongoing human interaction. Situation jokes are indicated as those which are *spontaneous* and have, to a major extent, their origin in the ongoing interpersonal (or intrapersonal) process. The practical joke category is defined as that made up of jokes which are both presented and spontaneous – in that the joker consciously contrives his joke, but must depend on the unfolding of an interpersonal (or intrapersonal) process for the presentation of his joke.' Fry, p. 43.

22. The reference is to Wittgenstein's discussion of the Augustinian description of language and his presentation of the idea of a language game, in L. Wittgenstein, *Philosophical Investigations*, translated by G. E. M. Anscombe (Oxford: Basil Blackwell, 1978) p. 3. 'Let us imagine a language for which the description given by Augustine is right. The language is meant to serve for communication between a builder A and an assistant B. A is building with building stones: there are blocks, pillars, slabs and beams. B has to pass the stones, and that in the order in which A needs them. For this purpose they use a language consisting of the words "block", "pillar", "slab", "beam". A calls them out; B brings the stone which he has learnt to bring at such-and-such a call. Conceive this as a complete primitive language.'

23. The incongruity of intellectualism and manual labour is given an added force in the following joke which also exploits the ethnic dimension in a reversal of the usual joke pattern:

> Irish labourer: I've come for the job, sir.
> Foreman (on building site): Have you any qualifications?
> Irish labourer: No sir, but you can ask me anything you like.
> Foreman: OK. What's the difference between a joist and a girder?
> Irish labourer: That's easy, sir. Joist wrote *Ulysses* and Girder wrote *Faust*.

(Acknowledgement due to Joseph A. Capstick of Swallownest, Sheffield for this.)

24. Davies, p. 394.
25. M. Douglas, *Purity and Danger* (London: Routledge & Kegan Paul, 1978) p. 121.
26. Douglas (1975), p. 97.
27. Ibid., p. 101.
28. Zijderveld, p. 10 defines a cliché: 'A cliché is a traditional form of human expression (in words, thoughts, emotions, gestures, acts) which – due to repetitive use in social life – has lost its original, often ingenious heuristic power. Although it thus fails positively to contribute meaning to social interactions and communication, it does function socially, since it manages to stimulate behaviour (cognition, emotion, volition, action) while it avoids reflection on meanings. *Summary*: The sociological essence of a cliché consists of the supersedure of original meanings by social functions. This supersedure is caused by repetitive use and enhanced by the avoidance of reflection.'

29. Douglas (1978), p. 147.

30. Ibid., p. 121. See also E. Leach, 'Magical Hair', *Journal of the Royal Anthropological Institute*, no. 88 (1958) pp. 147–63.

31. Douglas (1975), pp. 97*ff.*

32. See S. Hall, 'Encoding/Decoding', in S. Hall *et al.* (eds) *Culture Media Language* (London: Hutchinson, 1980) pp. 128–38.

33. In arguing this I am rejecting the distinction between myth and connotation observed by Heck: '... myth seems identifiable with the lexicons of very large groups, if not of society as a whole. Myth therefore differs from connotation at the moment at which it attempts to *universalize* for the whole society meanings which are special to particular lexicons. In the process of universalization, these meanings, which in the last instance are particular to certain lexicons, assume the amplitude of reality itself and are therefore "naturalized". Thus, we might say, *myths are connotations which have become dominant-hegemonic.*' Marina Carmargo Heck, 'The ideological dimension of media messages', in Hall *et al.* (eds) *Culture Media Language*, p. 125. This implies that sub-groups normally regard their sub-cultural meanings as having no more significance than at the level of their verbal formulation where they rub shoulders in plurality with other forms of jargon or slang, and do not regard them as having anything to say about universal and absolute reality. This reduces them to an inconsequential existence. It is ridiculous to assume that human beings labour to define the world and do not attribute some universal status, even if temporary, to their labours. As Vladimir says to Estragon, '... But at this place at this moment of time, all mankind is us whether we like it or not.' (S. Beckett, *Waiting for Godot* (London: Faber, 1956) p. 79. Also quoted by Golding, p. 763.) Myth is both inescapable and necessary to a degree; it is not a product of the ambitions of sub-groups.

34. See Golding, pp. 773–4, for a discussion of the 'sense of limits' which is manifested as a rule which blocks access.

35. See D. Hebdige, *Subculture: The Meaning of Style* (London: Methuen, 1979).

8 Racist Humour and Racist Ideology in British Television, or I Laughed Till You Cried

Charles Husband

HUMOUR AND 'RACE' IN IDENTITY

A capacity for humour and laughter seems to be a genuinely universal facility of human kind, one which transcends different cultures. However, the means of expressing humour, the stimuli which are potentially humorous and, indeed, the significance attached to the possession of 'a sense of humour' clearly vary with culture. In Britain, there are strong cultural sanctions for those lacking a demonstrable capacity for humour, and humour itself is valued as a medium of communication and a lubricant for social interaction. The benign, and even cathartic, properties of humour are celebrated in folk-wisdom through such utterances as 'if we can laugh together we can live together' and 'it's not so bad if you can laugh about it'. This is a position which has received support from psychologists of varying persuasions. There is the unqualified statement of Grotjahn (1957, p. viii):

> Everything done with laughter helps us to be human. Laughter is a way of human communication which is essentially and exclusively human. It can be used to express an unending variety of emotions. It is based on guilt-free release of aggression and any release makes us perhaps a little better and more capable of understanding one another, ourselves and life.

Or the more tentative conclusion of Gordon Allport who suggests that:

> [Yet] if the syndrome of the prejudiced personality is correctly defined in Chapter 25, we can easily believe that humour is a

149

missing ingredient; also that it is a present ingredient in the syndrome of tolerance. (Allport, 1958, p. 409)

Humour it seems is a force for good, a characteristic of 'tolerant' people and a benign presence in our life. It is one of the central purposes of this argument to suggest that the assumption of the benign nature of humour, ossified in folk-wisdom and sustained by social science, takes on a particular significance in Britain where it exists in a potent interaction with another widely held belief namely that Britain is a tolerant society.

The notion that Britain is a tolerant society is one of the cornerstones of the British self-image and its history has been repeatedly rewritten to sustain its credibility. School children are provided with partial truths regarding the tradition of succouring refugees; and politicians find it useful to embellish the myth in order to buoy-up current half-truths, deceits and political cowardice. A national concern to demonstrate toleration of minorities has, indeed, often been invoked to justify restrictions on the immigration of those same minorities on the grounds that their entry would jeopardise harmonious community relations. In 1938 the British government responded to the known plight of Jews in Nazi Germany (Sharf, 1964), with plans to admit some 'selected' adults and a limited number of children for training, prior to their dispersal to the colonies. This policy was justified by consideration of the possibility that to do more would lead to a 'definite anti-Jewish movement in the country' (Krausz, 1971, p. 63). More recently, *The Times* (leader, 14 August 1972) neatly and unintentionally encapsulated the current expression of this formula in its assertion that 'immigrants already settled here stand to suffer more than anyone else from a rate of new immigration greater than the social body of the host country can digest, or than its prejudices can tolerate'. Only a little later, in January 1973, Mr Carr, then Home Secretary, speaking after the reluctant acceptance of Ugandan Asian UK passport-holders, made it clear that any further entry of East African Asians with similar passports would be very severely restricted; this in order to maintain 'good community relations' (Humphry and Ward, 1974, p. 144).

The exact nature of 'tolerance' such as this has been highlighted by King who has pointed out:

It remains that the fundamental question underlying all discussions of tolerance is really to do with the legitimacy of the advantage

which tolerators may enjoy. If we look about us, wherever we are, we may readily perceive not merely unequal advantage, but *unjustifiably* unequal advantage. And if any forms of promotion of tolerance is confounded with the promotion of avoidable inequity, then we are confronted with a calamity wrapped up in a mistake. (King, 1976, p. 10)

The manifestation of British tolerance in the 1960s and 1970s in enacting discriminatory legislation against black immigration in order to promote 'good community relations' in Britain, and the creation of a toothless Race Relations Board to guarantee racial equality, were *prima facie* examples of the promotion of tolerance confounded by an ideological inability to perceive the extent of disadvantage; and a political unwillingness to compromise the economic benefits of cheap labour and the political benefits of a scapegoate 'alien' minority (cf. Dummett and Dummett, 1969; Foot, 1965; Sivanandan, 1976). Even the manner of interpretation of the immigration legislation showed just how alien 'toleration' was to white British consciousness (Moore and Wallace, 1975; Humphry and Ward, 1974; Akram, 1974; Gordon, 1981; Gordon, 1984). Any examination of British tolerance which goes beyond the verbal fabric to look at the historical reality rapidly exposes the mythical nature of this invaluable self-stereotype. And yet the myth persists. For example, in May 1976, Roy Jenkins, the then Home Secretary, invoked, 'Britain's historic role as providing refuge for the poor and repressed' (*The Guardian*, 25 May 1976), in a hypocritical attempt to counter a current expression of Enoch Powell's jaundiced anti-Asian sentiments. And in 1980 Harvey Proctor, MP, a right-wing member of the Conservative Party, was able to invoke his concern for 'racial harmony' in arguing for the possibly voluntary repatriation of black citizens (cited in Miles and Phizacklea, 1984, p. 108).

The essence of the power of tolerance as a value in British society is that it has no exclusive political affiliation. It is literally a subordinate value associated with such grand abstractions as social democracy and national tradition rather than the concrete pettiness of party politics. Thus its legitimacy as an important value and national characteristic is continually reaffirmed throughout the political spectrum. It has achieved a taken-for-granted status that allows it to be coopted into a wide range of discourses in an entirely unproblematic way. Hence the existent concern for its malign potential when, in the context of contemporary British race relations, it is fused with humour in a

mutually sustaining equation. This equation takes the form of:
(a) humour is a positive social activity;
(b) tolerance is a positive social value;
(c) therefore ethnic humour is a quintessential manifestation of tolerance in praxis.

The effect of this is to make unassailable the position of the ethnic joke-teller. To challenge the propriety of their actions is not only to be damned as a bad sport who cannot take a joke, it is also to define yourself as an extremist who is beyond the decency of the consensus politics of race relations; where tolerance is all things to all people, *you* are political. Increasingly it is likely that you would be typified as a particularly anti-British part of the 'Looney Left', namely an anti-racist who by definition takes everything to an indefensible extreme and is thereby intolerant himself.

Troyna (1981, 1982) has shown how the press, in discussing the activity of the Anti-Nazi League in opposing the fascist National Front, depicted the ANL as extremists of the Left who were equated with the National Front in being outside of the responsible middle ground of party politics. We have to remember that it has been this decent middle ground wherein successive governments have introduced discriminatory immigration legislation and have competed for the ever more demanding white racist vote (Foot, 1965; Husband, 1982). Seidel (1986) and Murray (1986) have detailed the development in the 1980s of, respectively, an intellectual and a populist reactionary nationalism which identifies the majority white population as the victims of the political products of anti-racists who violate the rights of this majority. Thus, over the last decade, the acceptability of ethnic jokes as 'tolerant humour' has become further reinforced by the growth of a new racism (Barker, 1981; Gordon and Klug, 1986) which has reified the ethnocentric and racist response of large parts of the white majority to the growth of black minority communities in Britain as the normal expression of their 'genuine fears'. Drawing on recent notions from sociobiology, including that of inclusive fitness and kin selection, this philosophy presents hostility to ethnic out-groups as a natural function of human nature in which individuals defend their own group interests. To the extent that this view has gained wide popular usage, and Barker (1981), Seidel (1986), Levitas (1986) and Murray (1986) would argue that it has, then the aggressive element of ethnic humour becomes more salient and legitimate.

It becomes more salient in that interethnic hostility has been a

continuing feature of experienced everyday life which has been occasionally given a specific focus in relation to major civil disturbances in the inner cities (Joshua and Wallace, 1983; Benyon, 1984), or in relation to specific disputes in relation to education, (Carby, 1982; Troyna and Williams, 1986), political representation, (Fitzgerald, 1984) or the inequitable rule of law, (Gordon, 1983; Smith and Gray, 1985). As Troyna (1981) has argued, for a large part of the white British population their concern with the 'immigration problem' of the 1960s was construed in terms of an external threat, whereas from the mid-1970s onwards this same sense of threat has been increasingly articulated in relation to 'the outsider within'. He observes (p. 80): 'As part of the media's representation of reality, cultural differences are disparaged and the black population seen as a problem to, and essentially different from the mainstream of the society.' The reality of objective ethnic conflict in a society with ubiquitous racist practices and evident racial inequality has made the subjective experience of ethnicity virtually unavoidable for black and white alike. This in turn has given significance to those criteria that mark ethnic boundaries and the cultural characteristics of different groups. Indeed as Barker (1981) has argued it is the perceived implacable nature of cultural difference which is central to the new racism. He says, in a way that disturbingly parallels Troyna's account of the press reporting of 'race' relations:

> This then, is the character of the new racism. It is a theory that I shall call biological, or better, pseudo-biological culturalism. Nations on this view are not built out of politics and economics, but out of human nature. It is our biology, our instincts to defend our way of life, traditions and customs against outsiders – not because they are inferior, but because they are part of different cultures. This is a non-rational process; and none the worse for it. For we are soaked in, made up out of, our traditions and our culture. (Barker, 1981, p. 24)

Thus ethnic humour has had an emotionally charged context in Britain since the 1960s when the white population initially felt itself to be threatened by an 'external threat', and increasingly felt itself to be under attack from an 'alien wedge' within. In this context cultural differences have had great visibility and significance. Not only this, but as indicated above, because of the development of racist philosophies which prioritised culture and made out-group hostility

'natural', the expression of racial antipathy through humour has enjoyed a particular legitimacy. It has made the subtleties and mediating powers of joke-work an artistic skill to be appreciated, rather than a social necessity to be enforced with sanctions.

ETHNIC HUMOUR THEORISED

Burma, some four decades ago, noted that much racial humour 'definitely can be related to racial competition and conflict and the social and cultural patterns which has arisen from them' (Burma, 1946, p. 714). Since that time La Fave (1972) and Zillman and Cantor (1976) have added to our understanding of intergroup humour and, more recently, Davies (1982) has written specifically about ethnic humour in Britain. Echoing early writings on the social functions of humour Davies notes that ethnic jokes police the social and moral boundaries between groups, and provide a vehicle for stating group power and expressing in-group perceptions of an anxiety toward the out-group. However, he goes beyond this to make a more novel point. He argues that:

> It is not, however, a simple question of dividing the world up into virtues and vices with the good qualities reserved for one's own group and the bad one's ascribed to the outsiders. In complex modern societies each individual will experience a conflict of goals and of values and will need to steer his way carefully between the competing claims of legitimate alternatives, such as work and leisure. Under these circumstances, the stereotypes that underpin ethnic jokes tend to occur not singly but in pairs of opposites. Thus in most western industrial societies the most popular ethnic jokes are those about groups supposed to be stupid and (in opposition to this) jokes about groups supposed to be canny (i.e. crafty and stingy). (Davies, 1982, p. 384)

This statement is most helpful in linking the specific nature of ethnic jokes to the specific context of particular ethnic minorities. It valuably moves ethnic jokes out of the static model of ethnic stereotypes, culturally transmitted, and locates ethnic jokes, with the ethnic community, in the midst of complex social forces. The ethnic stereotypes are still there and the act of categorising people in specific ways does, as social psychologists have demonstrated, have

consequences in identifying the personal and group attributes which are likely to feature in the policing of the group boundary (Tajfel, 1981; Turner, 1981). Yet what Davies is stressing is the social agenda of values and choices within which these stereotypes will be articulated. The stereotypical ethnic joke is thus more than the current repetition of an ossified cultural prejudice. It represents the continuity of stigmatising the out-group in relation to very salient immediate concerns. In this respect it is consistent with contemporary sociological analyses of racism in which racist thought and imagery is not seen as an independent theoretical monolith, detached from other concerns and ideas. Indeed Williams (1985) has provided a useful model of racism, in which its strength and pervasiveness can only be understood in relation to its interlocking relationship with other ideologies associated with class, parliamentary democracy or, for example, professional and bureaucratic practices. The agenda of concerns to do with work and the values of enjoyment, and with success and failure, identified by Davies, is clearly capable of extension and might easily contain, for example, the ambiguous polarity of progress – underdevelopment with its association of hi-tech consumerism and noble savage nostalgia. Sex, too, in Western capitalism has provided a continuum of restraint to excess which, in addition to its immediate physical reference, also has links to other powerful ideologies associated with the family and nation. Ethnic humour then must be seen in more sophisticated terms than the analysis of surface features provided by the stereotyping literature or the gross simplicities of identifying the social functions of ethnic humour. Yes, ethnic jokes may, amongst other things, serve to make statements about:

> the legitimacy of the situation of the majority relative to those ethnic groups above or below them. . . . Those ethnic groups who have failed economically and who provide the unskilled labour in industry and on construction sites . . . are labelled 'stupid' with the implication that they deserve their low place in the hierarchy of classes and occupations . . . Ethnic groups who have done better than the majority are labelled cheats and exploiters with the implication that *their* success is unfair and undeserved. (Davies, 1982. p. 390)

Quite so; but beyond the apparent truthfulness of such statements, what do we know of how this is possible? How do we account for the

existence of the social agenda of values and choices, the social relations within which humour fulfils these functions? Elsewhere, in his ex-cathedra commentary on Zijderveld, (1983), Davies has argued that:

> Zijderveld is entirely right to stress that ambiguity is the essence of humour (TR, p. 23), but we always need to specify what kinds of ambiguity are funny, in what social context and in what kind of society. Equally he is justified in stressing that 'the effect of the joke depends on the situation in which it is told and on the definition of the situation by the audience' (TR, p. 25). The key question though is 'What social forces determine why a particular audience adopts the definition that it does?' (Davies, 1984, p. 148)

Thus we are pointed to the necessity of employing a highly specific analysis of ethnic humour. Happily this makes sense not only in relation to our current state of knowledge regarding humour, but also, as indicated above, in relation to current analysis of the situational determination of ethnic consciousness (Wallman, 1978) and the complex determination of racism (Williams, 1985). Ironically, in order to attempt this in relation to ethnic humour in contemporary Britain it would be necessary to draw upon the body of literature which is anathema to Davies, namely neo-Marxist theory. See Davies (1984, p. 144) for a categorical rejection of this approach which constitutes a significant qualification to his conclusion that 'the study of humour and laughter has to be eclectic, based on many different sociological perspectives and on multi-disciplinary collaboration' (Davies, 1984, p. 156).

In relation to contemporary analyses of racism, and of the mass media, the extensive body of neo-Marxist literature lacks theoretical unity but does constitute an essential element in constructing a coherent analysis of ethnic humour in a Western capitalist society. Hall (1980) has usefully pointed out the contradictions and value of a neo-Marxist analysis of race, whilst Miles (1982) and the Centre for Contemporary Cultural Studies (1982) are but two of the valuable tests within this diverse paradigm. Equally in the analysis of the mass media, to deny oneself the insights derived from critical neo-Marxist informed analysis, which has spanned the range from discourse analysis of specific tests to macro analysis of international media markets, is to be perverse rather than eclectic. In summary, however, there is agreement that the analysis of ethnic humour requires multidisciplinary analyses of specific instances.

THE CONTEXT FOR BRITISH 'RACIAL' COMEDY SERIES

Bearing in mind the above comments, and the limitations of a brief chapter, it is appropriate to look again at Britain in the period from the mid-1960s to the latter years of the 1970s. Over the period in question there was an increasingly explicit demonstration of racism which, to some extent, paralleled the growth of real interethnic competition for scarce resources in housing, education and employment (cf. Rex and Moore, 1967; Moore, 1975; Sivanandan, 1976; Brown, 1984). Perhaps more fundamentally, growing class awareness and class conflict over a period of economic stagnation, and then recession, made the manufacture of a 'black immigration problem' a highly functional scapegoating strategy which deflected public attention away from anything other than an economistic critique of the distribution of social resources in the country (cf. Hartmann and Husband, 1974; Downing, 1975). Thus, stresses within the social relations of British society generated a situation in which the white majority population came to see itself as a legitimate and superior group which was threatened economically by the growing black presence in Britain. And threatened not only economically but also in more diffuse ways associated with cultural values.

Over this period there should have been no doubt in the world of humour that the white British audience would be keenly aware of its ethnic identity, hence implicitly its whiteness, and that this would be particularly evoked by racial jokes. Also over this period, the white hostility manifest in government policy and individual behaviour, as outlined above, resulted in an increase in militancy and the growth of black consciousness in the black communities. For example, 'West Indians' became progressively over the period less likely to respond as 'disappointed guests' and more as angry black parents or adolescents. They too came to television humour primed to respond selectively; and differently to the white audience.

One side-effect of the explicit racism of this period was that the injustice and prejudice characteristic of Britain's dealings with the black community became embarrassingly exposed, at least to the political elite. The embarrassment turned upon the fact that the exploitation and viciousness was visible, not that it occurred (Husband, 1982). The awareness that the white's superior status was based upon 'various forms of injustice' (Tajfel, 1974), generated a cruel conflict of values and hence 'British tolerance' became much paraded, verbally, in the hope that asserting the myth sufficiently

often might mask the reality. This heightened racial sensitivity and the salience of British tolerance may not have been irrelevant to the acceptability of the determinedly 'racial' television comedies such as *Till Death Us Do Part, Love Thy Neighbour*, or *The Fosters*. The symbiotic relationship of humour and tolerance had found its most supportive environment.

It was into this environment of racial conflict and heightened ethnic awareness that the television mandarins released a progression of comedy programmes containing explicit racial content. The first was *Till Death Us Do Part* which, following its first appearance in 1966, became a massive success whenever it reappeared over the subsequent years. In this series, Alf Garnett was intended to display the narrowness, stupidity and ignorance of the bigot and thereby serve as an attack on bigotry. However, the context in which his bigotry was displayed did nothing to reinforce the intended message. Within the family situation, Garnett was surrounded by a frumpish wife of possibly greater intelligence, a loutish son-in-law, who espoused the socialism of 'all that's yours is mine and all that's mine is staying mine', and a daughter who supported her husband rather than her father. There would be many who could empathise with the bitterness Alf felt in his extremis as an ex-soldier, a working man with nothing to show for his years of effort. Put into this man's mouth derisive comments about the blacks, or 'coons' and, for many of the white audience, in the political and social context of that period, you had an emergent folk hero. Like Enoch Powell after him, his great attraction was that he *said* what others thought. Against this there was no clear model for an alternative system of values to be found in the ranks of the other characters. For a white audience, no 'liberal' would wish to identify with the son-in-law and, for the intolerant, he was more a reinforcement of their biases than a challenge to them. Looked at from outside the ideology of humour-as-an-expression-of-tolerance, the notion that a programme with these internal dynamics and characterisations could constitute an assault on bigotry was grotesque. Certainly the BBC and Speight, the scriptwriter, were convinced of the positive educational potential of the series; and were seemingly simultaneously untroubled by the likelihood of a 'boomerang effect', in which well-intentioned propaganda reinforces the target audience's prejudices, which has haunted propagandists since the work of Cooper and Jahoda in 1947.

For the black audience, who could hardly be expected to share the white audience's psychological motivation for investing in the myth of

benign humour, this programme was a commentary upon their invisibility as an audience for the gentlemen of the BBC. The reintroduction of the word 'coon' to the British popular lexicon, and stimulating its use on the urban streets of Britain was but one of the more visible consequences of this series. For the black audience, the willingness of the BBC to continue the series after public expressions of outrage and concern had come from the black communities in Britain, represented an extension of the white-controlled media's facility for denying black integrity and distorting black experience. Just as the news media and cinema abused and assaulted black identity, so now television comedy made explicit its place within that white hegemony (cf. Hartmann and Husband, 1974; Husband, 1975; Leab, 1975; Pines, 1975; see also Friar and Friar, 1972). This position was expressed with particularly tasteless clarity by *Curry and Chips*, the comedy series which followed *Till Death Us Do Part* from the pen of Johnny Speight and which starred Spike Milligan as a blacked-up Pakistani–Irishman, Paki–Paddy.

Commercial television spawned its own answer to Alf Garnett in the more youthful character of Eddie Booth in *Love Thy Neighbour*. This programme more than any of the others illustrated the dilemma of ethnic humour in television comedy in as much as the same content may have very different meanings for different audiences. Thus, in 1972, *TV Times* reported that their own research showed that the programme was very popular among urban blacks. Well it might have been, for on a medium where blacks seldom occurred and less frequently starred, here was a black character beating whitey. Very little selective perception was needed to see Eddie Booth, the bigoted white, as constantly losing out in the competition with his black neighbours. 'Poor' Eddie with a plain wife living next door to a black man (Bill) of greater physical stature who is married to a 'very attractive' wife; and on top of that being bested in his most sacred territory, amongst his friends in the local pub. In that context the verbal abuse which Bill heaped upon this effigy of white working-class bigotry must have been satisfying viewing.

However, a probable large portion of the white audience could construe a different reality in these events. Eddie Booth could also be seen as the average working man embattled in his own house with the constant sniping of a pushy black who could buy a better car than him, who poached his friends and soured friendships, who even caused his own wife to mock him. For many whites living in multiracial areas, this reflected their feelings and resentments; for

whites in pristine enclaves of Caucasia who know of the immigration problem and the threat of blacks taking over (Hartmann and Husband, 1974), this was the shape of things to come. For them Eddie's bitter verbal assaults were potential expressive releases for their frustrations and fears. Thus, although this series was popular with urban blacks, and although, rare in British television, it occasionally contained a glimpse of the aggressively satirical comment described by Arnez and Anthony (1968) in US programmes, still to a large section of the white audience its likely impact must have been to reinforce racist assumptions.

More recently, *It Ain't Half Hot Mum* provided the novelty of stereotyped images of 1940s India as the background for a military situation comedy. The main Indian protagonist, played by a blacked-up Englishman, was a hybrid mixture of Mowgli and Gunga Din, at once wily and innocent, wheedling and occasionally wise. His highly orchestrated throat-clearing cued in to one of the prevalent white British complaints against the Asian immigrant. Similarly, his efforts to emulate the British were a source of comic incident, and also happened to reflect the essence of Enoch Powell's statement that an Indian, even born in Britain, remained an Indian. Unlike *Till Death Us Do Part*, it was the incidental detail rather than the central dialogue which was the medium whereby old Imperial and current racist stereotypes were likely to be reinforced. There was a cosy nostalgia about the programme which made the appearance of the Indians as servants and punka wallahs, gliding about in the penumbra of events, so inevitable; and acceptable.

'RACIAL' COMEDY SERIES: SOME DATA FROM THE 1970S

In these comedy series in which 'race' plays a significant part, the legitimating ideology of British tolerance and its manifestation in humour achieved a critical visibility in 1966 with the successful floating of *Till Death Us Do Part* as a comedy series specifically designed to challenge racial prejudice. Though the primary factor in guaranteeing the longevity of this series, and promoting the subsequent derivative 'racial' series, was its success in terms of audience size (16 million in 1972, BBC, 1975), surely a potent catalyst to the emergence of the derivative variants was this legitimating ethos for the series. Certainly the well-publicised intent

of the 'socialist' scriptwriter of the series was supported then and reiterated subsequently by the BBC. This legitimating ethos has been echoed since by those responsible for American and German variants of *Till Death Us Do Part*. Before going on to examine in some detail the available research data on *Till Death Us Do Part*, it will be useful to examine briefly the larger body of data on its American variant *All in the Family* – and see if this series vindicated those apologists who emphasised its positive educational function.

Vidmar and Rokeach (1974) in a study of an adult Canadian sample and an American adolescent sample, hypothesised that selective perception would be found in that prejudiced viewers would be more favourably disposed toward Archie Bunker, (the American Alf Garnett) and his views. Their data supported this expectation. However, a second hypothesis that selective exposure would be found in that more ethnocentric individuals would be more likely to view the programme was confirmed only with the American sample. Surlin (1974) and Tate and Surlin (1975) have shown data consistent with Vidmar and Rokeach's demonstration of selective perception in finding a positive relationship between high dogmatism, (a measure which tends to correlate with what is popularly called 'prejudice') and agreement with Archie Bunker. Wilhoit and de Bock (1976), in a more complex analysis of the impact of *All in the Family* in Holland, interpret their findings as indicating that *All in the Family* is unlikely to reinforce negative attitudes. However, their data does include examples of selective perception: for example, people who were highly ethnocentric or intolerant of divergent lifestyles were less willing than people low on these factors to say that Archie was usually responsible for trouble in the Bunker family; highly intolerant or authoritarian people were more likely to say that Archie usually had the situation under control; and people high on ethnocentrism, or intolerant of divergent lifestyles were more likely to see Archie Bunker's arguments as reasonable. On selective exposure, Wilhoit and de Bock's findings are completely contrary to those of Vidmar and Rokeach in that they found a tendency among highly intolerant and authoritarian people to avoid watching the programme. One of the problematic aspects of this competent study by Wilhoit and de Bock is the question of what their over-all findings would have been had the out-groups being disparaged in the series been the Surinamese and Amboinese rather than Poles and American blacks. Significantly, an indigenous Dutch series produced by the Catholic Broadcasting Organisation (KRO) in 1970, which

was closely modelled on *Till Death Us Do Part*, was withdrawn because of anxiety about its dubious impact.

In Germany, Alf Tetzlaff, their own anti-Semitic and anti-Social Democrat variant on Alf Garnett, had an embarrassingly unambiguous reception, for opinion polls of viewers showed them to be often agreeing with his frankly anti-Semitic, nationalistic and reactionary utterances. In a WDR poll of viewers taken after the Tetzlaff programmes which included references to Chancellor Brandt's illegitimate birth and an attack on Rosa Luxemburg, 1679 viewers approved of the programme, whilst only 3 were critical. The author of the Tetzlaff script said, 'In the first eight programmes we would never have dreamt that Alfred with his reactionary criticisms would get so much popular applause' (Terry, 1974).

Findings such as these suggest quite clearly that the therapeutic intent of authors and producers, and their faith in the benevolent power of humour, are not sufficient to guarantee the positive consequences they intend. Had these professionals been familiar with the growing body of research demonstrating that an individual's perception of, and response to, humour was significantly determined by the reference groups which were cued for that individual by the context and content of the joke, then they might have been more circumspect in their frequent use of derogatory ethnic jokes (cf. Priest, 1966; Priest and Abrahams, 1970; La Fave, 1972; La Fave, Haddad and Marshall, 1973–74; La Fave, McCarthy and Haddad, 1973; La Fave, Haddad and Maesen, 1976; Zillman and Cantor, 1976). The research data on *All in the Family* reviewed above indicates that, to an important extent, what you find in such a programme is a function of what attitudes and values you bring to it. In particular you cannot isolate a programme, or reactions to it, from the cultural milieu which sustains particular taken-for-granted worlds for the viewers. We may choose to remember here the introduction, in which the extensive development of popular and party political racism in the 1960s and 1970s, reflected in the increasingly discriminatory immigration legislation, was matched by official political declarations of tolerance. It was throughout this period that the BBC broadcast *Till Death Us Do Part*.

Disturbingly, as is argued elsewhere (Husband, 1977a), the BBC's own audience research challenged the complacent consensus regarding the positive effects of the series. In 1975 the BBC Audience Research Department published a summary[1] of research they had carried out three years previously on the series of *Till Death Us Do*

Part which had run from 13 September to 25 October 1972. The full report[2] had been prepared in 1973 and in conjunction with the summary provides a valuable example of the limitations of an analysis based upon an implicit acceptance of 'British tolerance' and the positive power of humour (Husband, 1977b).

The summary provided information on the audience's agreement with Alf Garnett thus:

As far as Alf is concerned, the greatest amount of support came for the statement 'Although his views are too extreme most of the time, some of the things he says are true'. Even half of the non-viewers gave Alf Garnett this qualified approval, whereas one half of the regular viewers of the series went further and claimed that he was 'Right more often than he's wrong'. (BBC, 1975, p. 30)

However, the relevant figures from the report (Table 8.1) show how significant is this difference between 'regular viewers' and 'non-viewers', a difference which disclosed an embarrassing degree of Vidmar and Rokeach's selective perception.

Table 8.1

		Regular viewers (%)	Occasional viewers (%)	Non-viewers (%)
'Although his views are too	*Agree*	84	74	50
extreme most of the time,	*Disagree*	10	15	24
some things he says are true'	*No opinion*	6	11	26
		100	100	100
'Right more often than he's	*Agree*	45	25	13
wrong'	*Disagree*	46	60	59
	No opinion	9	15	28
		100	100	100

SOURCE: BBC (1975, p. 26)

In order to qualify the implications of this data the summary went on to say:

However, the *great majority* of both groups apparently recognised him as something of a cipher, a harmless buffoon, agreeing with

one *or more* of the three statements, 'So extreme as to be just a joke', 'Unimportant and insignificant', or 'Misguided but harmless'. (Emphasis added.) (BBC, 1975, p. 30)

Once more the relevant data in the report, (Table 8.2) is illuminating in that it indicated that only by summing over all three statements could the phrase 'the great majority of both groups' be given any credibility.

Table 8.2

		Regular viewers (%)	Occasional viewers (%)	Non-viewers (%)
'So extreme in his views	*Agree*	62	63	58
that he's just a joke'	*Disagree*	33	27	15
	No opinion	5	10	27
		100	100	100
'Unimportant and	*Agree*	42	56	58
insignificant	*Disagree*	50	31	22
	No opinion	8	13	20
		100	100	100
'Misguided but harmless'	*Agree*	65	55	39
	Disagree	26	28	33
	No opinion	9	17	28
		100	100	100

SOURCE: BBC (1975, p. 26)

The necessity of this 'great majority' is revealed in the next paragraph of the summary where it is argued that:

it would seem undesirable that if a person regards Garnett as 'harmless and unimportant', this must take precedence over the fact that he also believes him to be 'right on occasions'. (BBC, 1975, p. 30)[3]

Though this argument could in part claim to be consistent with Surlin's (1974) hypothesis of congruence between liking of source and statement, it is argued elsewhere (Husband, 1975, pp. 33–5) that the

learning potential of racial humour may lie in the rehearsal of the assumption underlying the joke. Hence it would be possible to regard Garnett as a fool and still, in finding the humour funny, rehearse the latent assumptions.

It is possible to develop an argument completely contrary to that presented in the BBC summary; namely that their data indicates a classic situation where learning and reinforcement of existing beliefs can occur whilst defences are down (cf. Krugman, 1965). Given the legitimacy of racial humour (see above and Emerson, 1969), viewers may suspend moral monitoring and since the programme is categorised as entertainment they are able to rehearse racist beliefs in a situation where they are freed from moral sanction and responsibility to validate statements. Thus, particularly if Garnett is regarded as a harmless buffoon, the audience need feel no embarrassment and they may reject the man whilst accepting his views. However, it is his views which are the problem for they resonate with a long cultural tradition of racism and were voiced at a time when ethnic identity was particularly sensitised. This potential was increased by the fact that the data in the BBC's own report indicated that the 'regular viewers' of the series were somewhat less liberal in their views than a matched sample of 'non-viewers'.

An interpretation of the BBC report from within the assumptive framework of Vidmar and Rokeach, rather than that of Johnny Speight and the BBC, produces a case for arguing the dangerously negative impact of the series, based on selective exposure to it and selective perception of the programme content. The BBC summary states that: 'the regular viewers of the series were, *not surprisingly*, much more 'pro' [Garnett] than were the non-viewers of the series' (BBC, 1975, p. 30, emphasis added), and that:

> some of the large number who tended to regard Alf Garnett as 'on the whole reasonable most of the time' may, it seems, have had their prejudices confirmed; though the evidence suggest that very few of them went further and adopted his more extreme views. (BBC, 1975, p. 35)

The amazing implications to be drawn from this is that it had been anticipated that regular viewers would be more pro-Garnett and that, in some way, it was acceptable to merely reinforce existing prejudice. Belief in the benign function of humour seems capable of interpreting even the most awkward data.

In 1976, Ian Trethowan was asked if he would put on *Till Death Us Do Part*; he replied that:

the research on that at the time ... was that it didn't change attitudes either way. There is some evidence that it might have firmed up attitudes. Whether we would put it on now, I don't know. (*The Listener*, 1 July 1976, p. 832)

What we do know is that Mr Trethowan was probably prepared to firm up a few more attitudes with *The Melting Pot*, a further comedy starring Spike Milligan which revolved around two Pakistanis, illegal immigrants, who lived in an Irishman's boarding house. Milligan in a press interview said of this confection: 'It's all there. References to niggers, wops and wogs. That's what gets the laughs today.' (*Sun*, 21 August 1976.) And the rationale behind this series remained as before: the myth of the positive function of humour. Upset by Spike Milligan's suggestion that, 'This series won't do a thing to improve race relations, or make people more tolerant' (*Sun*, 21 August 1976), Ian MacNaughton, the producer of the series, replied, 'I do agree with co-writer, Neil Shand, who is optimistic about racial tolerance. And I do feel that the best way to attack idiotic bigots is through laughter' (*Sun*, 11 September 1976). Two years later at the Edinburgh Television Festival, Humphrey Barclay, the Head of Comedy for London Weekend Television, defended *Mind Your Language*, a series which consisted essentially of a range of gross ethnic caricatures who provided the 'humour' through a grotesque parody of supposed ethnic characteristics. With a suitable genuflection in the direction of concern for promoting racial harmony he said:

I don't think that series is socially damaging. I hope it is not; otherwise we really oughtn't to be doing it. What people get out of that is a lot of enjoyment. I don't think it is at the expense of the characters.

It will perhaps help to put the naivety and institutional racism implicit in these comments into perspective when we note that in the major government review of broadcasting published in 1977, *Report of the Committee on the Future of Broadcasting* (HMSO, 1977), the discussion of the treatment of racial minorities in the section on 'Programme Standards' takes up less space than 'bad language' and considerably less space than 'sex' or 'violence'. The sensibilities of the

media personnel responsible for television comedy did not, and do not, exist in a vacuum. To a large extent the unwillingness of television companies in the 1970s to develop a clear policy to counter racist practice was consistent with a wider reluctance in Britain to develop policies to challenge racism (Young, 1983).

THE EMERGENCE OF 'BLACK' COMEDY SERIES

Yet 1976 saw the introduction of the first all-black programme on British television and it was a comedy. A variant of the American programme *Good Times*, the British audience was provided with a family comedy centred on a West Indian family in *The Fosters*. For the liberal white audience it was dangerously easy to see *The Fosters* as a breakthrough, if only because it presented an all-black cast in a familiar format which may serve as a palatable means of introducing white Britain to the notion that blacks share many concerns and interests with 'ordinary' people in Britain. *The Fosters* depicted a warm, caring family and their particular difficulties as blacks, as for example in gaining employment, did receive mention. For reasons such as these, it is possible to argue that for some parts of the white audience *The Fosters* was a positive educational influence. But even there the programme operated at another level to reinforce racist stereotypes. True the casting was a breakthrough but what of the 'heavy racist undercurrents. The most obvious is the image that we all are "jive niggers" and that all Black fathers act like Mr Foster or his eldest clown of a son, Sonny' (Shabazz, 1976). It was true; Sonny was the most recent media portrayal of Sambo – the all-smiling, all-gibbering, eyeball-rolling clown. There was much in the behaviour of the Fosters which would cue existing white stereotypes, and selective perception would do the rest.

The best judges of *The Fosters* must be the West Indian communities for it is they who were being (mis)represented and perhaps it is they who, particularly, were supposed to be grateful for *The Fosters*. There clearly were West Indians who were regular viewers, and among these the fact that the actors were black seemed to be almost sufficient reason for viewing. In the current media environment this was not unreasonable. However, others were bitterly decrying *The Fosters* as a pastiche of their life-style and experience as blacks in Britain and it is this message which is crucial, for it identified *The Fosters* as yet another white comedy with racial

content (cf. reviews of *The Fosters* by Shabazz, 1976; and Rugg, 1976).

More recently, Channel Four's *No Problems* has attempted to continue to provide a situation comedy which reflects black experience and black culture. Its popularity with black audiences must reflect the extent to which the programme acceptably represents their world. Regrettably it will also partially be an artifact of black audiences preferences for programmes with black characters (Jones and Dungey, 1983), which continue to have relative scarcity value on British television (Anwar and Shang, 1982). However, to the extent that this programme accurately taps black life-styles and black experience, it may alienate significantly large sections of the white viewing audience who resent being challenged with 'alien' linguistic codes and who find their perception of an 'alien wedge' that will not assimilate being justified. A view which, as we have seen, is consistent with powerful contemporary racist currents. One problem with mass communications is the fact that there is no mass audience, but rather many highly partisan audiences. Indeed the attempt by Channel Four to develop an explicit policy of developing multicultural programming from within a white-dominated institution has attracted criticism from sections of the black community (Freeth, 1982; Cohen and Gardner, 1982; Saakana, 1982; Gardner, 1981; Gilroy, 1983).

Given the frequency of British television channels purchasing comedy series from the USA, the development of comedy series there with black characters is of some importance. Jones and Dungey (1983) have already demonstrated that *Different Strokes* was the most popular programme for the 'West Indian' boys and girls in their British sample, and was the third favourite for 'Asian' boys and girls. They also indicated the popularity of *Benson* among 'West Indian' parents. Indeed their research showed a strong preference for programmes with characters with whom the ethnic minority audiences identify. Hence given the continued relative absence of such characters from British home-produced programmes, these imports from America assume a very particular significance.

In this context Gray's (1986) analysis of black male images in prime-time situation comedy is most valuable. He examines in particular *Benson, Webster, Different Strokes* and *The Jeffersons* and notes that the male characters in these series represent black Americans who have achieved middle-class success, thus confirming the belief that:

in the context of the current political, economic and cultural arrangements, individuals, regardless of colour, can achieve the American dream. However, these images also exist in the absence of significant change in the overall position of black Americans as a social group. (Gray, 1986, p. 224)

British viewers, for example, will be familiar with the translation of Benson from being the butler in *Soap* to being the head housekeeper in the Governor's mansion in *Benson*, and his subsequent rise to State Budget Director and then Lieutenant Governor. In his analysis Gray notes that the imagery in these programmes emphasises individualism, professional competence, upward social mobility and the routinisation of racial issues; whilst racial conflict and struggle are peripheralised. He concludes his perceptive analysis by arguing that:

> Television's idealization of racial harmony, affluence and individual mobility is simply not within the reach of millions of black Americans. To the extent that different realities and experiences are not mentioned or addressed in television programmes featuring blacks, the effect is to isolate and render invisible social and cultural experiences of poor and working-class black Americans. In those instances where racial issues are addressed, they are often presented as expressions of deviance and function to confirm existing definitions of normal middle-class experience. With their emphasis on individualism and individual achievement in a supposedly colourblind society, the present generation of black male images offers popular legitimation for a narrow and conservative definition of race relations and racial interaction. The major impact of this narrow conception is to deflect attention from the persistence of racism, inequality and differential power. (Gray, 1986, p. 239)

While we cannot assume that these conclusions would identically apply to British viewing audiences, there is reason to assume that the emphasis on individualism, success and upward mobility, and the imagery of 'race relations' fostered in these programmes would be consistent with the contemporary nature of British racism sketched in the introduction to this chapter.

Yet another American situation comedy would on the face of it seem to fit Gray's sample, namely *The Cosby Show* in which the

Huxtable family are remarkably successful: the father is a gynaeco-
logist and obstetrician and the mother is a lawyer. They live in
considerable comfort with their attractive and achieving children in a
family that is a model of responsibility and openness. Interestingly,
in an analysis of *The Cosby Show* Downing sees important
differences between it and some of those programmes examined by
Gray. Particularly in relation to the stigmatisation of the Negro
family in contemporary America he argues that:

> The family's assured dignity and fundamental cohesion offer a
> powerful communication on several levels, countering the 'sham-
> bles' image of Black family life. (Downing, forthcoming)

He also argues that this programme's explicit attack upon sexism,
and its more implicit exploration of social class constitute a valuable
critique of the 'correlates' of racism which is likely to succeed
because it is embedded in such a successful show. Again we are faced
with the complexity of the potential variation of meanings which
different audiences may abstract from the same material. At one
reading *The Cosby Show* can be seen to reinforce those ideological
values identified by Gray; whilst at another level it may be that its
potential to subtly challenge is because it is framed within the
unproblematic consensus of this genre.

CONCLUSION: THE CURRENT SITUATION

Comedy series have become a staple ingredient in the television
company's battle over the carcase of the viewing audience; and a
major criterion in the creation and production of such series is their
ability to draw a large audience (Taylor, 1976). The format of these
series ranges widely over situation comedies such as *No Place Like
home*, *To The Manor Born*, *Only Fools and Horses*, and *Last of the
Summer Wine*, to the anarchy and *ad hoc*ary of *Monty Python*, or the
popular banality of *The Benny Hill Show*; and there remain those
programmes structured around comedians such as Dave Allen, Russ
Abbot or the black comic, Lenny Henry.
   Perhaps series like *Porridge* or *The Likely Lads*, which were
scripted by authors influenced by a documentary tradition, offered
locations and conflicts of interest of a structural nature which
provided the basis for social comment. But even in these program-

mes the dominant influence was nearer to empathy than social analysis since the humour was generated in the interaction of individuals who became virtually decontextualised. The social location of characters in comedy series serves only as a stage setting to provide the necessary props to augment the interpersonal dynamics which generates the humour. The different class identity of the protagonists in *Last of the Summer Wine* or *To The Manor Born* merely serves to situate the interaction within an identifiable milieu so that the humour may be accurately cued. The actual interpersonal dynamics of the plots are the focus of the action.

This dominance of the interpersonal plane of activity in situation comedy serves the dual function of providing a routine basis for humour, whilst simultaneously submerging any potential for political comment by reducing the context to an unproblematically familiar *status quo*. Given the known political proclivities of the British news media (cf. for example, Downing, 1975; Glasgow University Media Group, 1976; Hartmann and Husband, 1974), and the control and ownership of the media (cf. Murdock and Golding, 1974 and 1977), it should perhaps be no surprise that television humour too reflects the hegemony of capital in failing to cut through the taken-for-granted world of interpersonal relations to reveal an underlying structure.

It is the credibility, the taken-for-granted normality, of the location which is the basis for the linking of ethnic humour to the agendas of a racist society. It is here that the traditional ethnic stereotypes are revitalised by being firmly rooted in the contemporary familiar world. Thus, although we no longer have *Till Death Us Do Part*, the invective of the Alf Garnett character continues in *In Sickness and in Health* where his occasional racist remark ironically adds to the credibility of the character, since in the world he inhabits such remarks would be a 'normal' complement to his other views. Their very normality is part of their potency in confirming racist behaviour. In a different context the 'innocence' of such humour is invoked and rehearsed in the ease with which ethnic jokes are included in the patter of stand-up comics and in the *ad hoc* asides of competition comperes and chat show participants. However, whilst there is evidence in 1986 of a new sensibility in broadcasting which would not condone the gross racial abuse of *Till Death Us Do Part*, it remains the case that *Mind Your Language* was being broadcast for peak children's viewing in that year. Among television management, the public complacency of broadcasters toward their responsibility to

consider the implications of ethnic humour in their programming, as was demonstrated at the 1978 Edinburgh Television Festival, is no longer apparent. The issue has successfully been placed upon the professional broadcaster's agenda. Yet the current absence of any indigenous black comedy series may indicate that such sensitivity has generated withdrawal and paralysis, rather than positive experimentation. It seems likely, however, that imported series like *Different Strokes* or *Benson* are regarded as safe – doubly safe in that they have proven success in attracting an audience and in that they do not directly address British 'race relations'. Indeed to the extent that Gray's analysis does transfer to the British situation such programmes are ideologically compatible with contemporary racial discourse.

Several factors are likely to militate against the creative use of television comedy to expose racism in Britain at present. A sufficient reason to block it is the likelihood that it would offend the majority audience. A further reason is the current political assault upon the broadcasting media, which has been successful in engendering a nervous self-consciousness among programme producers regarding the 'political' tone of their programmes. And linked to this is the successful right-wing counter-attack upon the anti-racist initiatives of the last two decades. In both elite and popular discourse the Right have been successful in presenting the white majority as the segment of the British population whose values and 'rights' have been constrained by the actions of 'anti-racist zealots'. It is not a propitious moment to hope to anticipate anti-racist initiatives within British comedy series. Perhaps the oblique counter-images, and the displaced targets of sexism and class identified by Downing are all that can be hoped for in the immediate future. However, the current vogue for 'alternative comedians' on radio and television has provided a vehicle for occasional 'progressive' humour for a probably self-selected audience.

The calculus which will allow for an *a priori* identification of acceptable ethnic humour and socially damaging humour has not been devised, and given the mechanics of selective perception would not be applicable to any medium directing itself to a mass and multiple audience. The nature and content of comedy on British television must remain a matter of active concern for those opposed to the continuation of racism in Britain.

NOTES

1. 'Reports on Some *ad hoc* Research Studies', *Annual Review of Audience Research*, vol. 1 (1975) pp. 26–35.
2. *'Till Death Us Do Part' As Anti-Prejudice Propaganda*, BBC, March 1973. I am grateful to the BBC for access to this document.
3. It is of interest that the BBC summary received considerable press coverage in the national press and that, in particular, they were keen to stress this very point. The headlines alone provided this emphasis: *Daily Express* (17 March 1975): Nobody loves yer actual Alf; *Daily Telegraph*: Alf Garnett 'doesn't provoke prejudice'; *The Times*: T.V. viewers do not identify with Garnett; *Daily Mail*: Just harmless; *Guardian*: Alf, the 'harmless buffoon'; *Daily Mirror*: Alf, you're the silly old moo.

REFERENCES

Akram, Mohammed, *Where Do You Keep Your String Beads* (London: Runnymede Trust, 1974).

Allport, G. W., *The Nature of Prejudice* (Garden City, New York: Anchor Books, 1958).

Anwar, M. and A. Shang, *Television in a Multi-Racial Society* (London: CRE, 1982).

Arnez, Nancy Levi and Clara B. Anthony, 'Contemporary Negro Humour as Social Satire', *Phylon*, vol. 29 (1968) pp. 339–46.

Barker, M., *The New Racism* (London: Junction Books, 1981).

Benyon, J., *Scarman and After* (Oxford: Pergamon, 1984).

Bethel, N., *The Last Secret* (London: Futura, 1976).

Bridges, Lee, 'The Ministry of Internal Security: British Urban Social Policy 1968–74', *Race and Class*, vol. XVI, no. 4 (April 1975).

British Broadcasting Corporation, ' "Till Death Us Do Part" as Anti-Prejudice Propaganda', *Annual Review of Audience Research*, vol. 1 (1975).

Brown, C., *Black and White Britain* (London: Heinemann, 1984).

Burgest, David R., 'The Racist Use of the English language' *The Black Scholar*, vol. 5, no. 1 (September 1973) pp. 37–45.

Burma, John H., 'Humour As A Technique in Race Conflict', *American Sociological Review*, vol. XI, no. 6 (December 1946) pp. 710–15.

Carby, H. V., 'Schooling in Babylon', in Centre for Contemporary Cultural Studies, *The Empire Strikes Back* (London: Hutchinson, 1982).

Centre for Contemporary Cultural Studies, *The Empire Strikes Back* (London: Hutchinson, 1982).

Coard, Bernard, *How the West Indian Child is Made Educationally Sub-Normal in the British School System* (London: New Beacon Books, 1971).

Cohen, P. and C. Gardner, *It Ain't Half Racist Mum: Fighting Racism in the Media* (London: Comedia, 1982).

Cooper, Eunice and Marie Jahoda, 'The Evasion of Propaganda: How Prejudiced People Respond to Anti-Prejudice Propaganda', *Journal of Psychology*, vol. 23 (1947) pp. 15–25.

Davies, C., 'Ethnic jokes, moral values and social boundaries', *The British Journal of Sociology*, vol. 33, no. 3 (September 1982) p. 383.

Davies, C., 'Commentary on Anton C. Zijderveld's Trend Report on "The Sociology of Humour and Laughter"', *Current Sociology*, vol. 32, no. 1 (Spring 1984) pp. 142–57.

Davies, David Brion, *The Problem of Slavery in Western Culture* (London: Pelican Books, 1970).

Day, Beth, *Sexual Life Between Blacks and Whites* (London: Collins, 1970).

Downing, John, 'The (Balanced) White View', in Charles Husband (ed.) *White Media and Black Britain* (London: Arrow Books, 1975).

Downing, John, 'Ideology in Capitalist Society', unpublished manuscript, 1976.

Downing, John, 'The Cosby Show and American Racial Discourse', in A. van Dijk Teun and Geneva Switherman-Donaldson (eds) *Discourse Discrimination* (Berlin: Walter de Gruyter, forthcoming).

Dummett, Ann, *A Portrait of English Racism* (Harmondsworth: Penguin, 1973).

Dummett, Michael and Ann Dummett, 'The Role of Government in Britain's Racial Crisis', in Lewis Donnelly (ed.) *Justice First* (London: Sheed and Ward, 1969).

Emerson, Joan P., 'Negotiating the Serious Import of Humour', *Sociometry*, vol. 32 (1969) pp. 169–81.

Foot, Paul, *Immigration and Race in British Politics* (Harmondsworth: Penguin, 1965).

Fitzgerald, M., *Political Parties and Black People* (London: Runnymede Trust, 1984).

Freeth, T., 'TV Colonialism', in Cohen and Gardner (1982).

Friar, Ralph and Natasha Friar, *The Only Good Indian* (New York: The Hollywood Gospel Drama Book Specialists, 1972).

Gardner, C., 'Black Employment in the Media', *Multiracial Education*, vol. 9, no. 2 (Spring 1981) pp. 69–74.

Garrard, John A., *The English and Immigration 1880–1910* (London: Oxford University Press, 1971).

Gartner, Lloyd P., *The Jewish Immigrant to Britain, 1870–1914* (London: George Allen and Unwin, 1960).

George, M. Dorothy, *London Life in the Eighteenth Century* (London: Kegan Paul, Trench, Trubner, 1930).

Gilroy, P., 'C4 – Bridgehead or Bantustan', *Screen*, vol. 24, no. 4–5 (1983) pp. 130–7.

Glasgow University Media Group, *Bad News* (London: 1976).

Gordon, P., *Passport Raids and Checks* (London: Runnymede Trust, 1981).

Gordon, P., *White Law* (London: Pluto, 1983).

Gordon, P., *Deportations and Removals* (London: Runnymede Trust, 1984).

Gordon, P. and F. Klug, *New Right, New Racism* (London: Searchlight Publications, 1986).

Gray, H., 'Television and the new black man: black male images in prime-

time situation comedy', *Media, Culture and Society*, vol. 8 (1986) pp. 223–42.

Grotjahn, Martin, *Beyond Laughter* (New York: McGraw-Hill, 1957).

Hall, S., 'Race, articulation and societies structured in dominance', in Unesco, *Sociological Theories: Race and Colonialism* (Paris: Unesco, 1980).

Hartmann, P. and C. Husband, *Racism and the Mass Media* (London: Davis Poynter, 1974).

Humphry, Derek, *Police Power and Black People* (London: Panther Books, 1972).

Humphry, D. and G. John, *Because They're Black* (Harmondsworth: Penguin Books, 1971).

Humphry, D., and M. Ward, *Passports and Politics* (Harmondsworth: Penguin, 1974).

Husband, Charles, 'Racism in Society and the Mass Media: A Critical Interaction', in Charles Husband (ed.) *White Media and Black Britain* (London: Arrow Books, 1975) pp. 15–38.

Husband, Charles, 'The Mass Media and the Functions of Ethnic Humour in a Racist Society', in Antony J. Chapman and Hugh C. Foot (eds) *It's a Funny Thing, Humour* (Oxford: Pergamon, 1977a).

Husband, Charles, 'News Media, Language and Race Relations: A Case Study in Identity Maintenance', in Howard Giles (ed.) *Language, Ethnicity and Intergroup Relations* (London: Academic Press, 1977b) pp. 211–40.

Husband, Charles, 'Social Identity and the Language of Race Relations', in Howard Giles and Bernard Saint-Jacques (eds) *Language and Ethnic Relations* (Oxford: Pergamon Press, 1979).

Husband, Charles, *Race, Identity and British Society*, Units 5–6 of Block 2, Course E.354, *Ethnic Minorities and Community Relations* (Milton Keynes: Open University Press, 1982).

Johnson, Paul, *The Offshore Islanders* (Harmondsworth: Penguin Books, 1975).

Jones, M. and J. Dungey, *Ethnic Minorities and Television* (Leicester: Centre for Mass Communication Research, 1983).

Jordan, Winthrop D., *White Over Black* (Harmondsworth: Penguin, 1969).

Joshua, H. and T. Wallace, *To Ride The Storm* (London: Heinemann, 1983).

King, P., *Toleration* (London: George Allen and Unwin, 1976).

Krausz, E., *Ethnic Minorities in Britain* (London: MacGibbon and Kee, 1971).

Krugman, Herbert E., 'The Impact of Television Advertising: Learning Without Involvement', *Public Opinion Quarterly*, vol. 29, no. 3 (Fall 1965).

Kuepper, William, G., E. Lynne Lackey, and E. Nelson Swinterton, *Ugandan Asians in Great Britain* (Beckenham: Croom Helm, 1975).

La Fave, Lawrence, 'Humour Judgements as a Function of Reference Groups and Identification Classes', in J. H. Goldstein and P. E. McGhee (eds) *The Psychology of Humour* (New York: Academic Press, 1972) pp. 195–210.

La Fave, Lawrence, Jay Haddad and William A. Maesen, 'Superiority,

Enhanced Self-Esteem, and Perceived Incongruity Humour Theory', in Tony Chapman and Hugh Foot (eds) *Humour and Laughter: Theory, Research and Applications* (London: John Wiley, 1976).

La Fave, Lawrence, Jay Haddad and Nancy Marshall, 'Humour Judgements as a Function of Identification Classes', *Sociology and Social Research*, vol. 53 (1973–74) pp. 184–94.

La Fave, L., K. McCarthy and J. Haddad, 'Humour Judgements as a Function of Identification Classes: Canadian vs American', *Journal of Psychology*, no. 85 (May 1973) pp. 53–9.

Leab, Daniel J., *From Sambo to Superspade: The Black Experience in Motion Pictures* (London: Secker and Warburg, 1975).

Levitas, R., *The Ideology of the New Right* (London: Polity Press, 1986).

Miles, R., *Racism and Migrant Labour* (London: Routledge and Kegan Paul, 1982).

Miles, R. and A. Phizacklea, *White Man's Country* (London: Pluto, 1984).

Moore, Robert, *Racism and Black Resistance in Britain* (London: Pluto, 1975).

Moore, Robert and Tina Wallace, *Slamming the Door: The Administration of Immigration Control* (London: Martin Robertson, 1975).

Murdock, Graham and Peter Golding, 'For a Political Economy of Mass Communications', *The Socialist Register 1973* (London: Merlin Press, 1974).

Murdock, Graham and Peter Golding, 'Capitalism, Communication and Class Relations' in James Curran, Michael Gurevitch and Janet Woolacott (eds) *Mass Communication and Society* (London: Edward Arnold, 1977).

Murray, N., 'Anti-racists and other demons: The press and ideology in Thatcher's Britain', *Race and Class*, vol. xxvii, no. 3 (Winter 1986) pp. 1–20.

Phizacklea, A. and R. Miles, *Labour and Racism* (London: Routledge and Kegan Paul, 1980).

Pines, Jim, *Blacks in Films* (London: Studio Vista, Cassell, 1975).

Priest, R. F., 'Election Jokes: The effects of reference group membership', *Psychological Reports*, no. 18 (1966) pp. 600–2.

Priest, R. F. and J. Abrahams, 'Candidate preference and hostile humour in the 1968 elections', *Psychological Reports*, no. 26 (1970) pp. 774–83.

Rex, John and Robert Moore, *Race, Community and Conflict* (London: Oxford University Press/IRR, 1967).

Rugg, Aukua, 'Reviews: The Fosters', *Race Today*, vol. 8, no. 5 (May 1976) p. 117.

Saakana, A. S., 'Channel Four and The Black Community' in S. Blanchard, and D. Morley, *What's This Channel Four?* (London: Comedia, 1982).

Searle, C., *The Forsaken Lover* (Harmondsworth: Penguin, 1973).

Seidel, G., 'Culture, Nation and "Race" in the British and French New Right', in R. Levitas (ed.) *The Ideology of the New Right* (London: Polity Press, 1986).

Seymour-Ure, Colin, *The Political Impact of the Mass Media* (London: Constable, 1974) p. 114.

Shabazz, Menelik, 'The Fosters from embarrassment to insult' *Grass Roots*, vol. 4, no. 8 (September–October 1976) p. 10.

Sharf, Andrew, *The British Press and Jews under Nazi Rule* (London: Institute of Race Relations/University Press, 1964).

Sivanandan, A., 'Alien Gods' in B. Parekh (ed.) *Colour, Culture and Consciousness* (London: Allen and Unwin, 1974) pp. 104–18.

Sivanandan, A., 'Race, class and the state: the black experience in Britain', *Race and Class*, vol. XVII, no. 4 (Spring 1976) pp. 347–68.

Smith, David J., *The Facts of Racial Disadvantage* (London: PEP, 1976).

Smith, D. J. and J. Gray, *Police and People in London* (Aldershot: Gower, 1985).

Surlin, Stuart, H., 'Bigotry on Air and in Life: The Archie Bunker Case', *Public Telecommunications Review* (April 1974) pp. 34–41.

Tajfel, Henri, 'Social identity and intergroup behaviour' *Social Science Information*, vol. 13, no. 2 (1974) pp. 65–93.

Tajfel, H., *Differentiation Between Social Groups* (London: Academic Press, 1978).

Tajfel, H., *Human Groups and Social Categories* (Cambridge: Cambridge University Press, 1981).

Tajfel, H., *Social Identity and Intergroup Relations* (Cambridge: Cambridge University Press, 1982).

Tajfel, H., *The Social Dimension* (Cambridge: Cambridge University Press, 1984).

Tate, Eugene D. and Stuart H. Surlin, 'A Cross-Cultural Comparison of Viewer Agreement with Opinionated Television Characters', paper given to the International Communication Association, Intercultural Communications Division, Chicago, Illinois, April 1975.

Taylor, Francina, *Race, School and Community*(London: NFER, 1974).

Taylor, Paul, 'Laughter and Joking – The Structural Axis', paper given to the International Conference on Humour and Laughter, Cardiff, July 1976.

Terry, Antony, personal communication, 1974.

Troyna, B., *Public Awareness and the Media* (London: CRE, 1981).

Troyna, B., 'Reporting the National Front: British Values Observed', in C. Husband (1982).

Troyna, B. and J. Williams, *Racism, Education and the State* (Beckenham: Croom Helm, 1986).

Turner, J. C., 'The Experimental Social Psychology of Intergroup Behaviour', in J.C. Turner and H. Giles (eds) *Intergroup Behaviour* (Oxford: Basil Blackwell, 1981).

Vidmar, Neil and Milton Rokeach, 'Archie Bunker's bigotry: A study in selective perception and exposure', *The Journal of Communication*, no. 24 (1974) pp. 36–47.

Wallman, S., 'The Boundaries of "Race": Processes of Ethnicity in England', *Man*, vol. 13 (1978) pp. 200–17.

Walvin, James, *The Black Presence* (London: Orbach and Chambers, 1971).

Wilhoit, G. Cleveland and Harold de Bock, *Archie Bunker in a Foreign Culture*, A Panel Study of Selectivity Processes in the Dutch Television Audience, Colloquium at the 10th General Assembly and Scientific Conference of the International Association for Mass Communication Research, Leicester, September 1976.

Williams, J., 'Redefining institutional racism', *Ethnic and Racial Studies*, vol. 8, no. 3 (July 1985) pp. 323–48.

Young, K., 'Ethnic Pluralism and the Policy Agenda in Britain', in N. Glazer and K. Young (eds) *Ethnic Pluralism and Public Policy* (London: Heinemann, 1983).

Zijderveld, A. F., 'Trend Report: The Sociology of Humour and Laughter', *Current Sociology*, vol. 31, no. 3 (Winter 1983) pp. 35–59.

Zillman, Dolf and Joanne R. Cantor, 'A Disposition Theory of Humour and Mirth', in Tony Chapman and Hugh Foot, *Humour and Laughter: Theory, Research and Applications* (London: John Wiley, 1976).

9 Scriptwriters and Producers: A Dimension of Control in Television Situation Comedies

Paul Taylor

There are a great many factors which affect and determine the sort of comedy output seen on television and this chapter concentrates on just one aspect: the relationship between the writer of situation comedies and the producer of the programmes (largely as a company employee). There are three linked areas which need consideration here: the initial stages of planning a programme, control over the artefacts (cast, script and over-all process), and the judgement of success or failure seen in terms of relative contributions. That the *content* of programmes will be affected by these three factors seems beyond doubt but, while it is interesting and sometimes fruitful to analyse content, it is really approaching the matter from the wrong end. Decisions are taken at every stage in the process which affect the nature of the end product and unless some level of adequacy in explanation can be reached on this, discussions about form and content cannot proceed from the 'what' to the 'why'. There appears to be a need for an analysis similar to that undertaken by Goodlad (1971) who details the themes, motives, and plots found in televised and theatrical drama, though the work by Eaton (1978) suggests an alternative approach, specifically with regard to situation comedies, which may bypass the functionalism of Goodlad through appeals to what are interpreted as a semiology of television structure. There is, however, little room for content in what follows (and thus the picture given is necessarily one-sided) other than by implication.[1]

Unattributed quotes in this chapter are taken from interview material and much of the linking commentary is based on attendance at rehearsals and recordings of situation comedies; attributed quotes are identified in the usual way referring to the list of references at the end of the chapter.

179

PLANNING THE PROGRAMME

It may be as well to dent the impression that there is a pool of writers who submit their work to a pool of television companies from which a number of comedies result. Interaction is the keynote, with the television companies always retaining control and often acting as instigators rather than recipients of ideas. The pressure on filling schedules will always ensure that the companies have to take an active role; they cannot sit back and cream off the top percentage of unsolicited scripts (especially as the rejection rate of unsolicited material approaches 100 per cent).

The different ways in which a comedy gets into production should be seen as part and parcel of an obligation and need felt by the companies to provide entertainment according to a principle of returns for investment. The returns for the BBC are a demonstration that they are serving the public with popular programmes (always useful when the Corporation applies to renew its licence or increase the fee) and those for the commercial companies are the advertising revenues (especially as the fees are higher for more popular programmes). Situation comedies are expensive and such financial and artistic investment is only taken after due consideration at an executive level well above that of producer.[2]

The origins of *Hancock's Half Hour*, credited by many, including this author, as being the first British situation comedy in any developed sense, have been well documented (for example, Briggs 1979, Galton and Simpson 1961 and 1974, Hancock and Nathan 1975).[3] A very brief resumé may set the scene for a discussion of modern examples. Hancock had made several unsuccessful attempts to become a professional comic during the early years of the Second World War and, being called up in 1942, found some measure of success in concert parties and 'Gang Shows' under the direction of Ralph Reader. After the war he performed, mainly as a comic impressionist, in shows at the Windmill Theatre, in pantomime and in seaside variety. There were also occasional radio appearances in programmes like *Variety Bandbox, Workers' Playtime, Happy Go Lucky*, and *Forces All Star Bill*. He first met Galton and Simpson in October 1951; they had written a sketch for the comedian Derek Roy which Hancock admired and he asked them to write something for him which he could use in *Workers' Playtime*. The collaboration had started and continued with material for Hancock in *Forces All Star Bill*, produced by Dennis Main Wilson, and the series which followed

it *All Star Bill* and *Star Bill*. Galton and Simpson were not involved in Hancock's first big radio success; this was the role of the tutor in *Educating Archie* and the series was largely scripted by Eric Sykes.

As a writing team, Galton and Simpson had been in existence since 1948 and had made the break into radio through Gale Pedrick, then Script Editor at the BBC, who had passed one of their sketches to Roy Speer, then producer of *Happy Go Lucky*. When Main Wilson replaced Speer as producer he commissioned three programmes and while they continued to write for other comedians, notably Frankie Howerd and Dick Emery, the working relationship with Hancock increased. The idea to break away from short sketches, patter and structured jokes came from the writers:

> ... we wanted to do a half-hour situation comedy without funny voices and without jokes as such. The humour was to come out of the situation. Tony was in complete agreement and so was Dennis... The format we were after was a storyline not split up at all by other acts. Just go straight the way through like a half-hour play. (Galton and Simpson, 1974, p. 131)

The big influence, freely acknowledged by them, was the type of programme enjoying success in Britain but which originated in America – the domestic comedies like *Amos 'n' Andy* or *The Great Gildersleeve* – where the elements of variety were absent altogether or bracketed off.

The first edition of *Hancock's Half Hour* was broadcast in November 1954 with 12 per cent of the adult population listening; the series had built up a substantial following by early 1955. Hancock had appeared on the newly created Independent network in late 1955 with material by Galton and Simpson (under false names because of their contractual liability to the BBC). In 1956 suitable rewards were offered to Hancock by the BBC and the first television series of *Hancock's Half Hour* started on July in that year.

The two factors needing emphasis here are the role of BBC personnel in the process, and the opportunity for the writers to gear their material to a character with established appeal and popularity. Both these factors can be found in the following quote from a scriptwriter (with the series in question being an adaptation of some short stories):

> [The series] was really put together as a package by Jimmy Gilbert (then Head of Comedy at the BBC). I said I'd like to do some of

the stories, he said he couldn't sell them to the planners and potential American backers just on their own but we stood a chance if we could have the box-office appeal of _____. To my surprise, Jimmy was able to swing this. . . and the whole thing was a great joy.

Any assignment writer[4] will be faced with the same set-up – the package assembled without his contribution and the cast chosen or already in existence as a durable team – but the same may apply to other writers. In common mythology and in the opinions of television executives, the writer of situation comedies is a talented and creative individual who is much sought after for his expertise and rarity value. It is suggested here that the active part taken by television personnel may be crucial in not only determining the shape of the series as transmitted (see later) but also the initial concept. An example may help to demonstrate the possible source of the stimulus as the television professional rather than the writer.

A particular series was scripted by a partnership who had never worked together before but had situation comedy credits in their own right. According to the 'senior' partner the original idea came from an actor he knew socially as well as having written for him in the past. The opening conversations, as recalled by the writer, apparently ran along the lines of the actor casually remarking on his availability, his desire to find a series which reflected his appeal as a slightly pig-headed but likeable character, and the writer offering some ideas on basic plots and the way he saw a series shaping up around the character. Unknown to the writer (though later discovered), it was made clear from an interview with the producer of the subsequent series that the first moves had come from himself and the television company. The producer had long wanted to pair the actor with a certain actress (he felt they would spark off one another and form a popular 'team') and he discussed the project with his departmental head. Approval was obtained to approach possible writers, with the Head of Comedy actually suggesting the 'junior'. The junior agreed but asked to work with someone who had written for the lead actor to avoid possible clashes of ideas and personalities; he suggested the senior as the likeliest and favourite future partner. At this point a casual and unofficial approach was made to the proposed stars and after some preliminary discussion the lead actor agreed to approach the senior writer as mentioned above. It should be apparent that, even at the stage where the scripts had not been

started, key personnel other than the writers had definite ideas about how the series should look.[5]

A number of meetings were arranged by the producer to work out the over-all format of the series. These took place at the company's offices and present were the producer, senior and junior writers, the actor, and occasionally the actress and the Head of Comedy. It was decided to go for 13 episodes and various plots were considered which also meant that suggestions for the supporting cast were aired. The producer took the role of chairman and the actor took to himself, with the producer's agreement, an effective power of veto over the writers' suggestions as to plot or aspects of the character. From these meetings the writers put forward a pilot script which had to be agreed by the Head of Comedy (having already 'passed' the producer and actor) who, according to the senior writer, felt there were few risks and commissioned a full series subject to him selling it to the planners. Everybody seemed to feel confident about the proposed series and the producer started to prepare budgets, plan location filming, work out timetables, and organise the more mundane aspects of production. The first programme of the series was recorded about seven months after the first full discussion.

Two further examples from different programmes introduce new elements. In the first, the process is neatly compressed by the writer:

> [An actor], at my suggestion, was cast in 'A' in 1975 and was apparently impressed by my work in that he took the part. He had already agreed to do a series for Yorkshire TV later in the year based on a pilot written in 1974 by [another writer] who was not available to write the series and [the actor] asked for me. I spoke to Duncan Wood, Head of Yorkshire TV Light Entertainment, and he was happy to have me. End of story.

It should be explained that 'A' was not the series in question but a stage play which had been transferred to television as a series. The element of a writer picking up a pilot from someone else need not substantially alter the basic process which may be understood, from the writer's further comments, as the company approaching an actor and commissioning a pilot. Secondly, another writer talked briefly of the origins of his work.

> Both the current series came into being via the idea being talked about to the respective Heads of Light Entertainment, then a pilot show and subsequently a series being commissioned.

Other writers talked of ideas being given to them by companies as the most common way of getting a programme started. Here, certainly, the role of Comedy Advisers (employed by the company to generate new ideas, among other things) is instrumental, just as the Heads of Departments play an active part in appointing producers, inviting actors for lunch, and maintaining contacts with writers. The traffic of ideas is not, of course, just one way from the companies outwards but it should be emphasised that they are always involved at the earliest possible stage; if the original impetus comes from the writer rather than the company it will not be long before they exercise their discretionary powers.

A final example may indicate the process where stars are absent. As there was no possibility of interference by the performers (unchosen at the planning stage) the writers had a freer rein:

> Most of the parts we wrote with specific people in mind and we actually got the people we wanted because we were fortunate that they were available. I don't think that's general, though, it's just the way we did it.

It may be an elementary choice but it is a choice nonetheless: the difference between writing for a predetermined character and the opportunity of creating one while relying on a pool of known actors. There was, however, the expected early involvement of the company. The producer gave the story behind the start of the programme. He had been producing a particular comedy series when he was contacted by an agent representing a relatively new writer; the agent suggested he should watch an episode of another series which his client had written with his partner. It is assumed that this producer was not the only one contacted but he appears to have been the only one to have done anything about it. He watched the episode, remembered the names of the writers and the sort of dialogue, and had the opportunity some two years later to call upon them. He had been given a brief by his company to find a new series which would get away from a domestic basis and bring some new faces to television; according to the producer, the company had recently fallen out rather badly with one of their regular star performers and had decided, as a matter of policy, to try a new approach away from 'top billing'. The producer contacted the writers and asked them to submit draft ideas on any setting they chose as long as it was not domestic; they were also told not to write around any established

performer but to create a vehicle for new talent. Among the ideas submitted was the one later turned into the series – it fitted the brief and the producer liked it, but at first the producer had difficulty in selling it to the company who were only prepared to experiment so far. However, a change of departmental heads brought the producer a new ally; as part of the process of flexing his muscles, the Head of Comedy argued for the series on a point of principle (to establish the limits of his authority in relation to the company). The series was commissioned and production eventually started.

It is not suggested that the above descriptions are the only ways of getting a programme on the air but they do appear to be the most common; they are certainly more common than the successful submission of a new idea.[6] The early involvement of television professionals, especially as providers of ideas or creators of programme packages, may have two important consequences for the sort of situation comedies that appear. Firstly, the form and content of such programmes are largely determined to match the professionals' concept of entertainment.[7] Specific examples are easy to suggest but hard to substantiate; there are no rules or directives to include, for example, a plot at the expense of the GPO or a jibe at the Liberal Party. There is no conspiracy to ensure that certain issues are presented in such a way to esteem or disparage whatever beliefs or norms are given a comic treatment; there are no written guidelines informing producers what is and what is not considered preferable (or essential) in the way of material (and the infamous Green Book, which gave the maxim, 'If in doubt, don't', on dubious matters, has long disappeared). However the absence of formal and easily identifiable policy does not mean that television production takes place without restrictions or sanctions which directly affect the content of programmes.[8] On the most basic level there are inclusions and exclusions discoverable through content analysis; it would, one presumes, be possible to tabulate figures for types of plot, settings, class of main characters, and so on, to give statistics about frequency, emphasis, or type of motivation of the main characters. If this sort of content analysis can be linked to the process of production, through interviews and situational analysis, then some inner logic might be discovered which links the content of the programmes to a television ideology. It might, in short, identify those elements of an editorial grid through which the writer's script must pass.

Secondly, the role of the writer may be reduced to that of an artisan rather than an artist, a jobbing writer rather than an inspired

creative talent. Experience may teach writers that executive involvement with their script or concept leads in certain directions as a result
of the primary consideration of entertainment. Those writers with a
burning zeal to express an opinion are unlikely to be attracted to the
situation comedy as a medium or else, if they are attracted, find it
difficult to maintain momentum in the face of the need to be funny
and attract audiences. The relative lack of power enjoyed by a writer
emphasises that situation comedies are first and foremost television
products rather than a simple transfer of a writer's idea to the screen;
as such, they are subject to an organisational ideology which seeks to
maximise audiences. One method of approach would be to link
content with ideology (though the chances of finding simple
equations between the two are slim indeed); it would be preferable
here to leave content aside and concentrate on an aspect of
ideology. The most direct contact a writer will have with a television
company is in his relationship with the producer, as a representative
of that company, and it is this that I would now like to outline.

KEEPING CONTROL

The 'keeping control' refers to producers and not the writers, but
there are exceptions. The more experienced and established the
writer is, the more authority he can attach to himself and his work in
any subsequent discussions during production. From the 14 writers
interviewed, only two managed to keep a degree of editorial control
over their script, the first through a forceful personality:

> ... the writer has to be much more powerful [than in drama], at
> least in my experience. I go down there and play Hamlet and make
> a bloody nuisance of myself. I think writers far too often don't
> assert themselves in this field ... they know much better than
> anyone else how the thing should be done.
>
> I've never sent in a script without thinking that's the best I can
> do. When I send it in I don't expect them to muck it about. I've
> seen scripts sent in by other writers and I can see that it's straight
> off the typewriter and they know they're going to have to rewrite it
> several times. I do my re-writes before anybody sees it.

The second writer keeps control through great depth of experience
as writer, actor and theatrical director:

I can direct actors. I write something, I cast it. I know exactly what I want – what do I want some guy to come along and muck it up for me. I'm an exception, I dare say, to the rule. Supposing I do write something and [the producer] casts it wrongly – this can happen – and he's got no idea of what I want? If I lose control, the whole work goes up the spout. I've done hundreds of comedies and farces and this is my strength, I feel.

This quote raises the subject of casting, but before commenting on this aspect of control, there are some examples of the more common process of script negotiation which points to the two writers above as being somewhat exceptional.

The power of the producer can be clearly demonstrated, especially if he is working in close conjunction with a script editor,[9] in terms of how much of the writer's original intentions and script are represented in the final recorded version. Bearing in mind that the writer's creative preserve has already been eroded in the way that the programme concept is likely to have occurred, the percentage of that preserve kept intact may be low indeed:

I've done a script which everybody thought was terrific – when it actually appeared on the screen it was pretty lousy. I think I got about 30 per cent of the script on the screen, or less, because of everybody else's alterations and interference. This is when I first started, when I didn't have any say at all. If it's bad and it sinks, I'd rather sink on my own ship than on somebody else's.

It's a process of wearing down, it's a process of erosion. Speight was absolutely dogmatic – he would say, 'That's the way I'm going to do it, if you don't like it, don't have it.' And it paid off because in the end he got over his style of what he wanted to do ... I had terrible rows in the early days but with me it didn't pay off, so in the end I said, 'To hell with it.' You get what you can, you get as big a percentage as you can, you settle for 60 to 70 per cent in the end. You say, 'I know the other 40 per cent is not what I want', but what the hell can you do?

A successful series will obviously give the writer the power to bargain from a position of strength as no one in the business would willingly lose programmes which were attracting record audiences (though in the end, Speight and the BBC fell out rather badly). However, very few series could claim to be essential to the television

company, which leaves few options open to the dissatisfied writer. He can withdraw his labour on a point of principle but must, as a result, attract the kind of reputation of being unreliable which could severely restrict his future employment.[10] Other options may be effectively closed as the following quotation suggests. It comes from a writer who was then enjoying a success in the ratings but had had his relative failures in the past:

> You take the script along, God willing, some weeks or even months before the recording. It's rarely totally rejected, sometimes totally accepted, and usually accepted after some re-writes have been agreed. The size of these depends on the producer and often on how much he fancies himself as a creative writer. Mostly, they're fairly minor and obviously always agreed – though I must admit that I have sometimes agreed reluctantly to a re-write and found the producer to be right in the end. I'm speaking of my own experience here, of course. I know of cases where the script is put together by a sort of committee of writer, producer and star, and then sent out under the writer's name. I know of others where the writers turn up at rehearsal with a sort of blue-print for a script which is then kicked around by all present and ad-libbed into a final version.
>
> The writer is expected to turn up at the run-through on the first day of rehearsal for what should be only minor cutting and polishing. I have once had to go home to write a new scene overnight for length, but only once. I suppose writers could attend all the rehearsals but it's not encouraged and, personally, I find them boring. I don't go back until the final day in the studio for the run-throughs. Between those two attendances much may happen. Usually I find that bits have been cut for time and sometimes bits have been altered slightly. The alterations I can frequently change back if I feel strongly enough about them but sometimes, as with _____, you can arrive to find the script has been completely rewritten by the stars and the producer has allowed them to do it. On the first show, we had exactly four straight lines left of the original script. They'd even changed the number of the house they were living in. . .

The Writers' Guild could have been called in and pressure brought to bear on the television company, the writer thought, with some chance of success, though this could well be over-optimistic.[11] Anyway:

... when the producer is siding with the stars, it would mean endless arguments and bad performances from the actors who didn't want to perform the lines. In the circumstances, my co-writer and I decided to leave them to it, take the money and run. The end result was disastrous and the series vanished without trace... I'm not boasting but simply stating a fact when I say that the only successes I've had are those in which the actors were prepared to say my lines as written almost to the last comma and the producer was prepared to make them. Actors, and not just stars, are far too prone to tinker about with scripts, and producers are far too prone to let them. Any argument will usually produce only a sulky actor and a rotten performance for which the writer all too often gets the blame.

Physical attendance throughout the process is not easy, nor is it paid, and the writer cannot expect to attend every meeting, discussion or briefing; he is not party to the numerous conversations in corridors or backstage chats but even if he were, there is no guarantee that his words would carry much weight. The producer will always retain ultimate control and has at his disposal the threat of referral upwards if his decisions are questioned.[12] His authority may be compromised, however, through his company's decision to rely on star performers as supposed audience-pullers.

One writer, who coincidentally also gave the figure of 60 per cent as an average for getting his script through the process, described several examples where there had been major interference by leading actors including changing the script on the night of recording with the connivance of other members of the cast and, one presumes, the producer. Feeling that they had gone behind his back to present a *fait accompli*, he complained to the Departmental Head and company executives but got nowhere, being told jokingly but firmly that the producer was right and that such-and-such a star was, of course, an experienced performer who knew the business backwards, and in changing the script he only had the best intentions for the show, and so on. The bigger the star, the more the producer's control may be threatened. One producer recounted an occasion where the star of the programme prepared, in secret, some slapstick business which he brought out during the live recording to the amazement of the other actors and the hysteria of the gallery. He also complained but, as the company valued the star's services more than his, all he could do was accept the situation and be forewarned about what to expect should he work with that performer again.

Another writer felt his work had suffered by his not being in attendance throughout the process (unlike the producer whose physical presence is guaranteed and whose office may serve as a concrete base emphasising his link with the company); he had some trouble, during the early stages of writing a particular series, in trying to achieve what he saw as a balance between verbal and visual humour. The star saw his forte as the latter, the producer was prepared to comply, but the writer managed to keep some sort of pressure on for his original idea. Unfortunately, for the writer, he was hospitalised for a period of weeks and on his return found that what little control he once enjoyed had now vanished – the script had gone into rehearsal as a collection of pratfalls, walking into doors, and spilling drinks interspersed with gag-lines and name-calling. The producer and the star put up a united front and the crucial element of time (with recording a few days away) knocked out the possibility of considered rewrites or reasoned debate. [13]

All is not gloom from the writers' point of view. As the following quotes indicate, there may exist possibilities for negotiation, especially where the producer exercises his authority diplomatically rather than dogmatically or to keep a star happy:

In the best of possible worlds – and this does happen surprisingly often – decisions are a group thing. Once a crunch of any kind comes, the ultimate decision about a programme comes from the producer.

One has to work intimately with the producer and he must be able to produce the show in the way that the writers have conceived it. . . the script has to be produced and directed more or less as it is written.

You do have a sort of control because it doesn't end with just writing it. I go to rehearsals and you are there to suggest, change, alter, put in or take out lines. Although it's not always acknowledged by the producer the writer does have a certain amount of control.

Before starting the series I had a couple of meetings with [the producer]; long talks about the nature of the show, the qualities of the actors, the technical limitations we were working under, et cetera, et cetera. Similarly, before starting the second series,

trying to build on strengths, eliminate weaknesses, extend and develop in healthy directions. Now, I'm writing the scripts, I pass them to [the producer], he reacts, we'll meet to discuss possible amendments. [The star] and [the Head of Comedy] also see the scripts and have their say. My relationship with [the producer] is very friendly and easy-going. We laugh at the same things.

This last quote may serve to underline two points. Firstly, diplomacy and friendly agreements may be the order of the day not just because of the personalities involved but also because the writer accepts that he is not in full control of his script. Secondly, and certainly as far as situation comedies are concerned, the essential triviality of much of the material ('Is it worth the argument...') may release the writer from an obligation to fight for power in the face of a chain of authority ('...which you are likely to lose anyway'?) demanding regular supplies of what is deemed to be popular television entertainment. In short, the writer is working in a medium where the terms of reference are decided largely by television professionals whose job is to attract, keep and entertain as large an audience as possible rather than give opportunities to the expression of the creative and committed writer; where these two match, and this is a personal view, programmes like *Porridge* or *Steptoe and Son* may result. I would suggest they fail to match in the great percentage of occasions either because committed writers choose other types of programmes or media or because the creative writer cannot ensure that his intentions will reach the screen without alteration.

Producers may understandably articulate their roles in terms of diplomacy rather than bare exercise of authority or the expedient cooperation with stars. Those interviewed gave quotes which are essentially the same as the two given below:

I have the power, I suppose, to say, 'That line shall not go in' or 'You will say that that way', but my way is to create the atmosphere, to guide and to nurture the thing along.

The producer plays a very big part but obviously without the script you have nothing. You start with the egg and hatch it out. But as Granada always say – any programme is a result of teamwork. The writers originate the idea but the total creation involves a lot of other people, not least the people playing it. A good script can be ruined by miscasting – the casting is very much the producer's and

director's responsibility. Together with the writers, perhaps, but the producer has the last word in all of that.

The producer is bound to serve the television company to a greater extent than the writer and this may be the basis of many of his decisions on any number of levels from the straightforward desire to progress in his career to the more complex one of taking on of the attitudes and policies of the company. Obviously, many of his decisions are specific and related to the groundwork of producing a comedy show, as the following suggests:

> You get a script in and you read it and you think, basically, not of the jokes but of the plot and the construction of the plot . . . where it's weak or where it can be improved or in some cases you reject it entirely . . . I suppose you may reject one in thirteen totally. On the other hand, you tend to just make plot changes in those initial moments, perhaps stressing one character – this is before the cast have even seen it – and that will help to strengthen it. I've just been working with [a scriptwriting partnership] who are very good but they're not writers of situation comedy, they're sketch writers basically, and their plots were poor although their lines were good. Once you pointed it out, they saw it and there was no problem.

There must be an idea of what the final product should look like, a concept of what makes good television comedy; this was usually explained as a 'feel' for comedy, having a 'good ear', relying on instinct or gut reaction. It is equally plausible, and not contradictory, to pitch the level of explanation within television itself rather than the individual and his preferences or tastes. In short, the producer's own ideas (and those of the writer, for that matter) may not only reflect a television ideology but also ultimately derive from it through the processes of socialisation, experience, perceiving expectations and accepting as routine the numerous decisions that have to be taken to achieve a product which succeeds with both the audience and the companies; in the final outcome, the audience and the companies may be indistinguishable in terms of judgement of success or failure.

Davis (1960) and Thomas (1962, p. 100) give adequate definitions of the jobs undertaken by producers and directors[14] which were confirmed by the producers interviewed in this study:

> You are appointed to a specific programme and for that you have

to look after, as a producer, the financial and general structure of the programme. Basically, you are usually, but not always, handed a star and a subject.

Once it is decided to do a programme then you are responsible for getting that programme on to the air.

The word 'responsible' has commonly come to mean 'being in charge' but also carries the notion of accountability and these two strands are evident in how producers see their position. For example, one producer stated:

> If one is made a producer one of the reasons is that he is held in esteem as a responsible person – and you wouldn't employ irresponsible people to be producers because it's a very powerful position.

The most visible attributes of responsibility may be seen when situation comedies edge into possibly controversial ground – sexual innuendo, racial humour, 'serious' topics, and so on – where the chain of thought is circular but runs something along these lines: large audiences need to be attracted, entertainment is popular and shown during peak hours when most people who will watch are watching (including families); the obligation is to amuse rather than shock or provoke; the more families that are shocked the fewer viewers. The responsible producer is well aware of the ill-defined boundaries of good taste as settled by the companies (just as the scriptwriter who refers to 'self censorship' is, perhaps, reflecting the same ideology).[15] It is highly unlikely that they would be situation comedy producers if they wanted to make controversial statements; it is more unlikely that even if they wanted to they would be allowed it; it is verging on the impossible that if they managed to incite protests and outrage public opinion they would be allowed to do so again.

It would be naive to state that producers are the willing but unwitting exponents of a company ideology (such ideology being very briefly discussed in the conclusion) and this interpretation of a complex issue can only be implied here rather than fully supported. If such is the case, however, and producers have a large degree of control over scripts, as suggested above, then it may be fruitful to widen the picture here to include the matter of casting and what sort of control the producer enjoys thereover. As may be expected,

casting decisions reflect the power relationship between the writer and the producer and whoever can exercise authority over casting can alter the terms of that relationship in his favour. The really powerful writer may demonstrate his status in this field; in answer to a question about how much say a writer has in choosing the cast, one replied:

> One hundred per cent. I wouldn't be interested in writing otherwise. I couldn't write for anybody if I didn't have complete say because I write for the cast. I cast from actors when I'm writing, I cast the parts in my mind because I know so many actors; as I'm writing the characters more, I see the characters playing the parts.

Another writer had a clause in his contract which ensured a say in the matter, and added:

> On the running characters they should always consult you because if they use someone you just don't like, you can't see them playing your character . . . you've got to write six more with this man you can't even see saying your lines. Then, they're asking for trouble.

The less experienced the writer, the more meetings and discussions with 'joint' decisions take place. One writer praised London Weekend Television because they always invited him to their casting conferences (unlike the other commercial companies for which he had worked), but he realised that he was effectively a non-voting member and could only argue for a particular actor through requests rather than demands. The usual process is one of negotiation along a continuum of experience with the producer having the final say in all but the rarest of cases. A fairly typical comment from writers is represented by the following:

> [I] usually [have] some say, yet. Certainly, as far as the leads are concerned agreement is generally reached between the producer/ director and me. Clearly, a director would be barmy to cast someone I hated (or who hated me) in the lead for a series I was writing. Featured players, unless I get a flash of inspiration, I usually leave to the director. He knows more of them than I do and most directors have their own little rep of supports they consider dependable. I have squashed a few *bêtes noires* and boosted a few unemployed mates but, on the whole, there's hardly any nepotism as far as I'm concerned.

The producers interviewed all reflected this attitude of friendly cooperation but, when pressed on the point, admitted that they had the ultimate authority – it was just that discretion was the better part of valour and it was sensible policy to let a valued writer have his head as far as was practical, while less established writers might need to be led a bit more. The fact that producers, as employees of the company, might be subject to other pressures than finding the right actor for the role, was suggested strongly by one writer who has suffered, according to himself, a succession of bad casting decisions:

> The casting departments at the television companies have a kind of chip on their shoulder. They don't like other people doing their job. Their job, in fact, is just to assist; a casting director is to help the producer find the right people. He should submit a short-list of people and make a recommendation and occasionally say, 'I think so-and-so would be perfect for this part'. A casting director is a kind of assistant, he's useful in the same way as a stage manager is useful, or a secretary. However, they have an inflated status at the television companies and particularly we found with _____ it was virtually impossible to get anyone that we wanted into the show because they felt that it was the writers infringing on their department. And the producer, he works at the company, we don't as it were, although we write the show we're not there every day, we're not part of the politics that any office has – it was politically wise for the producer to keep the casting department happy, we used to feel, to the extent of casting the wrong people.

The producer's right to cast may well be tempered, also, by diplomacy and gentle persuasion which is subject to, and supports, the common mythology of the situation comedy scriptwriter as a *rara avis* which should be well nurtured and rewarded.[16]

RELATIVE CONTRIBUTIONS: JUDGEMENT OF SUCCESS[17]

As may be expected, the writers interviewed saw their own contribution as the crucial element in creating a successful programme or series – the more of their original script and casting intentions that were reflected in the final product, the better that product would be – though this may lead one to assume, within a framework of control by producers, that the script matches company expectations.

Oddly enough, the producers also stressed the importance of the
script and tended to play down their own contributions:

> Basically a successful comedy is dependent on script and the
> artists. If you've got a good script and a bad cast you've got
> nothing; if you've got a bad script and good cast you've got
> nothing. You've got to have a good script and a good cast (then)
> there's nothing much you can do to ruin it.

> People say you've got to have ideas for comedy. Rubbish – the
> ideas are not the important thing. The important things are the
> comedy writing and the comedy casting and the direction as such.
> In that order – scripts first.

These sort of comments match those given by writers:

> Above everything you've got to have a good script, above
> everything else. A good script will just about carry a show. I've
> never seen a bad script carried by a good cast.

> I'd put the percentages at: scriptwriter, 50 per cent; producer, 20
> per cent; cast, 20 per cent; and sheer luck, 10 per cent. I think
> everybody agrees that you can do nothing without a good script,
> but even the best script needs the alchemy of the rest. And if that
> 10 per cent is missing, you haven't got a 90 per cent good show. At
> best, it'll just be passable.

> First, a good script, second a good and sympathetic producer, then
> a good cast. Last, and hardest to achieve, an empathy between the
> people involved which results in everybody working for the good
> of the show and not their own egos.

Either the producer's role *is* minimal (which seems unacceptable)
or it has been drastically underestimated by producers and scriptwriters alike. There are a number of reasons for this apparent anomaly.
Firstly, there may be a dimension of modesty/immodesty – the
producers' preferment of the soft glove, the writers' claims to be
artists – though this offers a very limited level of explanation.
Secondly, it rather depends on which script one is talking about. If it
can be assumed that the 'good script' or 'comedy writing' refers to the
finished and polished article as recorded and transmitted, then the

anomaly disappears altogether. Finally, a common occurrence is that of the largely acceptable script which is kept intact (or very nearly so); this need not mean that the scriptwriter has fought long and hard to preserve his artistic integrity but merely that he has understood the kind of output on which the companies rely and can write to an ill-defined standard of what makes a model situation comedy. This view is, perhaps, rather cynical though not quite as justifiably cynical as that of Powdermaker. Her comments on Hollywood screenwriters can usefully close this section:

> The problem remains essentially one of knowing how to achieve the best conditions for creative story-telling in a mass-production system. This cannot be done by men whose drive is for domination rather than creativity, who think in formulas and in clichés, and who have no realistic concept of the audience... Writing for the movies becomes the means to wealth or comfort, which eventually becomes the goal. The writers take over the executive and producer's values more successfully than the latter take over the artists' goals... In Hollywood, the writer does not write to be read. Nor do most writers write because they have something to say, or to express a point of view but rather in order to earn large weekly salaries. (Powdermaker, 1950 pp. 110, 149, 151)

There may be no direct parallel between Hollywood and Borehamwood (where ATV made so many of their programmes) but similarities might well outweigh any differences in the market-place of attracting audiences.

CONCLUSION

It has been suggested in this chapter that something or somebody invariably intervenes between the writer or his idea and the end product, the televised situation comedy. Nothing has been said of what consequences might arise from the fact that this end product is comic with the intention of provoking laughter. Although this affords a good entry into the subject (through, say, the work of Bergson, 1911), it is beyond the scope of this chapter to indicate the differences that may exist between the production of a situation comedy and, say, a documentary or a new programme.

The 'something or somebody' may exist in three areas. Firstly, the

original idea for a series is likely to be framed according to the perceived expectations of what the companies want. Obviously, if the package is put together by the company executives this must necessarily be the case, but even where the idea comes from 'outside' the type of material that may be suitable is now so well known to prospective writers that established patterns are more likely to be followed than broken. To get a series on television the writer must, at some point, obtain the sympathy of the executives who will make the investment. Secondly, the idea will be subject to a producer's understanding of what his company wants to appear.[18] Thirdly, the companies wish to attract large audiences by entertaining them.

This is not to suggest that the process is simple or linear (nor is it necessarily so that an increase in the writer's control over his material would lead to a significantly different output), but if a certain ideology from above informs on decision-making, then that ideology at least deserves some recognition. The closing comments are confined to a brief discussion of how television executives see the function of entertainment, with the preceding sections serving to indicate how this may be engineered through structure and organisation. Tom Sloan, Head of BBC Light Entertainment[19] throughout most of the 1960s, is forthright about his duty:

> As far as I am concerned, the purpose of television light entertainment is to help people relax, to make them feel that the world is a pleasant place. (Sloan, 1964, p. 22)

Or, more specifically:

> Personally, I believe that *all* television must be entertainment and, although it is reasonable, I think that what is known as light entertainment may have a slightly thinner intellectual content than other programmes; I see nothing wrong in this. I am sure the average viewer bought his television set for enjoyment rather than as a means of education or information, and I take the view that if after watching one of my programmes he feels a little more content with his human lot, then I have done my job. Of course, I want to stimulate him and interest him by our work, but if I more often simply relax him I do not consider I have wasted my time. (Sloan, 1965)

The same themes are repeated elsewhere (Sloan, 1970) and expanded to include the following observations: light entertainment

will tend towards conservatism; as a national network catering for audiences between 10 and 20 million there is no place for experimentation; light entertainment is geared totally to the idea that the majority of people want television to provide escape with a consequent onus on the department to provide that.

Bill Cotton, former Head of Comedy and Head of Light Entertainment with the BBC until his promotion to Controller of BBC1, has also indicated the twin themes of relaxing/amusing an audience and making sure the audience is of a large enough size. The sorts of programme that will deliver an amused audience are:

> ... good-humoured humour: 'Dad's Army', Corbett and Barker, Morecambe and Wise. I don't think you can opt out by using comedy to carry a message – particularly if the message is stale. I think comedy has a job now to keep a sense of balance, bringing us back to the fact that life isn't that bad. People aren't awful. (*Radio Times*, 18 January 1975)

And the size of the audience?

> ... any entertainment programme that attracts an audience of around 10 million is more than earning its keep. (*Stage and Television Today*, 13 January 1977)

One must assume that higher figures would be preferable but the equation is plain. Philip Jones, then Controller of Entertainment at Thames Television, has this to say on the subject:

> I like to think that the thought of the ratings does not stop us doing certain things ... they must be done with discretion because, sharing one channel among all the ITV contractors, our job in this department is to make programmes that do two things – not necessarily in this order. One is to capture a large audience; the other to make programmes as well of their kind as you can. It's a joint exercise: what will please the public and please light entertainment professionals at the same time. (Jones, 1977)

The responsibility to catch an audience and amuse it is, of course, not quite the same as amusing an audience through which you capture it but it is somewhat in the nature of a chicken-and-egg distinction and, mixing metaphors, it depends on which side of the

fence you sit. There is no need to ascribe to entertainment an element of 'narcotizing dysfunction', or to see it as a 'broadcast aspirin tablet';[20] nor is there any need to subscribe to a conspiracy theory. The end result, however, is that content may be affected by an interpretation of entertainment as that which must attract a large audience and keep it amused. One possible consequence, much debated in the 1950s and 1960s, is that conservatism becomes the norm as topics which might provoke or challenge are held back for 'serious' programmes with their supposed balance and evenhandedness. Dexter, for example has the following suggestive comments:

> Partly because people generally treat the mass media as entertainment – and entertainment ceases for most people to be entertaining if it challenges what they already believe – the mass media most of the time reinforce whatever people are inclined to believe. (Dexter, 1964, p. 12)

Probably, yes; but there is also the case where those in control of the programmes treat the mass media as entertainment and nothing more. Entertainment then becomes homogeneous, and not necessarily from the glib equation that if 12 million people watch it, it must be right. The individual choices and preferences of the creators and executives are bound through tradition, background, organisation and policy (both official and unofficial) to present a certain view of society. Situation comedies may not be as they are because such is the nature of comedy; they are as they are because such is the practice of television.

NOTES

1. Leaving 'content' out of this chapter may be a more basic fault than mere omission. While I am aware that suggestions about editorial policy affecting content are very much weakened by ignoring the latter, this is not the place to attempt a full-scale analysis linking production to content.
2. Curran (1979) gives the cost per hour of situation comedies as £49 000 (for the BBC); only drama is higher, at £56 000.
3. Claims for the first 'real' televised situation comedy in Britain have been made for *Fast and Loose* (for example, Black, 1972, p. 196 and Briggs, 1979, p. 716). The programme was shown in 1954, before *Hancock's Half Hour* but a personal communication from Bob Monkhouse, star and co-writer, clearly puts the series into a revue or variety mould:

Denis [Goodwin] and I attempted to invent an entirely new kind of structure for the show, making use of just a little film to link the songs and situation sketches. Each show began with an alarming opening gag for my entrance.... and then [I] did an opening monologue and gags which moved logically to the first sketch.

The show was, apparently, closer to a Crazy Gang type of stage act than existing radio or television forms; it also ran for 45 minutes per episode.

4. Assignment writers are those contributing separate episodes to an existing series. The structure of the programme is already determined and the characters developed; the assignment writer has to deliver a script which is consonant with established patterns and is likely to lose any control over his material:

> If you're in the situation of writing your own show which is successful and has been running for a long time, you're in a position to go down to rehearsals and to influence quite a few things. If you're contracted to work on somebody else's series you hand the script over to the producer and, in my experience, working it that way, if you get 60 per cent on to the screen of what you intended in the script, you're very lucky. (Scriptwriter)

5. See the conclusion to this chapter. Whether or not it is useful to see these personnel as 'gatekeepers' (see Lewin, 1947 and White, 1950 for the original articulation) is a moot point. The concept has been most widely applied to new programmes and newspapers where the flow of items through certain channels comes up against 'gates' and is either admitted or turned away according to the decision of the gatekeeper. While producers of situation comedies may well be gatekeepers, they are also instigators of ideas in the same way that executives put together programme packages. Although the concept of gatekeeping need not have an element of passivity I believe it is best restricted to its original use; as the concept has grown wider, it has lost some of its worth.

6. The 'new idea' of a series about the Home Guard turned into *Dad's Army*; Perry and Croft (1975) give brief details of the origins of the programme. There are other processes of getting a programme on the air: two popular methods are the adaptation of a book and the 'spin-off'. Of the first, recent examples include *No – Honestly, The Rise and Fall of Reginald Perrin, Wodehouse Playhouse* and *I Didn't Know You Cared*. This last series came from three novels by Peter Tinniswood who also wrote the television scripts. He is quoted (in *Radio Times*, 23 August 1975) as saying that the transfer from book to screen was relatively easy, but a perceptive article by Hunt (1976) demonstrates that the transfer involved considerably more than mere transcription. Differences include, for example, the hero Carter Brandon losing his virginity on a works outing in the books but remaining intact on television, and Uncle Staveley dying in print but recovering on the screen. Spin-offs include *Yus, My Dear* (from *Romany Jones*) and *Robin's Nest* and *George and Mildred* (both from *Man About the*

House), with a proposed regeneration of *It Ain't Half Hot Mum* in production at the present. This recycling of material from an old series to start a new one seems to be largely as a result of two pressures: to hang on to a proven success but to revitalise the schedules.

7. Almost without exception, the writers I interviewed stressed that they 'wrote for themselves' – if they found something humorous, then so would the audience – and little support was found for the suggestion that the medium intervenes between the artist and his craft, at least from the writers themselves. However, as Murdock and Halloran (1979) have suggested with regard to televised drama:

> Established writers . . . are expected to recognise the parameters of the situation and to cut their cloth accordingly. This means turning in work that fits the dominant style and is likely to attract audiences. Hence, they . . . are likely to play safe. (p. 280)

While the idea of the inspired writer, committed to the sanctity of his work, may be an attractive one it is likelier that the market demands of television will affect supply.

8. Such sanctions as do operate may be positive or negative with the rewards of promotion or increased status just as important as the punishments of dismissal or being placed in a backwater.

9. The role of the script editor was usefully summarised by one writer from his own experience:

> [As script editor] I'm responsible for collating everything, I'm responsible for the ultimate production of the script. I'm there to make sure it comes in on time, that it contains what we want it to and that any re-writes are done and done within the time required, that if the writer isn't getting the scene right then I'll have to re-write it. . .

On the most basic level, the job means ensuring that the submissions of assignment writers keep the characters true and do not invent plots which would be unbelievable or compromising to the series as a whole.

10. Reliability is a very highly regarded attribute, at least by the television companies. Schedules are planned several months ahead (if not a year or more) and series are an excellent way of filling in the blanks of weekly slots. A writer who regularly delivers a script to a good standard may well be preferred to one who delivers an exceptional script but outside the deadline.

11. The Writers' Guild was viewed with a certain amount of disrespect by the writers. Its powers to argue on behalf of its members are limited as the following suggests. The quote is taken from the official paper (*Writers News*, September 1976) and the author is a member of the Censorship Appeals Committee:

> . . . we don't pretend that protection under our Agreement is all that solid. The wording of the relevant clauses is vague and indefinite. The Independent Companies may make 'such reasonable alterations' as they 'shall consider necessary in the interests of good television production'. The BBC may, after a script has been

accepted, make 'minor alterations'. . . and before accepting a script may require 'certain alterations'. . . to make it acceptable for television use.

There is little doubt where the power lies.

12. Not only will scripts be seen at Departmental Head level, they are also subject to a second line of control – if the producer is in any doubt about content or style, he can 'refer up'. The likelihood of a producer being overruled by those above him is slim indeed and a fairly common ploy is for producers to use the threat of referral to establish their authority in the face of, say, a challenging writer. Garnham (1973, p. 28) has noted that the process of referral works to inhibit the producer – if he uses it too much he may be marked as lacking individual initiative, if he fails to use it he may be deemed irresponsible – and forces him to err on the side of safety.

13. Most programmes have only four half-days of rehearsal prior to recording. Once the script is in the hands of the actors on, for example, a Monday afternoon it would be a very self-assured and confident writer who would press the issue over control with recording looming on the horizon of Friday evening.

14. Full accounts of the role of the producer can be found in Cantor (1971), Elliott (1972) and Shubik (1975).

15. The boundaries of good taste were once clearly defined. The Green Book, referred to earlier, was issued by Michael Standing as BBC Director of Variety in 1949 and its contents are reprinted in Took (1976, pp. 86–91). Hood (1976, pp. 207–8) writes of light entertainment personnel as being able to judge, with the utmost precision, the boundaries of good taste and whose guiding principle is the depoliticisation of all situations (such act being, of course, political). Tunstall (1970, p. 27) has usefully commented on the ability of comedy programmes to carry political values.

16. The common mythology has been expressed on numerous occasions by television executives. See, for example, Muir (1966), Wheldon (1976), and Cotton (1977).

17. Other measures of success come from audience research, opinions of colleagues, television critics, instinctive feelings and the reaction of the studio audience. All of these are unreliable in their own way with the last a very poor indication indeed, see Taylor (1979).

18. Many writers somewhat bitterly pointed to the technical rather than creative backgrounds of producers (supported by the interview data here). See Wood (1976) for how this may help to generate comedy through, for example, the proper use of camera angles.

19. The organisation at the BBC comprises a Department of Comedy (mainly producing situation comedies) and a Department of Variety (producing the Val Doonicans and Harry Secombes). Both departments come under the umbrella of Light Entertainment.

20. 'Narcotizing dysfunction' and 'broadcast aspirin tablet' come from Lazarsfeld and Merton (1964, p. 465) and Muir (1966, p. 10) respectively.

REFERENCES

Bergson, H., *Laughter: An Essay on the Meaning of the Comic* (New York: Macmillan, 1911).

Bigsby, C. (ed.) *Approaches to Popular Culture* (London: Edward Arnold, 1976).

Black, P., *The Biggest Aspidistra in the World* (London: BBC, 1972).

Briggs, A., *The History of Broadcasting in the United Kingdom*, Vol. 4 *Sound and Vision* (London: Oxford University Press, 1979).

Cantor, M., *The Hollywood TV Producer* (New York: Basic Books, 1971).

Cotton, B., 'The BBC as an Entertainer', in *And They Call It the Good Life* (London, BBC, 1977).

Curran, C., *A Seamless Robe: Broadcasting Philosophy and Practice* (London: Collins, 1979).

Davis, D., *The Grammar of Television Production* (London: Barrie and Rockliff, 1960).

Dexter, L., in L. Dexter and D. White, *People, Society and Mass Communications* (New York: Free Press of Glencoe, 1964) pp. 3–25.

Eaton, M., 'Television Situation Comedy', *Screen*, vol. 19 (1978) pp. 61–89.

Elliot, P., *The Making of a Television Series* (London: Constable, 1972).

Fischer, H.-D. and M. Melnik, (eds) *Entertainment: A Cross Cultural Examination* (New York: Hastings House, 1979).

Galton, R. and A. Simpson, 'Writing for Hancock', *The Twentieth Century*, vol. 170 (1961) pp. 91–5.

Galton, R. and A. Simpson, *Hancock's Half Hour* (London: Woburn, 1974).

Garnham, N., *Structures of Television* (London: BFI, 1973).

Goodlad, J., *A Sociology of Popular Drama* (London: Heinemann, 1971).

Hancock, F. and D. Nathan, *Hancock* (London: Coronet, 1975).

Hood, S., 'The Dilemma of the Communicator', in C. Bigsby (ed.) *Approaches to Popular Culture* (London: Edward Arnold, 1976).

Hunt, A., 'A Slice of the Media', *New Society*, 3 June 1976, pp. 537–8.

Jones, P., 'The Serious Business of Sit Com', *Stage and Television Today*, 10 June 1977, p. 13.

Lazarsfeld, P. and R. Merton, 'Mass Communication, Popular Taste and Organized Social Action', in B. Rosenberg and D. White (eds) *Mass Culture: The Popular Arts in America* (New York: Free Press of Glencoe, 1964) pp. 457–73.

Lewin, K., 'Channels of Group Life', *Human Relations*, vol. I (1947) pp. 143–53.

Muir, F., 'Comedy in Television', BBC Lunchtime Lectures (London: BBC, 1966).

Murdock, G. and J. Halloran, 'Contexts of Creativity in Television Drama', in H.-D. Fischer and M. Melnik (eds) *Entertainment: A Cross Cultural Examination* (New York: Hastings House, 1979).

Perry, J. and D. Croft, *Dad's Army* (London: Hamish Hamilton, 1975).

Powdermaker, H., *Hollywood: The Dream Factory* (Boston: Little, Brown, 1950).

Rosenberg, B. and D. White (eds) *Mass Culture: The Popular Arts in*

America (New York: Free Press of Glencoe, 1964).

Shubik, I., *Play for Today: The Evolution of Television Drama* (London: Davis-Poynter, 1975).

Sloan, T., *Contrast*, vol. 4 (1964) p. 22.

Sloan, T., 'The Business of Light Entertainment', *Ariel*, vol. 10 (1965).

Sloan, T., 'Television Light Entertainment', BBC Lunchtime Lectures (London: BBC, 1970).

Taylor, P., 'The Studio Audience for Television Situation Comedies', in H.-D. Fischer and M. Melnik (eds) *Entertainment: A Cross Cultural Examination* (New York: Hastings House, 1979).

Thomas, H., *The Truth About Television* (London: Weidenfeld and Nicholson, 1962).

Took, B., *Laughter in the Air* (London: Robson, 1976).

Tunstall, J., *Media Sociology* (London: Constable, 1970).

Wheldon, Sir H., 'The British Experience in Television', *The Listener*, 4 March 1976, pp. 265–90.

White, D., 'The Gatekeeper: A Case Study in the Selection of News', *Journalism Quarterly*, vol. 40 (1950) pp. 283–90.

Wood, D., 'The Situation Comedy Situation', *Independent Broadcasting*, no. 8 (June 1976) pp. 15–17.

10 The Comedian as Portrayer of Social Morality

George E. C. Paton

Although historically the pedigree for the modern role of professional comedian is about a hundred years old,[1] there is very much less appreciation of his role in terms of the mutual expectations of his behaviour in interaction with other significant role players, especially his audience in contemporary society. At the very least, of course, in the consistency of his orientation to his audience, the comedian is expected to make them laugh. We can, then, say simply that the role of professional comedian is to elicit or invoke laughter in other persons by telling jokes about subjects, objects, or human situations which his listeners can cognise or perceive as being humorous. This role, in fact, can better be seen as consisting of a range of role-types as indicated by the designations of 'comedian', 'clown', 'satirist', etc., in its more professional or occupational guise. (see Table 10.1 below).

Whereas literary criticism, philosophy and psychology abound in analyses of what is comic, humour, laughter, etc., there are, unfortunately, few sociological studies of these phenomena and of comedians *per se*.[2] There is, however, a growing number of serious newspaper and journal articles on comedians who are currently in vogue, an increasing number of autobiographies and biographies of famous professional comedians past and present, in Britain and the USA, and even films and stage plays about the more celebrated or notorious 'folk hero' comedians – all of which provide a rich source of sociological material on their role in modern society. Amidst such variety it might be tempting to suggest that this makes sociological generalisations about their role even more tenuous, especially if this is coupled with the differing role-styles of comedians when permuted with different role-types. However, it is here suggested that, as in all social interactions, there is a tendency to 'typification', to use a Schutzian term, as well as a strong normative element governing the role relations between the professional comedian and the members of

his audience, particularly as the comedian, as a type of humorist, can be seen, following Bergson, as a 'disguised moralist'.[3] In her study of the burlesque comedian in American night clubs, Salutin further observes that because of his role distance he can 'play on what he perceives to be the sexual hypocrisy prevalent in our culture'.[4] It is suggested that this can also be extended to all forms of hypocrisy and prejudice or double-standards extensively present and displayed in society – between the sexes, ethnic groups, generations – which the comedian can play on and expose in his jokes and joking behaviour. Koestler's[5] 'bisociation' theory of humour, in stressing the way in which humorous stories – in our case the comedian's jokes – permit the perception of a situation or idea in two self-consistent but habitually incompatible frames of reference, neatly points up the wider ranging possibilities for the professional comedian to expose and play on double-standards in official morality or legitimated moral codes and actual moral behaviour; and also the shifting borderline between the two as morality becomes more 'permissive' with social change.

Here, then, it is possible to suggest that one facet of the role of the comedian with regard to listeners' expectations of him is that he legitimates a situation whereby, in laughing with him at the stereotypical patter of his jokes depicting the humour of a morally stressful social situation in real life, e.g. living with a mother-in-law, being discriminated against because of one's race, ethnicity, etc., this distances the listener from or temporarily suspends involvement in a real-life situation which clearly would be stressful, intolerable or insufferable for social actors themselves in reality, especially if they expressed such unvoiced resentments in non-joke form in real-life situations in which social tensions exist. Similarly, the comedian articulates and expresses linguistically the moral sentiments, attitudes, opinions, etc., which his listeners perceive as meaningful or recognisable and which they are inhibited by normative conventions from saying or cannot articulate/express so readily or so well. One is reminded here of the old saw, 'Many a true word is spoken in jest'.

Whilst this may suggest a social conservation function for the joking behaviour of the professional comedian, it should also be borne in mind that certain types of comedian tread more dangerously, especially in verbally manipulating the cognised and generally accepted boundaries between different and incompatible frames of reference in public morality. Thus, for example, Alan Brien, in reporting his visit to the Soviet Union, observed that the nation's top

comedy duo, 'In their patter . . . plough a satirical furrow across the Soviet landscape, reading items from the local press, explaining to each other situations the natives all understand but rarely discuss. It is a therapeutic act of social soil ventilation calculated never to go deep enough to hit an unexploded mine.'[6] The professional comedian may therefore, in his joking behaviour and verbal art be seen sociologically to linguistically mediate bisociated and incompatible frames of reference concerning social reality as linguistically understood by his audience. In so doing he performs a central function of the tension-management of morally problematical interpersonal situations in society. This can be contrasted with the tension-release functions of laughter highlighted by the psychologist.

THE VERBAL ART OF THE PROFESSIONAL COMEDIAN AND THE COMEDIAN'S WORLD

The professional comedian is, of course, a performing artist and his verbal art form or 'expressive activity'[7] is that of joking, i.e. the telling of jokes to an audience. Liam Hudson emphasises that the performance and the art, however ephemeral, of public figures such as famous comedians is deserving of the title 'work of art' which, in his words, is '. . . any expression of the imagination that is internally coherent and publicly negotiable – negotiable in that it becomes part of the coinage that a community uses in ordering its own longings'.[8] The successful comedian as a verbal performer requires to know what the community and culture from which his audience is drawn considers humorous if his jokes are to become part of its coinage. Although now increasingly rare, the one-time 'catch-phrase' was the stock-in-trade of countless professional comedians on the music hall and variety stage which was instantly recognised and reiterated by members of their audience to form part of the coinage of everyday humorous conversation in different communities throughout Britain. Humour, and its expression in joke form, has a particular place in the 'culture code'[9] of such communities and, in either consciously articulating and eliciting the longings – particularly the taboos[10] surrounding the moral longings of members of such communities – or unconsciously venting[11] the moral anxieties of such communities, the comedian can in his style of joking be seen as adopting the alternative role-types suggested by Fletcher[12] of 'conservative' or 'radical', dependent upon whether he is respectively articulating or ventilating

either an existing/traditional morality or a new/emergent morality. Thus the comedian's joke 'can be judged conservative or radical if, in its implications, it tends to reinforce the arrangements of society as it stands, or it protests against current arrangements'.[13]

Bauman[14] interestingly notes that folklore – which in its modern derivation may be said to include the verbal art and performance of the public figure or professional comedian – as largely a study of 'residual culture' looks backward to the past for its frame of reference and this clearly is reinforced by the stand-up comic adopting the conservative stance in joking about a community's morality and its taboos. By contrast the radical comedian's stance may be said to illustrate 'emergent culture', with its continuous creation of 'new meanings and values, new practices, new significances and experience'.[15] How the comedian will perform and exercise his verbal art of joking in relation to the targets or 'butts' of the humour encapsulated in his jokes – be they located in either the residual culture or emergent culture of his audience and himself – will depend not only on the 'surface properties' relating to the comedian's personal attributes (sex, ethnicity, etc.) but also his or her particular 'style' properties (principally fluency factors and personal hostility factors).[16]

In terms of the conservative/radical comedian role-types advanced above, it is of further interest to note the possible respective conjoining of two different role-styles, the first of which Pollio and Edgerley see as focusing 'the individual audience member on the here and now ... of his experiences, and a second ... which allows the individual member to transcend the situation and to roam in a sensibly-nonsensical world'.[17] They further suggest that this dichotomy distinguishes the comic from the humorist. Thus, the former '(and some of his near relatives – the nasty clown and the sarcastic wit) all focus the person on his immediate situation thereby making group structure and group solidarity a key issue. The humorist (and his relatives – the story-teller and the fabulist) all focus the audience member on himself and his experiences outside of the present context.'[18] In both cases, then, it is plausible to suggest that the comedian's verbal art of joking is essentially directed at either the residual or the emergent morality of a community with which he identifies and interacts professionally, or is identified by his audience as so directed towards. That the comedian's world is an essentially moral domain is further reinforced not only by the social control function performed by the comedian in the realm of social morality

but also the normative constraints (formal and informal) placed on him in his role-relationship with his audience in the social setting and 'focused activity'[19] of his joking performance.

JOKING FRAMES AND THE JOKING BEHAVIOUR OF THE PROFESSIONAL COMEDIAN

Handelman and Kapferer, in emphasising joking behaviour, note that apart from its function as an expressive and focused social activity, it is conducted in two types of 'joking frame'.[20] Whilst their emphasis derives but differs from the traditional anthropological interest in joking relationships in more informal settings, it can usefully be employed in the sociological analysis of the more formal entertainment setting in advanced societies in which the professional comedian performs and which helps to account for the adoption and development of either conservative or radical role-styles by the comedian. Essentially these joking frames suggest limits or social controls of a normative and linguistic nature which govern both the comedian's joking behaviour and his audience's receptivity to it. Thus Mary Douglas, in discussing social control of cognition and perception with special reference to joking and the permitting of joking, states that, 'social requirements may judge a joke to be in bad taste, risky, too near the bone, improper or irrelevant. Such controls are exerted either on behalf of hierarchy as such, or on behalf of values which are judged too precious and too precarious to be exposed to challenge.'[21]

In extending the analysis of the social control aspects of joking Handelman and Kapferer[22] suggest that in effect the auditors of the joker, the professional comedian in our case, 'issue' a 'license to joke' which establishes a frame around the subsequent joking behaviour of the joker or comedian. The first type of joking frame – '*setting-specific*' – is highly fragile depending as it does primarily on resources derived locally within the setting in which the activity occurs and the joking behaviour follows an indeterminate course. '*Category-routinised*' joking frames are anchored in the common recognition that particular categories of person can joke with one another and, accordingly, they are anchored in more general social conventions and are more resistant to subversion and to retransportation to overtly serious activity. This latter joking frame, unlike the former type suggestive of intergroup joking behaviour, also suggests

that it is more appropriate to joking relationships at the intragroup
or in intracommunity level in society and the social control function
of humour in the forms of joking about such relationships, especially
in hierarchically organised and socially stratified society. In this
connection it is interesting to note Duncan's illustration of joking
about the category-routinised stereotyped characteristics of European immigrants to the United States in the early part of this century
which he sees as a feature of their socialisation for membership in the
American community, so much so that, 'Such joking is really a form
of instruction, a kind of social control directed at those we intend to
accept once they learn to behave properly – that is like us.'[23] As
mouthed, for example in the form of the ethnic jokes of the socially
esteemed professional comedians operating in the category-
routinised joking frame, we can also perhaps subscribe to the view
that for appreciative listeners in the non-target community or public,
they constitute 'teachers we like'.[24] To summarise, then, we can see
that in exercising social control in both these joking frames, 'humour
may function to express approval or disapproval of social form and
action, express common group sentiments, develop and perpetuate
stereotypes, relieve awkward or tense situations, express group
sentiments, and express collective, sub-rosa approbation of action
not explicitly approved.'[25]

Such joking frames, then, insofar as they are formalised in our
case for the professional comedian and his audience, are evidenced
and effected principally through the language form of jokes and the
symbolic and meaning structures or 'culture codes' associated with
the joking behaviour of the comedian and cognised and compre-
hended by his auditors. It is suggested here that we can regard the
comedian's jokes as humorous verbal gestures (a form of what
Goffman calls 'sign vehicles'[26]) transmitted within joking frames
constituting the symbolic framework of language, the jokes being
seen by Granfield and Giles as a form of transmission of ideas
(especially, in our view, about social reality and morality) through
language. For them humour, like language itself, 'can possess
referential and expressive functions. Hence a humorous episode
functions referentially to represent a funny incident but also
expressively in providing implicit information on how we feel about
the target of the humour.'[27] As an expressed linguistic form or verbal
art form, joking both encourages and reinforces the development of
what the philosopher Perry calls 'intercognitions', which linked to a
community of objects yields communication or consciously shared

knowledge.[28] Joking, then, is an important linguistic mediating process and jokes are major sign vehicles in generating, developing and mediating intercognitions between the professional comedian and his audience by communicating or decoding implicit information or consciously shared knowledge or 'sets of meanings'[29] about the target in social reality of the humour expressed in joking, be it social situations, role-types, beliefs, social and individual behaviour, objects, events, etc. In terms of their sociological functions in relating jokes to social reality, differing joking frames are operative and the comedian's joke 'is only meaningful in the interaction between human beings. It is also in this interaction that the joke is born.'[30]

For our purposes, however, it is further necessary to distinguish potentially differing joking frames for our role-types of 'conservative' and 'radical' comedian. In expressing epigramatically the notion that the joke is the short-cut to consensus, Tom Burns[31] perhaps best sums up the significance for the 'conservative' comedian of the 'category-routinized' joking frame. The more obvious stereotypical aspects of this joking frame can be seen in the 'hot chestnut' jokes and the reliance of the stand-up comic on such stereotypes of social groups or more specific roles which are in some measure perceived by him and his audience as socially distanced–artificially, normatively, legally, etc. Obvious examples include the English comedian's 'Irish' jokes, jokes about 'mothers-in-law' and those referring to politicians and professional roles, eg. doctors, teachers, lawyers, etc. The truly radical comedian is the 'satirist' who can either adopt a setting-specific joking frame or a category-routinised one, or switch between them with great facility or verbal dexterity. However, what marks the satirist off from the 'conservative' stand-up comic is that essentially, in the brilliant insight of the theatre critic Harold Hobson,[32] the former is in collision, not collusion, with his audience.

Table 10.1   A Typology of Professional Comedians Operating Within Two Main Joking Frames

| | | Type of Comedian | |
		Conservative	*Radical*
Joking frame	Setting-specific	Ad-lib comic	Surreal comic
	Category-routinised	Stand-up comic	Satirist or burlesque comic

This, in effect, means that the satirist takes risks and his humour follows a more indeterminate course, whereas the stand-up comic flatters the general social conventions and prejudices of his audiences.[33]

The typology given in Table 10.1, then, is suggestive of the four main types of professional comedian who differentially operate, implicitly or explicitly, within the two main types of joking frame.

TWO ARCHETYPAL BRITISH COMEDIANS: LES DAWSON AND SPIKE MILLIGAN

To illustrate the way in which professional comedians operate within the different joking frames as typologised above, we have chosen two polarised exemplars: Les Dawson as representative of the category-routinised, conservative type of comedian on the one hand and, on the other hand, Spike Milligan as typifying a radical setting-specific comedian.

Les Dawson

Although, like a high proportion of the older generation of famous contemporary British comedians, Les Dawson retains links with the older music hall and variety tradition via the Working Men's Clubs in which he started his career, he has become a TV comic, certainly the first, as one critic has noted,[34] to be developed by Yorkshire Television. Whilst Eric Midwinter has perceptively noted that he is effectively one of the first 'atomic age comedians', at the same time Dawson, in the same author's view, maintains comic traditions, and historical and geographical strains as well, of some lengthier standing, so much so that 'his pedigree is Coronation Street out of Hindle Wakes. It is a reminder that the character of the thirties we associated with George Formby pushed hard for many into the forties.'[35] This is further reflected in the category-routinised or 'standard' and 'conservative' types of jokes he utilises as a stand-up comic and, in particular his seemingly anachronistic portrayal (in an age of greater equality between the sexes) as a 'hard man, anti-feminist in the fashion of W. C. Fields (a comedian he reveres)'.[36] Further evidence of his category-routinised joking framework is revealed by his statement: 'I think you have to choose your audience. You can't be loved by everybody.'[37]

ional indication of the category-routinised conservative
wson's comedy can be obtained from a content analysis of
n of his standard jokes[38] which, following the pioneering
of jokes by Winick,[39] can be divided into 'joke families', as
sho. in Table 10.2. As can be seen, by far the largest category of
jokes told by Les Dawson reflect the themes of sexism and the more
specific framing of joke families about wives, mothers-in-law and
other women. Many of these jokes are 'one-liners' typically
represented by the following:

> I'm not saying my wife's thick ... but she was late for work the
> other day because she got stranded on an escalator during a power
> failure.

> She tries to improve her appearance, but it's all to no avail. In fact,
> she's had her face lifted so many times that in future they'll have to
> lower her body. (Mother-in-law)

> A lass I know went to the pictures not so long ago.
> 'It was awful', she told me afterwards, 'I had to change seats twelve
> times.'
> 'What was wrong', I asked her. 'Did some bloke try it on?'
> 'Yes,' she said 'Eventually.' (Other woman)

Apart from the second largest category of 'miscellaneous', which
contains longer and less categorisable jokes with a number of
encapsulated themes, places as well as people and jokes based on
misunderstandings (mainly cross-purposes jokes), jokes on nationality (mainly Irish), racial (mainly Jewish) and regional (mainly North
versus South of England) themes are prominent in this comedian's
repertoire. The following are representative of the genre:

> There was a bad accident in the high street not long ago. This
> Jewish bloke was crossing the road when he got knocked down by a
> bus. A small crowd gathered and a young policeman dashed up to
> the scene, folded his cape up and put it under the head of the chap
> who'd been run over.
> 'There', said the policeman, 'is that better? Are you comfortable'.
> 'Well,' said the Jewish chap, 'I make a living.'

> They're supposed to be smarter in the South. I'm not so sure,
> though. I heard recently about a chap down there who invented an

Table 10.2 Joke Families and Social Morality Themes of Les Dawson's Jokes

Joke family	Social morality* theme	Number and (%) of jokes in each category
Wife, mother-in-law and other women	sexism	78 (31.7)
Miscellaneous	mixture of themes	34 (13.8)
Irish, Jewish	nationalism, racism,	29 (11.8)
North/south, neighbourhood	regionalism	27 (10.9)
Infants/children (own and others)	ageism	24 (9.8)
Animals (esp. parrots)		11 (4.5)
Relatives (other than wife, children and mother-in-law)	familism (kinship)	10 (4.1)
Drinking/pub-life	alcoholism	8 (3.3)
Golf		6 (2.4)
Doctors, lawyers, vicars	professionalism	6 (2.4)
Other (show business, policemen, shaggy-dog story)		13 (5.3)
Total		246 (100)

*I am grateful to Ernest Cashmore, Research Fellow in the Department of Sociology and Social History, for suggesting these broad social morality themes for joke analysis. Independently of my more specific reliance on Winick's concept of joke families, he devised a number of these broader categories (principally, sexism, nationalism/racism, ageism) and analysed the same source of Dawson jokes. Allowing for difficulties of precise categorisation of a number of jokes, his analysis broadly confirms the main thematic phases of this comedian's jokes as that derived from the use of more specific joke families based on the Winick pattern devised by the author of this paper.

electric car. It goes from London to Leeds on only £3-worth of electricity. But the flex costs £15 000.

The vast majority of Dawson's jokes play on outmoded stereotypes of and attitudes towards women, the Irish and Jews, for example, which articulate the conservative category-routinised joking frame of

his listeners who recognise them as such or consciously/unconsciously subscribe to them. Similarly, other themes such as animals as well as those about children (indicating their precocity or peculiar (to adults) logic), drink and golf are all well-tried and category-routinised themes from everyday life subject to humorous observations by audiences as well as comedians. Such jokes, then, represent the coinage of traditional community life, particularly that of the working class in the North of England and its cultural code and social morality with their attendant traditional social controls, which the verbal art of professional comedians such as Les Dawson both ventilates and reinforces.

Spike Milligan

In suggesting Milligan as an exemplar of the radical setting-specific comedian, it is important to observe initially that the substantiation of such a categorisation is more difficult than in the case of the contrasting category-routinised type of comedian. It is far more difficult to analyse and categorise the written comic material of this comedian as it appears in the form of scripts for the radio show he wrote for as well as performed in, i.e. the celebrated *The Goon Show*.[40] Although such representative selections of scripts for these shows are now available in printed form, they are more difficult to analyse by content analysis methods than is a standard collection of jokes which can be analysed using the schema applied above to Les Dawson's comic material. Nevertheless, if we follow Handelman and Kapferer's elaboration of a setting-specific joking frame – taking this to be, for our purposes, the specific aural nature of a radio comedy show situation with specific characters in the particular settings, however surreal, suggested by the programme titles – this can be judged an appropriate classification in the case of Milligan. We can also follow these authors' reasoning that in this joking frame, 'cues may have a cultural or normative basis, but they are not primarily prescribed by cultural categories. Because of this, the establishment of joking activity involves a high degree of uncertainty and joking follows an indeterminate course. Setting-specific joking frames are highly fragile and unresilient, and participants are rarely able to sustain the original definition of the frame in the face of attempts to end the joking discourse, attempts which we term subversion. This is so because these frames do not have routinised or established

behaviour cues or roles to follow through in joking activity.'[41]

A careful analysis of the format of the *Goon Show* scripts and a hearing of the recordings of the shows indicates the indeterminate course of the plots and the bewildering switching and timing of events and actions depicted in each episode. This confirms the subversion of any attempt to sustain the original definition of the joking frame, highlighted by Waterman[42] as the sheer speed and lightning about-turn of language in Milligan's scripts. The setting-specific joking frame is further reinforced by the story-telling format of *The Goon Show* and the fabulist nature of each scripted episode in the sensibly-nonsensical world created by Milligan. This surreal form of satire marked a radical departure in both the verbal and non-verbal (in the use of sound effects) art of humour, especially in radio comedy in Britain.

In contrast, then, to classifying joke families and breaking jokes down into what he calls 'jokemes', *qua* Winick, we have in essence in the comedy script a whole succession of jokes, as well as social morality themes, story-lines or plots to comprehend and unravel, not to mention, as in the case of the aural humour of the Goons, the heavy emphasis on sound effects as integral non-verbal reinforcements of the comic language and situations portrayed.[43] To attempt to grapple with this problem a more ambitious analysis, especially of techniques of humour, developed by Berger[44] is employed below even though it has not been operationalised by that author and is only partially so in this chapter. This is a particularly relevant schema for our purposes in that Berger notes the intimate connection between humour and cultural codes which in gestalt terms feeds on incongruences in figure/ground relationships. These, as he further suggests, provide useful insights into society's values and, more especially in our case, societal norms and morality.

Berger lists no less than 45 different techniques to create humour which he groups into four categories: language (humour is verbal); logic (the humour is ideational); identity (the humour is existential); and action (the humour is physical). One major problem is that under each of the first three categories there are no less than thirteen to fifteen different techniques which not only present problems in the absence of definitions of such terms as irony, satire, absurdity, grotesque, parody, etc., but give no suggestion (other than by means of a limited example of the author's analysis of one joke!) of how these are operationalised in joke analysis. Nevertheless they are suggestive enough to permit a basic analysis and pilot study of the

main techniques for creating humour employed by Milligan in his
Goon Show scripts.

(i) The Language and Anti-language of the Goons

One initial problem is that the language of *The Goon Show* is
essentially, as suggested by Halliday, an 'anti-language'.[45] This is a
metaphor for an everyday language which is generated by what he
calls an 'anti-society' which is 'set up within another society as a
conscious alternative to it. It is a mode of resistance, resistance which
may take the form either of passive symbiosis or of active hostility
and even destruction.' He cites in particular, examples of the
counter-cultures of vagabonds in Elizabethan England, the under-
world of modern Calcutta and the sub-cultures of Polish prisons and
reform schools. More technically, Halliday suggests that the anti-
languages developed in such anti-societies are 'relexicalised', i.e. new
words partially replace old ones, and in its manifestation in slang,
with its never-ending search for originality either for the sake of
liveliness or humour, seems somewhat larger than life, i.e. it is
'overlexicalised'. Of particular importance for the purposes of this
chapter are descendants of the Elizabethan anti-languages which he
calls 'music-hall languages' (or in America 'vaudeville languages')
and especially gobbledygook, in its original sense of a 'secret
language' of Victorian working-class humour, a genre exemplified in
more recent years by Spike Milligan in his creation of Goonery in the
1950s.

Furthermore, an anti-language reflects not only an alternative
reality but a counter-reality set up in opposition to some established
norm and which is a means of realisation of a subjective reality: not
merely expressing it, but actively creating and maintaining it. As
such, then, as Halliday concludes, 'The antilanguage is the vehicle of
... resocialization. It creates an alternative reality: the process is one
not of construction but of reconstruction.'

Sociologically speaking, we would affirm that such realities have to
be socially shared, i.e. are inter-subjective, and that the social
construction (*qua* Berger and Luckmann) of such alternative or
counter-realities is associated with the bisociation of social perceptions integral to the appreciation of the radical comedian's humour,
in this case that of Milligan and the Goons. It should be noted here
that Goonery emerged at a momentous period of social change in
British society in the decade after the Second World War, marked by
the end of the British Empire and the implementation of a modern

Welfare State. The inevitable social pressures for resocialisation to alternative realities and the reconstruction of social reality in British society at that time also permitted the ventilation and articulation of emergent cultures and their culture codes in anti-language forms. In such a *fin-de-siècle* situation the inevitable bisociation of social moralities embedded in residual/conservative cultures and emergent/radical cultures is highlighted and this fosters the emergence of satiric humour with its subversion of social controls. A radical comedian such as Milligan is thus enabled to use setting-specific joking frames of a surreal kind which are shared with his audience in the peculiarly receptive medium of radio comedy and which clearly reflect and express shared perceptions of the highly fragile and indeterminate nature of the social construction and reconstruction of reality in British society at that time. This is particularly well captured by Waterman who notes that in Milligan's writing for *The Goon Show*, and more recently for the 'Q' series of television programmes, his view of the world has been remarkably constant (hence reflecting a setting-specific joking frame?)

> It is a world which is literally crazier than the respectable pretence we are most of the time asked to believe in; where the people are Hieronymous Bosch figures, and the action is by Salvador Dali; where, in particular, the final sunset over the British Empire is still taking place, at the same time as the 1914–18 and 1939–45 wars are still both being fought simultaneously with the publication of endless military biographies which continue to remove the image farther and farther from whatever truth existed in the first place. And somehow, James Bond has become inextricably mixed up with John Buchan, Soldiers Three with The Wooden Horse and, somewhere along the line, With The Flag To Pretoria has got mixed up with the act.[46]

The elements of anti-language exploited by Milligan are reflected in his extensive use of slang, colloquialisms and idioms as an alternative to and in contrast with 'standard' English. Thus his scripts indicate in Waterman's words, his 'interest in and preoccupation with fragmentation of the English language, as well as his fascination with the fun to be had with literal meanings, idiotic idioms, and phrases that career off the rails in mid-sentence'.

Respective illustrations of these three aspects of linguistic fragmentation used to comic effect in Milligan's *More Goon Scripts* are:

(From 'The Scarlet Capsule', *The Goon Show*, No. 255 (9th series, No. 14, p. 94)

Crun: No no no. This is a vital brown archaeological site sir, it could be that on this very spot, the first men existed, you see this we dug up just now? Do you recognise it?
Bill: It appears to be a piece of mud.
Minnie: And there's more where that came from!

(From 'The Tay Bridge Disaster', *The Goon Show*, No. 256 (9th Series, No. 15 p. 110)

Seagoon: Thank you sir, a dud Burmese sixpence? Scotland for ever sir!
Ray: Och Aye and Oi Vay Mon, it's a warum bracht moonlacht nacht for the Schidduch the noo mon.
Seagoon: And Bless old Ghana too!

(From 'Ned's Atomic Dustbin', *The Goon Show*, No. 251 (9th Series, No. 10, p. 54)

Seagoon: Don't cry Bottle, here, have the suspender off my sock.
Bluebottle: Oh thanks ... no ... no! That suspender is just a glittering Western prize to make me forget my mission. Now Seagoon, look into my eyes, toot toot toot ... little daggers come out and point all the way along my eyes to his, toot toot toot ... the secrets of Bottles, mesmerism is bending Ned to my will ... strainnnnn strainnnnn power of eyes, power of eyes ... ohh squint, squint, squinteeee ... squin ... ohh, my nose has started to bleed.

   Some six of the thirteen linguistic techniques of humour listed by Berger are extensively employed by Milligan in these scripts, viz. allusion, exaggeration, puns, repartee, ridicule and satire. Allusion is well illustrated by the numerous double-entendres and cockney rhyming slang sprinkled throughout the scripts but more important-ly, in its lexical sense of implicit reference to the 'essence which serves as a criterion for devaluation'[47] this is directed at a specific target which is 'invariably pomposity or some hidebound aspect of

the Establishment'.[48] Thus policemen, bureaucrats, the military and, more fleetingly, MPs and even the Prime Minister are all alluded to and devalued or ridiculed in expression of the 'spontaneous sense of derision'[49] of the principal characters in *The Goon Show* and the comedians including Milligan playing them. Whilst every episode was, however tenuously extended, originally taken from life it was transcribed into the 'sensibly-nonsensical world' of the Goons and endowed with the 'illogical rationalizing'[50] of the anti-language of Milligan's scripts. Thus:

> If you could climb Everest from the outside you could do it from the inside. The story of the Bristol Brabazon aeroplane led naturally to the Bristol Brabagoon. If there was a North and South Pole it was obvious there had to be an East and West. When a newspaper reported that Westminster Pier was gradually sinking into the Thames mud and that someone had waded out and nailed an 'out of action' notice on the superstructure, it was inevitable that a programme would be built around it. When the QE2 was launched it provided the idea for a story 'The Building of the Goonitania', an 84,000 ton super-liner, and the problems involved in getting it out of its bottle.

Allusion was heightened by exaggeration, especially in the voices and language of the archetypal characters, or 'inspired defectives'[51] which regularly people the sketches – Eccles, Bluebottle, The Hon. Hercules Grytpype-Thynne, Henry Crun, Minnie Bannister, Major Denis Bloodnok, etc. The accompanying sound effects as forms of aural exaggeration were also an integral part of *The Goon Show* as 'image-building and image-shattering' techniques of radio comedy (see discussion of 'Action' below).

A particular technique of exaggeration accompanying the Goon's form of radio comedy and a particularly effective method or means of linguistic accentuation used in the comic dialogue between characters for satiric purposes, constitutes what Goffman[52] has called 'response cries'. Thus, exuded expressions such as 'Oops!', 'Ouch!', 'Wheee!' are seen by him as exclamatory statements allied to imprecations, which are not fully fledged words but constitute 'a natural overflowing, bursting of normal restraints, a case of being off-guard' (p. 99). These 'roguish utterances' or 'verbalisations' constitute forms of exposed self-talk or 'blurted vocalisations' uttered by what Goffman prefers to call a 'vocaliser' or 'sounder'

rather than a speaker. Insofar as respone cries become ritualised as conventional utterances, they importantly relate the vocaliser in sociolinguistic terms not merely to conversations but to social situations with bearings on a passing event with a limited course in time. Such a situation involving performers and listeners clearly exists and is accentuated by and in the setting-specific joking frame of a half-hour radio comedy show such as *The Goon Show*.

Goffman illustrates the more classical exercise of exposed self-talk as a response cry in dramatic terms as the soliloquy, and in popular culture a long-established form of comedy routine is that in which the butt of joking is made vulnerable by having to sustain a full-blown discussion with someone who is hidden from general view. More importantly for the study of humour, and radio comedy in the context of this chapter, is his further insight that, 'response cries themselves are by way of being second-order ritualizations, already part of the unserious, or less serious domain' (p. 114). For humorous purposes, then, in our case the radio listeners are placed in the social situation of a gathering of unacquainted members of a radio audience of intended recipients or overhearers hidden from general view. As Goffman graphically puts it, 'the audience are supernatural, out of frame eavesdroppers' (p. 83) on the dialogues and monologues of characters in radio comedy shows made vulnerable as the butts of joking.

Thus all the major characters in *The Goon Show* at some time or another in the bizarre and surreal situations in which they are depicted in each episode are supplied by Milligan with a gamut of blurted verbalisations and response cries in the form of the exposed self-talk of signalled asides to the radio listeners. This enables the characters to be heard as striking 'a self-defensible posture in the face of extraordinary events' (p. 109) or managing a tricky, threatening set of circumstances by deflecting 'into nonlexicalised sound a dramatization of . . . their reliefs and self-congratulation in the achievement' (p. 101).

In keeping with Halliday's observations noted above there are also over-lexicalised sounds manifested in the form of response cries of *Goon Show* characters. Examples of various types of response cries outlined by Goffman and which appear in *The Goon Show* scripts and on record, many of them in the form of anti-languages, semi-words and taboo words or their synonyms, are 'pain cries' such as 'Owwww!', 'Ooooh!' and 'Ohhhhhhhh!' uttered by characters subjected to scripted hits on the head; 'transition display' is expressed

in such semi-words as 'Phew!', 'Ohh ... Ahha!' and 'Ahhhh ...
Ahhhh, ahh!', especially in response to a scripted whoosh of wind;
and 'audible glee' expressions such as 'Whoopee!' and 'Ha hee!'.
There is also a liberal use by Milligan of what Goffman calls 'mocked-
up response cries' in the form of mock curses such as 'Blast!', the
French imprecation 'Sapristi!' and the more effete rendition of
'Curses!'. In terms of comic asides, one of Milligan's characters –
Bluebottle – frequently presaged this form of self-talk with 'Thinks!',
whilst another – Seagoon – was frequently party to the celebrated
'little does he know' routine. This is well illustrated in one recording
in which, after asides of this nature directed at each other via the
audience between Bloodnok, Moriarty and Grytpype-Thynne and
Seagoon, the latter concludes with:

> Great heavily whispered aside! 'Little do they know how little I
> know about the little they know. If only I knew what the little they
> know I'd know a little.'[53]

And finally, using soliloquy to comic effect, Milligan again has
Seagoon engage in phantasizing self-talk:

> I can see it all now, I'll fight till me ammunition's gone. I'll say to
> the other men; 'Lads, make your way back as best as you can ...
> me? I'll stay on, I'll fight 'em barehanded until I'm overpowered,
> and then I'll swallow my secret code. They'll torture me, I won't
> speak ... it'll mean the firing squad, ha ha. So what?
> They'll say: Any last request? I say yes, damn you, I want evening
> dress ... I'll take my time and put it on with my full miniatures ...
> blind fold they'll say ... ha ha ha ha, the rifles come up, the click of
> the cartridges rammed home, they're taking aim ... ha ha ha ...
> I'll be smiling, that ... that carefree daredevil smile, the officer will
> raise his sword ... the volley will ring out, and I'll slump smiling to
> the floor – dead![54]

With reference to Berger's fifth linguistic technique of humour,
Wood[55] has highlighted the ever-present puns in the show, the worse
the better, as exemplified in the following: 'You're not the famous
Evelyn Waugh, are you?''Heavens, no, I wasn't born till 1918.' 'Then
you must be the famous 1918 Waugh.'
  The dialogue between the principal characters also contains
elements of repartee, such witty retorts being frequently framed in

the linguistic forms of colloquialisms, slang, idiotic idioms and response cries noted above. But it is above all the use of ridicule and satirical techniques, especially in the use of language by Milligan, which marks him off as the exemplar of the radical setting-specific comedian. If we accept the basic conception of satire as being directed against the self-satisfied, as challenging accepted notions by making them seem ridiculous[56] and as intending to be damaging to the object of ridicule,[57] we can see this exemplified in Milligan as revealingly noted by the journalist Herbert Kretzmer,[58] who saw in the comedian's conversation, 'Hatred for bureaucracy and snobbery. Hatred for mediocrity and the cruelties of man. Hatred for phoney patriotism.' Milligan himself, asked to analyse the humour of *The Goon Show*, stated: 'Essentially it is critical comedy. It is against bureaucracy, and on the side of human beings. Its starting point is one man shouting gibberish in the face of authority, and proving by fabricated insanity that nothing could be as mad as what passes for ordinary living.'[59]

(ii) The Logic of Goon Show Humour

The first pertinent point to make with regard, especially, to the ideational nature of humour, is the insight into the *Goon Show* brand of humour made by one of its founder members, Michael Bentine who, in contrasting it with his own 'logical nonsense', described it as 'nonsensical logic'.[60] More generally, under the title 'logic', Berger lists a range of techniques from absurdity to theme and variation. Following Nagel[61] we can see the absurd, as a form of nonsensical logic, in real-life situations as including a conspicuous discrepancy between pretension or aspiration and reality. In linguistic or verbal art forms such as the radio comedy of *The Goon Show*, reliant on aural perception, we can further note that the surreal depiction of such a discrepancy results in laughter deriving 'from words and nothing but words; this is linguistic comedy, the *vis comica* of word-play – puns, spoonerisms, alliteration and assonance employed methodically, not just for a questionable joke (according to classical standards) or a witticism, but for hundreds of pages'.[62] All of these forms of word-play, as indicated in the above section, are staple constituents of the hundreds of pages of Milligan's *Goon Show* scripts, displaying, as they do, a nonsensical logic and absurdity which is achieved by 'the sheer speed and lightning about-turns of language'.[63]

The absurdity of the humour in the scripts and broadcasts is

revealed in the themes and variations covered in the seven series after 1953 when the programmes were titled for the first time. Thus a random selection of such titles reveals 'The First Albert Memorial to the Moon', 'The Dreaded Batter Pudding Hurler', 'The Trans-Africa Aeroplane Canal' and 'The Ten Snowballs that Shook the World',[64] which attest to the absurdity and zany phantasy of the themes and variations satirised in each programme. This is further emphasised by the typical synopsis of the plot of one such *Goon Show* classic, 'Ned's Atomic Dustbin', which reads:

> Another explosive drama of espionage and futility, in which the British Government is nearly overthrown by a security leek. Mrs Gladys Smith, the doubtful heroine, is disguised both as Major Denis Bloodnok and 'Mad Dan' Eccles and infilthtrated into the Russian Secret Service. Under her code-name Bluebottleski, she prevents single-handed the Russian Sabotage of Neddie's atomic dustbin. Her escape over the Vulgar Rapids, with the prototype strapped to her Union Jack underwear, was later classified as unfit for children. This story has been previously dramatised by Newton Abbot Wolf-Clubs, and is now moored off Portsmouth Point.[65]

Again, as expressed in the language and depicted actions of the principal characters in the surreal setting-specific situations in which they find themselves, each programme illustrated Milligan's extensive use of the humorous techniques of nonsensical logic listed by Berger as accident, ignorance, mistakes, repetitions and reversal.

(iii) Identity and Character Representation in the Goon Shows
Under this heading Berger refers to the existential aspects of humour and techniques of humour from before/after through to unmasking. Here perhaps the fullest range of humorous techniques is employed by Milligan in the *Goon Show* scripts, and especially in his cast of main characters with whom the radio listeners were required to identify. These clearly represent Milligan's use of Berger's central humorous techniques of imitation, impersonation and mimicry. So much so that without *The Goon Show*, as Waterman[66] puts it, 'where would a whole generation have been for imitation voices?'. All three techniques are particularly suitable to characterisation in comedy shows on radio, appropriately described by Milligan[67] as the 'great mind medium', in that it creates an incomparable verbal resource

allowing infinite possibilities of intonation and other prosodic variations of the human voice[68] crucial to imitation, impersonation and mimicry. In particular such techniques give free rein to the great communication wealth of phonemic expression in the forms of speech incorporated by Milligan, as illustrated above, into the dialogue of *The Goon Show*, especially in the sound gags using slang, puns and gobbledygook.[69]

The impersonation, particularly by the master exponent of the art – Peter Sellers – and mimicry was of readily identifiable real-life stereotypes or 'archetypal dunderheads',[70] all of whom were represented as grotesque anti-heroes at a time – the immediate postwar period in Britain – when there was still an aftermath of hero-worship. Milligan[71] himself describes Bluebottle as 'a cardboard cut-out liquorice and string hero'; The Hon. Hercules Grytpype-Thynne as 'a plausible public-school villain and cad'; Comte Toulouse-Moriarty of the House of Roland as 'French scrag and lackey to Grytpype-Thynne'; Miss Minnie Bannister as 'spinster of the parish'; and Major Denis Bloodnok, Ind. Arm. Rtd., as 'military idiot, coward and bar'. Thus, as Fisher brilliantly sums-up:

> The Goon world of flamboyant anarchy is a world most readily conjured up by its inhabitants, a bizarre mixture of upper-crust snobs and sub-human simpletons: the suave, patronizing Hercules Grytpype-Thynne; the Machiavellian Moriarty; twittering Minnie Bannister and niggardly Henry Crun; vocally-myopic Bluebottle, given to mouthing his own stage directions, and the lugubriously demented Eccles; the oppressive Major Bloodnok, of the same Anglo–Indian line as Colonel Blimp, and ... Neddy Seagoon ... Seagoon was the futile, flag-waving British idiot with the garbled Welsh accent punctuated at irregular intervals by manic giggle or exultant shriek. He represented at once catalyst, chorus figure, and scapegoat in his relations with the inspired defectives created by Milligan and Sellers ... His emotions just kept in check, he was the goon with whom the audience identified. He represented the Odysseus on the madcap expedition, who, however moonstruck himself, came face to face with its ordeals as the audience would have had to. And, as scapegoat, he underlined the theme of persecution which ran throughout the show, the embodiment of all institutions and individuals ever hated ... Their voices through an impression of startling originality, inveigled their way cunningly into the subconscious of the whole country.[72]

(iv) Sound Effects as Action Components of Goon Show Humour
The techniques of humour in the Berger schema are, in this case,
more limited and relate to the physicality of humour. Although
Berger does not discuss this aspect of humour he presumably implies
the more familiar forms of visual and non-verbal genres of silent film
comedy, e.g. the 'chase' and slapstick. Of particular interest here in
the case of radio comedy is the aural nature of humour conveyed by
sound effects relating to the depicted actions of the characters
involved and the situations in which they find themselves. In his
discussion of response cries, Goffman also points up what he calls
phonotactic aspects of social situations and the ways in which audible
indicators are involved as well as visual ones in maintaining a sort of
'communication tonus'. Thus:

> In our society . . . it is generally taboo in public to be drunken, to
> belch or pass wind perceptibly, to daydream or doze, or be
> disarrayed with respect to clothing and cosmetics – and all for the
> same reason. These acts comprise our conventional repertoire, our
> prescribed stock of 'symptoms', for demonstrating a lack of
> respectful alertness in and to the situation, their inhibition our way
> of 'doing' penance and thereby self-respect. [73]

Thus the scripts contain full references to audible indicators in the
form of instructions for tapes (GRAMS) and sound effects (FX)
which are crucial to actions depicted in *The Goon Show*, and
especially the speed and timing of the humour. Milligan's employment of sound effects for phonotactic purposes emphasises the
radical nature of his use of radio and audible indicators in comedy
challenging taboos and conventional repertoires extant in real life.
Thus, in addition to the standard sound effects of jelly sploshes, door
knocks and door opening as well as horses galloping off very fast or
resounding whacks on head (interestingly referred to in FX as
'Slapsticks'!), there is a whole gamut of colossal explosions, howling
winds, thunder flashes, thuds of falling trees, etc., which indicate
that *The Goon Show* 'was a violent show, achieving its effect through
an explosive barrage of barrier-breaking sound effects'. [74] The
following instructions for combined GRAMS and FX in the script of
'The Scarlet Capsule' (*The Goon Show*, No. 255) well illustrate this:

> Long series of smashing door down. Goes on and on . . . Give it
> variation, i.e. first confident crashes on door with axe. These all

very loud. Fail then renewed. Then furious . . . Then frenzied . . .
Then heavy full blows . . . Furious sawing . . . Then hammering on
door with fists . . . rattling of the door knob . . . Then four or five
heavy blows . . . Then furious hatchet attack on the door.

Those off-beat sound effects and reactions were an integral part of
the image-building, image-shattering technique that is the basic tool
of radio comedy which reached 'stratospheric heights'[75] in Milligan's
hands as he made more and more demands on the BBC Sound
Effects Department. Thus they were asked to produce such sound
effects as 'a Wurlitzer organ being hauled across the Sahara desert,
the pace of the music swelling with the engine revs. Playing a wave-
tossed piano across the Channel. A wall being driven away at high
speed'.[76] The scatological nature of sound effects as audible
indicators of taboo-breaking and expression of derision as used in
The Goon Show is well brought out by Peter Eton, the BBC
producer of the early shows. He describes the birth of a particular
sound effect, now known as 'Fred the Oyster', for the show 'The
Sinking of Westminster Pier' as follows:

> This old oyster-sexer goes down with the pier and is brought up
> from the river-bed with an oyster on a table and we built up the
> tension and you heard the oyster creak open slowly and then came
> the most frightful raspberry. Actually, it was a donkey farting. It
> was a fiendish noise and it brought the house down. It was made
> up for me out of three or four donkey farts played slowly and
> speedily, then edited. It's the most revolting noise you ever heard.
> And it was the most brilliant thing we ever did. We used it for four
> or five years. There was the announcement, 'This is the the Home
> Service', then came Fred.[77]

CONCLUSION

We have attempted in this paper to establish and develop a
conceptual schema for identifying types of professional comedian.
This has been based on the view that the verbal art of joke-telling is
conducted by the comedian within two major types of joking frame
which reflect basically the social morality of either a conservative
residual culture or a more radical emergent culture. For the sake of
parsimony it clearly has not been possible here to explore the

schema's alternative pairings of the *ad lib*. comic, representing the conservative setting-specific comedian, and the satirist or burlesque comic, as depicting the radical category-routinised comedian. The increased availability, however, of a wide range of aural and written expressions of the professional comedian's art in such forms as records, films, published scripts, as well as audio and video-tape material should enable the sociologist studying humour to attempt at the same time both a more comprehensive and a more penetrating analysis of their role-types, role-styles and functions in contemporary society.[78] By incorporating the more sophisticated forms of sociolinguistic analysis now available to the researcher, some of which have been employed above, such a typology as advanced in this chapter can further be employed and modified where necessary to focus the sociological examination of the full range of humorous techniques and material used by professional comedians to elicit favourable audience response.

It has been the main thrust of this chapter that the professional comedian has increasingly become a central portrayer of the social morality or the moral sense of social groups in modern society. The greater catholicity of taste in humorous entertainment now available in such societies has both crystallised and fluidised the cultural codes and modes of humour in such groups and joking frames in which the normative communication via the publicly negotiated exchange of humorous stimuli and responses between the comedian and his audience is conducted. Thus elements of residual morality as well as an emergent morality, and the inevitable social tensions between the two, are socially ventilated or played on in both category-routinised and setting-specific joking frames by comedians. Of particular interest is the emergence of radical comedians such as Spike Milligan in periods of social reconstruction represented by *fin-de-siècle* periods in a number of advanced societies especially in the last hundred years or so. This suggests that the typology developed in this chapter might also be usefully applied to re-examine social historical exemplars of radical comedians in a given society over time and for some fruitful contemporaneous comparative studies of the role of comedians and joking frames in various national and, especially, popular cultures.

Finally, whilst associated with feelings of liberation, humour is equally to be seen sociologically as constituting a form of tension management, social resistance and social control in human relationships. The legitimised expression of ridicule in humorous form,

therefore, especially in periods of rapid social change and the accompanying cultural changes in morals and morality challenging cultural codes, are of central interest here. In such periods of resocialisation and reconstruction of social reality, modern society requires its comedians to reflect and remind us of the bisociation of our perceptions of social reality. In so doing, and by humorously reminding us of our human frailties, they preserve and enhance their unique status as 'teachers we like'.

NOTES

1. Anon., 'The Benny factor', *New Society*, 21 May 1981, p. 299.
2. For a rare contribution in the sociological literature see M. Salutin, 'The Impression Management Techniques of the Burlesque Comedian', *Sociological Inquiry*, vol. 43 (1973) pp. 159–68. See also notes 12 and 16 below.
3. H. Bergson, 'Laughter', in W. Sypher (ed.) *Comedy* (New York: Doubleday, 1956) p. 143.
4. Salutin, p. 160.
5. A. Koestler, *The Act of Creation* (London: Hutchinson, 1964) p. 35.
6. A. Brien, 'Volga Jokemen', *Sunday Times*, 23 September 1973.
7. D. Handelman and B. Kapferer, 'Forms of Joking Activity: A Comparative Approach', *American Anthropologist*, vol. 74 (1972) p. 484.
8. L. Hudson, 'Life as Art', *New Society*, 12 February 1976, p. 319.
9. A. Berger, 'What Makes People Laugh? Cracking the Cultural Code', *ETC (A Review of General Semantics)*, vol. 32 (1975) pp. 427–8.
10. J. Emerson, 'Negotiating the Serious Import of Humour', in A. Birnbaum (ed.) *The Sociology of the Familiar*, p. 269.
11. A. Dundes, 'Projection in Folklore: A Plea for Psychoanalytic Semiotics', *MLN*, vol. 91 (1976) p. 1503.
12. C. Fletcher, 'Fool or Funny Man: The Role of the Comedian', mimeograph, no date.
13. Aristedes, 'Jokes and Their Relation to the Conscious', *American Scholar*, vol. 47 (1978) p. 306.
14. R. Bauman, 'Verbal Art as Performance', *American Anthropologist*, vol. 77 (1975) p. 306.
15. R. Williams, cited in Bauman.
16. H. Pollio and J. Edgerly, 'Comedians and Comic Style', in T. Chapman and H. Foot (eds) *Humour and Laughter: Theory, Research and Applications* (London: John Wiley, 1976) p. 230.
17. Ibid., p. 238.
18. Ibid.
19. Ibid.

20. Handelman and Kapferer, 'Forms of Joking Activity'.
21. M. Douglas, 'The Social Control of Cognition: Some Factors in Joke Perception', *Man*, vol. 3 (1968) p. 366.
22. Handelman and Kapferer, pp. 484–5.
23. H. Duncan, *Communication and the Social Order* (London: Oxford University Press, 1970) p. 389.
24. G. Gordon, *Persuasion: The Theory and Practice of Manipulative Communication* (New York: Hastings House, 1971) p. 319.
25. R. Stephenson, 'Conflict and Control Functions of Humour', *American Journal of Sociology*, vol. 56 (1951) p. 570.
26. E. Goffman, *The Presentation of Self in Everyday Life* (Harmondsworth: Penguin, 1969) p. 11.
27. A. Granfield and H. Giles, 'Towards an Analysis of Humour Through Symbolism', *International Journal of Symbology*, vol. 6 (1975) p. 18.
28. R. Perry, *Realms of Value* (New York: Greenwood Press, 1968) p. 139.
29. A. Lindesmith, A. Strauss, and N. Denzin, *Language Differentiation and the Learning Process*, 4th edn (Illinois: The Dryden Press, 1975) p. 161.
30. A. Zijderveld, 'Jokes and Their Relation to Social Reality', *Social Research*, vol. 35 (1968) p. 287.
31. T. Burns, 'Friends, Enemies and Polite Fiction', *American Sociological Review*, vol. 18 (1953) p. 657. This should be contrasted with the somewhat optimistic assertion more appropriate to the radical comedian that every joke is a tiny revolution: G. Orwell, 'Funny But Not Vulgar', in Sonia Orwell and Ian Angus (eds) *The Collected Essays, Journalism and Letters of George Orwell, Vol. 3 As I Please, 1943–1945* (New York: Harcourt Brace Jovanovitch, 1968).
32. H. Hobson, *Sunday Times*, 20 April 1975.
33. L. Adler, book review in *Sunday Times*, 18 May 1975.
34. P. Oakes, *Sunday Times*, 15 December 1974.
35. E. Midwinter, *Make 'Em Laugh: Famous Comedians and their Worlds* (London: George Allen and Unwin, 1979) pp. 176–90.
36. Oakes, *Sunday Times*.
37. Ibid.
38. L. Dawson, *The Les Dawson Joke Book* (London: Arrow Books, 1979).
39. C. Winick, 'A Content Analysis of Orally Communicated Jokes', *The American Imago*, vol. 20 (1963) pp. 271–91.
40. S. Milligan, *More Goon Show Scripts* (London: Sphere Books, 1974).
41. Handelman and Kapferer, p. 485.
42. J. Waterman, 'Walk Back with Milligan', *The Listener*, 13 April 1978, pp. 465–6.
43. There are, at the time of writing (1986) ten recordings (two shows on each) available as BBC gramaphone records of a selection of the 153 titled broadcasts of *The Goon Show* relayed between October 1954 and January 1960. In addition there are Parlophone and one EMC records of further *Goon Show* excerpts. Of these only one show ('The Scarlet Capsule', 2 February 1959) is available both as a recording and

in written script form in S. Milligan, *More Goon Scripts*. Ideally, to savour the true essence of the *Goon Shows* the reader should listen to the recordings, and for analytical purposes the sociologist can check with the written source for such research as is attempted here. These scripts are particularly useful in that they contain full details of instructions for tapes (GRAMS) and sound effects (FX) for all shows selected and thus permit additional analysis of the use of non-verbal humour especially under Berger's 'action' heading as in the examples cited in this chapter.

44. A. Berger, 'Anatomy of the Joke', *Journal of Communication*, vol. I (1976) pp. 113–15.
45. M. Halliday, *Language as Social Semiotic: The Social Interpretation of Language and Meaning* (London: Edward Arnold, 1978) Chap. 9.
46. Waterman, p. 465.
47. C. Perelman and L. Olbrechts-Tyteca, *The New Rhetorica: A Treatise on Argument* (Notre Dame: University of Notre Dame Press, 1969) p. 330.
48. A. Draper, *The Story of the Goons* (London: Everest Books, 1978) p. 179.
49. J. Fisher, *Funny Way to be a Hero* (London: Paladin, 1976) p. 241.
50. Draper, pp. 29–30.
51. Fisher, p. 243.
52. E. Goffman, *Forms of Talk* (Oxford: Basil Blackwell, 1981) pp. 78–122.
53. Transcript from recording of 'Tales of Old Dartmoor', from the BBC Recording, 7 February 1956, available on Parlophone long playing record (PMC II08), 'The Best of the Goon Show'.
54. Milligan, p. 63.
55. M. Wood, 'Kinds of madmen', *New Society*, 5 April 1973, p. 26.
56. J. Bronowski, *The Western Intellectual Tradition from Leonardo to Hegel* (London: Hutchinson, 1960) p. 252.
57. C. Gruner, 'Wit and Humour in Mass Communication', in T. Chapman and H. Foot (eds) *Humour and Laughter: Theory, Research and Applications* (London: John Wiley, 1976) p. 288.
58. H. Kretzmer, *Daily Sketch*, 1957.
59. Draper, p. 21.
60. Ibid., p. 20.
61. T. Nagel, 'The Absurd', *Journal of Philosophy*, vol. 68 (1971) p. 718.
62. H. LeFebvre, *Everyday Life in the Modern World* (London: Allen Lane, 1971) pp. 139–40.
63. Waterman, p. 466.
64. Milligan, pp. 14–15.
65. Ibid., p. 40.
66. Waterman, 'Walk Back with Milligan'.
67. Cited in D. Nathan, *The Laughtermakers: A Quest for Comedy* (London: Peter Owen, 1971) p. 50.
68. E. Martinez, 'Extraverbal Language', *Cultures*, vol. 6 (1979) p. 112.
69. For elaboration on this point with reference to another famous British radio comedy show, *Round the Horne*, and literary uses of phonemes

by Lewis Carroll, see S. Castagna, 'Oh You, Naughty Phoneme!', *La Linguistique*, vol. 15 (1979) pp. 31–42.
70. Fisher, p. 242.
71. Milligan, pp. 6–7.
72. Fisher, pp. 241, 243–4.
73. E. Goffman, (1981) p. 85.
74. Fisher, p. 240.
75. Nathan, pp. 41–2.
76. Draper, p. 57.
77. Cited in Nathan, p. 51.
78. For such a pioneering attempt based on a sample of American professional comedians see Pollio and Edgerly, 'Comedians and Comic Style'.

11 Representations of Women and Men in *Playboy* Sex Cartoons
Gail Dines-Levy and Gregory W. H. Smith

Playboy magazine occupies a remarkable place in the publishing history of the English-speaking world. It is, first of all, the premier publication of a now much-imitated genre, variously known as the 'girlie' or 'soft porn' or 'men's entertainment' magazine. This last, more euphemistic, designation accords with *Playboy*'s own proud boast on its contents page that it is 'the men's entertainment magazine'. It is also the advocate and disseminator of a widely-desired style of life: well-heeled, urbane and sophisticated. This style of life is not merely recommended through the pages of the magazine but has been actively promoted through the establishment of *Playboy* clubs, casinos, hotels and the wide range of personal goods bearing the distinctive 'bunny' logo. The special cast and appeal of *Playboy* has been very much shaped by one man's preferences and vision, Hugh M. Hefner, who has edited and published the magazine since its first issue in October 1953. For many years Hefner took the final decisions on matters large and small concerning the image and content of *Playboy*. Yet it is equally clear that the wide appeal and success of the magazine speaks also to important changes occurring in American and other Western societies in the postwar world: as Thomas Weyr put it, 'in the early 1950s the world was waiting for Hugh Hefner – or someone just like him' (1978, p. 3).

Judged in commercial terms, *Playboy* was the proverbial 'overnight success', a 'phenomenon'. The total print run of 70 250 for the first issue was a sell-out and with its notorious Marilyn Monroe centrefold it is now a collector's item. *Playboy*'s impressive early impact was sustained through to the mid-seventies. Circulation passed the one million mark in 1959 and two million in 1963. By the beginning of the 1970s, the period of special interest to us, *Playboy*'s worldwide circulation stood at around six million (Miller, 1984, pp.

45*ff*; Brady, 1974, p. 83). By the early sixties it was evident to many that the magazine was a major cultural force, but it is interesting to note that theologians, rather than social scientists, were the first to give *Playboy* serious and sustained attention (see esp. Weyr, 1978, pp. 93 *ff*).

The intention in this chapter is to consider the sex-role stereotypes evident in single frame *Playboy* cartoons. Our approach is informed by (a) feminist concern with images of women in the mass media (King and Stott, 1977; Tuchman and Daniels, 1978), and (b) an interest in the sociological uses of documentary materials (Platt, 1981; Glassner and Corzine, 1982). Cartoons, of course, are only one element of *Playboy*'s content. A typical issue will also contain fiction, articles, interviews, photographic layouts, reviews, comic strips, jokes, advice and letters columns, not to mention advertising. One reason for studying the cartoons (we have excluded comic strips from consideration) is that they occupy a not-insignificant proportion of *Playboy*'s total content. Approximately 20 pages in a typical mid-1970s issue of 250 pages were given over to cartoons which is rather less than the space devoted to female pictorials, but not much less. Indeed, *Playboy* has been described as America's 'chief humour magazine' (Greenberg and Kahn, 1970, p. 557) on the grounds that no other mass circulation magazine contains so much cartoon humour.

Cartoons, as newspaper and magazine editors the world over know, have a special appeal to very many readers. They are designed to be humorous, a diversion from life's serious concerns, and since they are presented in pictorial form they make small demands on the reader's attention and intellect (cf. Bogardus, 1945). Because cartoons are such light and readily digestible fare they are more likely to grab the reader's attention than the 'heavier' kinds of newspaper and magazine content (of which there is no shortage in *Playboy*). Specific empirical support for the popularity of cartoons is provided by Stauffer and Frost's (1976) study of readers' ratings of the content of *Playboy* and *Playgirl* magazines. They found that the cartoons received the highest interest ratings for both male and female subjects, achieving levels in excess of even the centrefold and the fashion pages. The cartoons were clearly the most widely interesting aspect of the magazines for the readers in this research study. Now whilst it is true that the cartoon may only hold the reader's attention for a short span of time, the very triviality of this graphic form makes for an insidious source of imagery. Our special concern in this chapter

is to examine one aspect of that imagery, the sex-role stereotypes of the principal cartoon characters in *Playboy*.

From the magazine's inception, cartoons were regarded as much more than page fillers. Hefner possessed a modest talent for cartooning and has recalled that he formed the ambition of becoming a professional cartoonist during army service at the end of the Second World War (Brady, 1974, p. 32). As an adolescent he would occupy himself making up coloured cartoon strips detailing personal events and topical issues. These were bound up into volumes which Hefner entitled his *Comic Autobiography* (by 1953, apparently, he was up to volume 52 of this enterprise). Hefner contributed cartoons to his high school magazine and later, when he enrolled at the University of Illinois, to its student paper. It was through his cartooning skills, then, that Hefner had his first contact with the world of journalism. In 1950, after dropping out of the masters programme in sociology at Illinois, he attempted to interest publishers in a collection of cartoons about Chicago life entitled 'That Toddlin' Town'. When none of them expressed interest, Hefner went ahead and published it himself. Further attempts to make a living out of cartooning met with little success, but the failed cartoonist was soon to become a highly successful editor and publisher. Even before the first issue of *Playboy* appeared, the *American Cartoonist* journal recommended the magazine as a useful outlet for their readers' work, providing Hefner with much-needed recognition and publicity. Early editions of *Playboy* used some of Hefner's own cartoons, but he readily abandoned cartooning in face of the much more demanding challenge of editing the magazine. As editor, however, he maintained a special fondness for the cartoon input. He once sent the renowned cartoonist Jules Feiffer a nine-page, single-spaced typed memo on how a cartoon strip he had submitted could be improved, advice which Feiffer was apparently grateful to receive (Brady, 1974, p. 123). Towards the end of the 1960s, when Hefner relinquished some of his absolute editorial control, he nevertheless continued to select the *Playmate*, choose the cartoons and edit the Party Jokes page (Miller, 1984, p. 148). The over-all character of *Playboy* was, it is widely agreed, very much the product of Hefner's vision, enterprise and devotion, and it is clear that the cartoons were an integral part of the philosophy and world view he wished to advance.

THE *PLAYBOY* IDEOLOGY

What are the elements of this world view? What was the 'ideology' *Playboy* promoted? Hefner and his associates devoted much thought and discussion to the image to be projected by *Playboy*. Hefner's editorial for the first issue is an obvious starting point:

> If you're a man between 18 and 80, PLAYBOY is meant for you. If you like entertainment served up with humour, sophistication and spice, PLAYBOY will become a very special favourite.
> We want to make it very clear from the start, we aren't a 'family magazine'. . .
> Within the pages of PLAYBOY you will find articles, fiction, picture stories, cartoons, humour and special features culled from many sources, past and present, to form a pleasure-primer styled to the masculine taste. . .
> We like our apartment. We enjoy mixing up cocktails and an *hors d'oeuvre* or two, putting a little mood music on the phonograph and inviting in a female acquaintance for a quiet discussion on Picasso, Nietzsche, jazz, sex. . . (Miller, 1984, pp. 44–5)

Initially, *Playboy* was regarded in some quarters as a thoroughly disreputable publication, not least because of its 'daring' coverage of 'girls', but also because of the negative connotations then attached to the term 'playboy'. To counter this image Hefner wrote the following for the April 1956 issue, which provides a thumbnail sketch of what he saw as the 'ideal reader':

> What is a playboy? Is he simply a wastrel, a ne'er-do-well, a fashionable bum? Far from it. He can be a sharp-minded young business executive, a worker in the arts, a university professor, an architect or an engineer. He can be many things, provided he possesses a certain point of view. He must see life not as a vale of tears, but as a happy time, he must take joy in his work, without regarding it as the end of all living; he must be an alert man, a man of taste, a man sensitive to pleasure, a man who – without acquiring the stigma of voluptuary or dilettante – can live life to the hilt. This is the sort of man we mean when we use the word Playboy. (Miller, 1984, pp. 64–5)

Playboy's ideology might be summed up as a libertarianism in

which hedonism, especially of the sexual kind, looms large. According to Hefner, *Playboy*:

> described an urban world and the play and pleasure parts of life. If you had to sum up the idea of *Playboy*, it is anti-Puritanism. Not just in regard to sex, but the whole range of play and pleasure. (Brady, 1974, p. 75)

Having fun, enjoying oneself and sampling the good things in life were accorded a primacy never before seen in a magazine.

Chief among the good things in life is sex. Hefner could sometimes speak with evangelical fervour on the subject:

> sex is more than simply a good and positive part of life. It is a key and touchstone of life. Sex, not religion, is the major civilizing force on this planet. Clearly and obviously, it is the best part of us. It is the part that brings us together, the beginning of the family, the tribe, of cities, of civilization. (Weyr, 1978, p. 222)

As Weyr has argued, Hefner saw sex as good in itself so that abstinence was paramount to a moral wrong. Not surprisingly, Hefner's touching beliefs about the world-historical significance of sex applied only to heterosexual activity. Homosexuality was treated sympathetically and the rights of gays supported, but as a sexual practice it was seen, in the end, as an aberration.

The robust endorsement of heterosexuality is evident throughout *Playboy*. Hefner again:

> *Playboy* is a combination of sex . . . and status . . . the sex actually includes not only the Playmate and the cartoons and jokes which describe boy–girl situations, but goes right down in all the service features . . . there's no confusion with *Playboy*. It is devoted to the boy–girl relationship, to heterosexual activity in a modern society. And in the best sense *Playboy* is sexual like a sports car can be sexy . . . We suggest these things in a context of boys and girls together. (Brady, 1974, p. 95)

What infuriated Hefner about the rebirth of feminism was that it was 'anti-sexual, unnatural'. The new feminists were 'unalterably opposed to the romantic boy–girl society that *Playboy* promotes' (Weyr, 1978, p. 231).

In turn, what infuriated feminists about *Playboy* was its reduction of women to a commodity, literally a plaything of men. *Playboy* portrayed a world of 'boys' 'playing' with, among other things, 'girls'. Feminists complained that women came to be seen as diversionary things reduced to a toy status. The connection can be made by considering the following comments by Arthur Kretchmer, *Playboy*'s Editorial Director:

> Hef helped the world discover toys. I mean, that's one of the most critical things about him – that he said 'play, it's okay to play' . . . Hef's central message . . . was celebrate your life. Free it up. Your sexuality can be as good as anybody else's if you take the inhibitions out . . . Part of our package is to say . . . that there is a world of objects and toys out there. (Weyr, 1978, p. 56)

Quite naturally feminists have been greatly concerned about the way *Playboy* so readily assimilated women into this 'world of objects and toys'.

Sex then, is placed very firmly in a hedonistic context. Hefner apparently wanted *Playboy* to show 'life as a celebration without being too self-conscious or too patronizing about it' (Weyr, 1978, p. 26). Taking away the constraints, removing the inhibitions is a central motif. For this reason Hefner was long opposed to his editors marrying (Brady, 1974, p. 134). Hefner once stated:

> *Playboy* is dedicated to the enjoyment of the good life, instead of settling for job security, conformity, togetherness . . . and slow death. (Brady, 1974, p. 89)

Small wonder that *Playboy*'s circulation achieved such phenomenal growth in the 1960s and that it is now faltering in the very different climate of the 1980s.

THE SEX CARTOON IN *PLAYBOY*

In the light of our sketch of *Playboy*'s ideology, it is no surprise to find that around two-thirds of the magazine's cartoons are concerned with sexual activity. But these cartoons are not simply a collection linked only by the common theme of sex. They have their own

consistent and distinct tone and ambience that is entirely in keeping with the *Playboy* world view. Obviously, Hefner's tight editorial control over the cartoon content partly explains this consistency, as does the use of work by the same dozen or so artists for nearly all the full-page colour cartoons.

When a large number of *Playboy* sex cartoons are viewed it becomes apparent that the collection as a whole is circumscribed by certain aesthetic and moral boundaries. However, it is not easy to specify exactly where these boundaries lie. The following is an attempt to approximate the characteristic features of these cartoons.

The artwork of these cartoons is quite literal, completely lacking in the use of visual metaphor for satirical purposes that is commonplace in political cartooning. In consequence, the humour of the cartoon is 'played straight': there are no hidden meanings awaiting excavation by the reader, or at least none that are required simply for the reader to comprehend the joke. Also in contrast to political cartoons we find that *Playboy*'s are peopled by anonymous characters, 'social types' rather than identifiable individuals. The large majority of cartoons are captioned with a single-utterance punchline, a device which according to social psychologists enhances the cartoon's humorous potential (Jones, Fine and Brust, 1979; McKay and McKay, 1982). Sexual themes are dealt with, but not in an explicit way. The portrayal of nudity is fairly limited and there is a virtual absence of profanity in the captions (again, research shows that cartoons with profane captions are rated funnier by men; see Sewell, 1984). The cartoons tend to be populated by middle-class characters and the jokes predominantly focus on the vicissitudes of sexual relations. There are no 'toilet jokes' and lewdness and crudeness are kept under tight rein. The cartoons, like the female pictorials, are infused with the same 'antiseptic sex imagery' (Michaelson, 1970) which has become *Playboy*'s hallmark.

In short the cartoons portray a world of male sexual pleasure largely uncomplicated by work and family demands, emotional ties and biological realities – a tasteful comic 'pornotopia' (Marcus, 1966). The substantive interest for this chapter lies in the images of women, men and their relationship employed in the construction of this comic world. But before discussing the findings of the content analysis, it is necessary to examine some fundamental issues about cartoons in general and *Playboy* sex cartoons in particular. Our first concern is with the important distinction between cartoon and caricature.

CARTOON AND CARICATURE

The term cartoon is often confused with caricature but they are distinct notions (Johnson, 1937; Kris and Gombrich, 1962; Bogardus 1945; Harrison, 1981). Broadly speaking, the cartoon is a *form* of artistic expression (like painting, musical performance, sculpture) whilst caricature is a *style* of artistic expression comparable to realism, expressionism and so forth. The cartoon has its origins in the full-scale drawings used as patterns for the construction of frescoes, mosaics and mural paintings, but since the eighteenth century it has come to denote a humorous drawing or, more recently, a film made from such drawings. Caricature is a style of artistic expression which, according to Kris and Gombrich involves 'the deliberate distortion of the features of the person for the purposes of mockery' (1962, p. 189). As we shall show, *Playboy* sex cartoons extensively use the caricatural mode of drawing.

Although caricature is as old as the graphic arts themselves, portrait caricature as an artistic style is a much more recent development, originating in Italy at the turn of the sixteenth and seventeenth centuries. The seventeenth-century commentator, Baldinucci, captured the style in the following terms:

> Caricaturing among painters and sculptors signifies a method of making portraits, in which they aim at the greatest resemblance of the whole of the person portrayed, while yet for the purpose of fun, and sometimes of mockery, they disproportionately increase and emphasise the defects of the features they copy, so that the portrait as a whole appears to be the sitter himself while its component parts are cheaper. (Kris and Gombrich, 1962, pp. 189–90)

The beginnings of the modern cartoon are found in the merging of the caricature tradition with the vindictive pictorial symbolism that had also become popular in the sixteenth and seventeenth centuries. Kris and Gombrich point out that it was in eighteenth-century England that:

> caricature portraits were first introduced into political prints, that the cartoon in one sense was born and caricature was given a new setting and a new function ... Caricature had become a social weapon unmasking the pretentions of the powerful and killing by ridicule. (Kris and Gombrich, 1962, p. 194)

In the classic political cartoon the object of ridicule was usually a powerful political personality. Later, similar methods of distortion and ridicule came to be used against the anonymous members of recognisable social groups. Indeed, Kris has argued that caricatures are aimed at an identifiable individual or at a type which is portrayed by exaggeration of particular features. Thus there is the caricature stereotype of blacks with big lips and rolling eyes, of Jews with large noses and stooped backs, and of women with large breasts and excessively curvacious hips. Although the actual individual portrayed in these caricatures is unknown, the exaggerated features have become stereotyped to the point where they are symbols of that group.

When caricature is used to establish social identity, as in *Playboy* cartoons, the cartoonist will tend to rely on popular prejudice and stereotypes to provide the requisite recognition tags. In this respect cartoons are inherently reactionary since they trade on the most reliable marks of social identity that are encapsulated in popular prejudice. The cartoon that embodies current stereotypes thus becomes an instrument of social control (Hines, 1933) defining the 'essential nature' of particular types of persons. The reductionistic method of caricature serves as a persuasive device for the reproduction of stereotypes. Our content analysis will show that, in line with what might be expected from a magazine of its kind, female characters are more likely to be subjected to caricatural portrayal than male characters.

THE CARTOON FRAME AND THE 'SERIOUS IMPORT OF HUMOUR'

Cartoons possess a capacity to engross a reader, albeit often for only a second or two. The competent reader has little difficulty in recognising a cartoon and in appreciating the special range of contingencies and possibilities belonging to the cartoon realm. Plainly, the cartoon is one type of make-believe but this does not preclude sociological interest in the genre as such. To begin with, the commonsense understanding pertaining to this realm can be given sociological treatment by means of the application of some of Goffman's (1975) frame analytic ideas. Frame analysis addresses the organisational features of the experiential modes that members of society employ in establishing what is going on in the world. We shall

speak of the 'cartoon frame' as the framework of understanding generated by the activity of reading cartoons. (Note that this usage stands in contrast to the vernacular where the frame is the lined box marking the border of the cartoon.) An initial frame analytic question that must be addressed is, how are cartoons recognised as such? How is the cartoon frame established?

William F. Fry, Jr, has remarked that 'it is awesome when one thinks objectively about it, how few mistakes are made in cartoon recognition' (1968, p. 143). There are several reasons for this. For the general public at least, cartoons are found in periodicals such as newspapers or magazines. The cartoon has a distinct form: it is a caricatured drawing designed to be humorous which may or may not be accompanied by a caption. The caption of the *Playboy* cartoon is typically a short utterance made by a single speaker which is placed in inverted commas immediately beneath the drawing. The cartoon is also recognisable as such by virtue of the distinctive space it occupies on the printed page. It is demarcated from the edge of the page and from adjacent print by one of two devices: a lined box or a blank border. *Playboy* prefers the latter device but many newspapers operate with the former. Through these cues readers are able to distinguish cartoons from other kinds of printed-page content and especially other kinds of graphics (news photographs, illustrations, explanatory diagrams, advertisements).

Cartoons are one example of what Goffman terms 'dramatic scriptings', that is 'strips of depicted personal experience made available for vicarious participation to an audience or readership' (1975, p. 53), typically through the principal mass media outlets. Cartoons, like plays, novels and films provide 'a mock-up of everyday life, a put-together script of unscripted social doings' (Goffman, 1975, p. 53), yet they are regarded as sharply separate from real life and considered to stand in marked contrast to it. Thus far, Goffman's argument about the status of dramatic scriptings differs little from the better-known analyses of the properties of fictional realms conducted by William James and Alfred Schutz. But unlike James and Schutz, who would consign cartoons to a special fictional realm albeit with its own 'cognitive style' and 'motivational relevancies', Goffman proposes that dramatic scriptings have systematic links with unscripted reality. The cartoon along with other dramatic scriptings is a 'keying' of ordinary unscripted social activity; that is, it presents a transformed version of activities that are already intelligible in terms of a primary framework. Thus a cartoon which features a boss seducing

his secretary can only be found intelligible because readers are able to make sense of real office life as holding out the possibility of a seduction between a real boss and a real secretary. Without prior understandings of office life and a multitude of other social situations mediated by primary frameworks, the cartoon would be meaningless. The often ludicrous and absurd situations depicted in cartoons are appreciated as such in contrast to our prior understanding of the normal and typical. It might be added that when a person fails to 'get' a joke, then what is being referenced is a lacuna in his unjoking social experience (cf. Sacks, 1978). Thus, the experiences depicted in the cartoon frames are not *wholly* peculiar to it. They do not make sense only in the terms of this realm, but are parasitic on the reader's wider interpretive competence. It is a mistake to think of the cartoon frame as a realm only amenable to understanding and analysis in its own terms, a kind of caricature equivalent of Winch's conception of primitive society.

Some care needs to be exercised in the development of this argument. Cartoon characters are admittedly inventions, products of the artist's imagination and skill, and have life only in the viewing of the printed page. Cartoons in themselves bear no obvious and necessary relationship of correspondence to the world 'out there'. At best, in reading a cartoon, as in other kinds of make-believe, the reader 'treats the depicted world as if it were real-like but of course not actually real' (Goffman, 1979, p. 15). This accomplishment bears further scrutiny: how is it possible for a reader to treat a depicted world as 'real-like'?

The solution is that both actual and depicted reality is interpreted in terms of a single viewing and reading competency. Members of society decode lived social reality and various pictorial representations of it (such as cartoons) in much the same way, picking out the same socially relevant features. Goffman notes how, particularly in public places in urban settings, the individual lives in a 'glimpsed world' (Goffman, 1979, p. 22). The individual may know little of the biography of strangers encountered on his way, but by paying attention to self-presentational conventions can make reasonable inferences about the category of the other, mood, current undertakings and so forth. These 'glimpsings' provide information which is truncated and abstract but which is quite adequate to the task of dealing with a world of strangers. The same sort of categories that the individual uses to glimpse others and their activities are also used to decode cartoons. In the case of cartoons, however, the task of

decoding is made easier because readers are given a glimpse of drawn action that is unambiguous and constructed in such a way as to allow the reader access to everything relevant.

It is widely acknowledged that matters can be broached in a humorous frame that cannot be readily handled in a serious frame. Emerson has spoken of 'the serious import of humour' to describe the introduction of serious topics of conversation in a humorous guise. 'For the very reason that humour officially does not "count" ', Emerson writes, 'persons are induced to express messages that might be unacceptable if stated seriously' (1969, pp. 169–70). Emerson emphasises how the joke can thus be used as a *sub rosa* form of communication that provides, as part of its frame, a let-out clause should the serious topic turn out to be unfavourably received, allowing the joker the defence that only a joke was intended, nothing serious. Underpinning this form of communication, Emerson argues, is a process of negotiation which 'may be regarded as bargaining to make unofficial arrangements about taboo topics' (1969, p. 170). The protagonists are seen as involved in negotiating how much licence may be taken under the guise of humour. In some instances however this negotiation is hindered by lack of face-to-face interaction between the involved parties which can lead to the joker over-stepping the mark, as where the cartoonist has offended the butt of the cartoon. King Louis Philippe imprisoned a nineteenth-century caricaturist, Philippon, for ridiculing him. In 1902 Governor Penny-packer attempted to protect himself against cartoonists by getting a law passed which curtailed their power to draw anything that they liked. In addition anti-cartoon laws were posted in New York (1897), Indiana (1913) and Alabama (1915) (see Wilson, 1979). Clearly the argument that cartoons should not be taken seriously because they are 'make believe' does not explain why cartoons have been taken very seriously in the past.

Sociologists generally point to two major functions that humour serves: social control and social conflict. The conflict function of humour includes such forms as irony, satire, sarcasm, caricature and parody (Fine 1983, Zijderveld 1968) which serves to separate an out-group from an in-group and may even provoke hostility from the out-group. Stephenson maintains that one of the advantages of humour is that it may 'conceal malice and allow expression of aggression without the consequences of overt behaviour' (1951, p. 569). If, as sociologists have argued, the cartoon is a potential vehicle for covert, aggressive and hostile communication and, moreover, if it is possible

for recognised butts to feel threatened by caricatured depictions, then we are dealing with an art form which may have implications for the standing of persons in the real world.

THE PORNOGRAPHIC CONTEXT

A thorough analysis of *Playboy* sex cartoons demands that we take into account the context in which they appear in *Playboy* magazine for, as Berger argues, 'the meaning of an image is changed according to what one sees immediately beside it or what comes immediately after it' (Berger, 1972, p. 29). The context that *Playboy* provides is essentially a pornographic context.

Moye in his article discusses some of the substantive differences between soft and hard-core pornography but argues that the common element is that women are depicted 'as limited beings with a restricted sexual presence subservient to apparently specific masculine desires' (Moye, 1985, p. 56). This view has been echoed by much feminist research which has argued that in pornography the essence and dignity of women are reduced to the provision of sexual services for men, that females are depicted as passive and sexually subordinate to men, that what pleases women is the use of their bodies to satisfy male desires (Dworkin, 1981; Lederer, 1980). Anyone reading the readers' letters or the fiction in these magazines will find these points are reiterated again and again. 'Within these fictions women's desire is centred on wanting, if not craving to be penetrated by the male protagonist' (Moye, 1985, p. 56).

A major selling point of any pornographic magazine is the pictorial display of nude women. One *Playboy* editor admitted that what sells the magazine is not the prestigious fiction or the highly acclaimed interviews but rather the 'girls'.

We could have all the Nabokovs in the world and the best articles . . . without attracting readers. They bought the magazine for the girls. We couldn't take the sex out. The magazine would die like a dog. (Weyr, 1978, p. 35)

The 'girls' in *Playboy* pose in diverse ways, but there is one theme which runs throughout; 'there remains the implication that the subject (a woman) is aware of being seen by a spectator' (Berger, 1972, p. 49). Berger is in fact not referring to pornography but rather

to the traditions of nude painting, but his argument is equally if not more relevant. Moye observes the way the gaze of the model is directed to return the reader's gaze: 'this gaze emphasises the woman's presence in a manner which is personalized and colluded with the reader's intent' (Moye, 1985, p. 55). The woman in the centrefold is in actuality offering herself sexually to the male reader, very often her genitals are sexually displayed for him, her body is arched towards him, in fact as Berger notes, 'everything is addressed to him, everything must appear to be the result of his being there. It is for him that the figures have assumed their nudity' (Berger, 1972, p. 54). The magazine speaks in a single idiom of tamed female sexuality in which the fiction, the advice and letters pages, and the nude layouts form an integrated whole.

If, as Berger proposes, our perceptions of images are affected by their surroundings, a brief description of the layout of a typical issue of *Playboy* magazine is required.

By the 1970s, *Playboy* had a well-developed standard format: centre stage obviously occupied by the centrefold of the 'Playmate of the Month', a couple of other pictorials either side of Playmate but interspersed with fiction and articles. Most issues ran to well over 200 pages but the first cartoon would rarely be encountered before p. 70 and the overwhelming majority of them appear in the final hundred or so pages. Clearly a variety of editorial and commercial decisions are involved in this format but it is perhaps noteworthy that the more serious regular features such as the advice column, letters page and reviews appear near the beginning of an issue, whilst most of the cartoons come after the 'girls' in the second half of the magazine. In *Playboy*, weighty matters are discussed early on in a typical issue, while more 'diversionary' concerns – 'the girls', the cartoons – figure later.

Thus the average *Playboy* reader makes sense of the cartoon images using the same mental set that has been gained from the accompanying letters, editorials and pictures whose 'central motif ... is the presentation of women's bodies, or parts of them, for consumption by men' (Root, 1984, p. 43). This, however, tells us more about the context of the cartoons than their content. What the present study aims to do is to analyse the content of the female and male stereotypes depicted in the cartoons. What we want to emphasise here is that a proper analysis of the cartoons must take account not only of the details of character and action within the cartoon frame but also the nature of the surrounding magazine

content. Other commentators have proposed a broad consonance between the values implicit in political cartoons and the editorial policies of newspapers (Seymour-Ure, 1975). We suggest that the same consonance is evident between the values embedded in *Playboy* cartoons and the magazine's more explicitly articulated values.

STRUCTURE OF THE STEREOTYPES

Previous studies of cartoons in magazines have concentrated their attention on only one or two aspects of this art form. Cantor's (1976) study of cartoon humour found in *Playboy, Cosmopolitan, Ladies Home Journal* and *Esquire*, coded the cartoons according to whether their main theme was sex, violence or hostility. In a further study of cartoons in the same four magazines, Cantor (1977) focused on the sex of disparager and victim. Since these studies were designed to advance understanding of tendentious humour and disparagement theory, entire cartoons were coded in terms of one of the three main themes. The more subtle elements of the cartoons, the particularities of person, scene and relationship were not addressed save for a concern with the ridiculer–ridiculed relationship. The same general complaint can also be levelled at Palmer's (1979) content analysis of the 'eight-pagers', a genre of pornographic comics popular in America in the 1930s and 1940s. A variety of comics were analysed to ascertain the extent of certain 'pornographic themes' and sexual activities. Palmer's system of categories does reveal the range of sexual behaviour evident in the eight-pagers but tells us little about the social setting, the social characteristics of the cartoon characters or the non-sexual aspects of their relationships. Similarly, Greenberg and Kahn's (1970) study of the appearance or non-appearance of blacks in *Playboy* cartoons contains only a small amount of information about the manner in which the black character is portrayed.

It can be seen that existing research has been somewhat limited in scope and is focused on a narrow range of concerns. The design of the present study utilises a rather more complex system of categories. The categories were devised in order to construct a profile of female and male *Playboy* cartoon characters which would highlight personal characteristics, sexual activity and the nature of the relationship with the other character(s). The aim was to develop a more comprehen-

sive analysis of differences in female and male representations in *Playboy* sex cartoons.

The Categories

The sample consisted of some 1400 cartoons containing 2412 cartoon characters. The main protagonist of each sex only was coded. The cartoons were drawn from an average of nine months of issues for each year between 1970–79. Only those cartoons which had a sexual theme (approximately 65 per cent) were used.

(i) Sex of Cartoon Characters
Of the 2412 cartoon characters coded, 1249 (51.8 per cent) were female and 1163 (48.2 per cent) were male. The fairly equal distribution of males and females in *Playboy* sex cartoons is a sign that much of the humour deals with the interaction between the sexes. This is to be expected given that a common feature of the cartoons was some form of heterosexual activity. Where only one sex was depicted, the humour was often contained in the captions with the cartoon protagonist relating the events of the sex act to the cartoon other(s) of the same sex. Thus, while not being depicted, the essence of the humour still focused on sexual activity.

(ii) Major Defining Role (MDR) of the Cartoon Character
This category was created in order to establish the role enacted by the cartoon characters. The sub-divisions within this category present the reader with information about the social status of the cartoon character and his/her relationship to the cartoon other. The original content analysis schema had fourteen MDR sub-divisions. However, after coding it was found that this number of sub-divisions was too extensive for the chi-square test to be valid. This resulted in the number of sub-divisions being reduced to five: spouse, employee, employer, sex partner, prostitute/client.

The original MDR sub-divisions had included both female employer and male employee. However, these sub-divisions had to be deleted as only thirteen cases of female employers and seventeen cases of male employees were found – evidence of *Playboy*'s adherence to standard sexist stereotypes of occupational roles. It could be argued that *Playboy*'s depictions are merely reflective of the present position of women in society. However, as we shall argue, *Playboy* is not so much in the business of reflecting reality as

Table 11.1   Sex by Major Defining Role

	Spouse	Employee	Employer	Sex partner	Prostitute/ client	Stranger	
Female	17.6	9.8	deleted	51.2	5.9	15.5	n = 1181
Male	18.1	deleted	11.2	49.3	4.9	16.5	n = 1077

$\chi^2 = 240.2$ DF = 0.5 $p < 0.05$ Missing cases = 154*

*Missing cases are those which were initially coded but are not included in the final tables because they fell into those sub-divisions deleted in that particular category, or those cartoon characters which did not fall into any of the sub-divisions.

presenting its own caricature brand of widely-current sexist stereotypes. One such stereotype is that women are sexually subordinate to men and that they exist merely for the sexual desire of men. Thus women are often depicted as sexual toys for males. In the workplace, they are portrayed not as workers but as sexual playthings, providing not productive services but light sexual relief from work. This argument is reinforced by further analysis of the female employee sub-division which shows that 52 per cent were seductively dressed, 30 per cent partially undressed and 5 per cent naked. Thus some 87 per cent of female employees were dressed (or undressed) in a manner quite inappropriate for work, but appropriate for sexual play.

Other than employer/employee sub-divisions there are no major sex differences in this category. It is worth noting that the original formulation had sub-divisions for mother/father, female pregnant/ male with female who is pregnant and daughter/son. However, because we found only six mothers and eleven fathers, three cases of pregnancy, and 23 daughters and sons, it was necessary for the purposes of statistical testing to delete these sub-divisions. These small numbers suggest that *Playboy* cartoons do not tend to portray longstanding intimate relationships which have emotional ties. This is indeed borne out by the finding that the single largest sub-division was sex partner which was defined as involving a sexual relationship where no other relationship is discernible. It appears therefore that we are dealing in the main with transient, temporary relationships with no sense of history or commitment or obligation. Although the second single largest sub-division was spouse, which suggests some long-term relationship, further analysis found that 71 per cent of all married cartoon characters were either betraying or being betrayed by their spouses.

(iii) Age of Cartoon Characters

It is particularly instructive to consider male and female representations in terms of age since a range of expectations about behaviour and attitudes, and especially sexual behaviour, are associated with this variable.

Table 11.2 Sex by Age

	Up to adolescence	Young/ middle	Middle/ old	Old	
Female	3.5	81.4	11.9	3.2	$n = 1248$
Male	2.2	43.2	45.4	9.2	$n = 1163$

$x^2 = 420.3$ DF = 0.3 $p < 0.05$ Missing cases = 1

Female cartoon characters were concentrated in the young to middle sub-division, whereas male characters were more evenly distributed between the young/middle and middle/old sub-divisions. Thus male cartoon characters often have the dual status advantage of being male and being older than the female characters depicted. We also find that there are more old males than old females. The difference is not only one of numbers but also of presentation. Whereas *Playboy* depicts a number of different caricatures for the old man, for old females there is but one major caricature. This appeared at regular intervals (always drawn by the same cartoonist, Buck Brown) usually as the last cartoon towards the end of the issue (see also Posner, 1975). The character was regularly depicted (in 85 per cent of these cartoons) as a sex-starved predator attempting to seduce males of all age ranges. Further analysis showed that old males met with very little female resistance (only 5 per cent of old males failed to consummate the sex act due to female avoidance or resistance). The old female in contrast was avoided or resisted in 60 per cent of cases. Thus the converse of the young sexually desirable female stereotype is the old predator who repels the majority of her potential partners. Given that the currency of worth in *Playboy* prizes youthful sexually desirable females it is not surprising that the old woman is no longer considered legal tender, and is therefore ridiculed.

(iv) Clothing

The clothing category provides further information about the identity of the cartoon character since it is a key indicator of financial and occupational status as well as the more localised relevancies

pertaining to the cartoon action, in particular whether the female cartoon character is to be cast in the sex object role. Originally there were six sub-divisions for females and males but as only thirteen cases of female costume were found it was necessary to reduce the female sub-divisions to five.

Table 11.3 Sex by Dress

	Conser-vative	Conven-tional	Seductive	Costume	Partial undress	Naked	
Female	3.3	9.9	38.6	deleted	40.9	7.3	$n = 1236$
Male	24.1	27.9	5.7	14.1	27.6	0.6	$n = 1161$

$x^2 = 855.5$ DF $= 0.5$ $p < 0.05$ Missing cases $= 15$

The majority of females (87 per cent) fell into those sub-divisions (seductive, partial undress, naked) which were most suitable for sexual play. Thus once again the female roles were essentially reduced to one, i.e. the sexual. Of the female cartoon characters, 87 per cent were garbed in a manner which circumscribed their activity, for being portrayed in a sexual manner precludes being taken seriously in any other role they may perform. The male cartoon characters were not similarly limited, however, for over 50 per cent were portrayed in conservative or conventional dress which allows them to be seen as fulfilling a wide range of roles.

This theme of female as sex object could be seen running throughout the cartoons. Irrespective of her major defining role, the female cartoon character was overwhelmingly portrayed as available for sexual play. Thus it is not surprising to find that the female's body was depicted naked nearly fifteen times more than the male body. Nakedness, of course, is depicted in a stylized way in *Playboy* cartoons. The conventions of *Playboy* cartooning are rather coy: the detailed depiction of genitalia characteristic of more explicitly pornographic publications is avoided. It is particularly amusing to note the great lengths to which *Playboy* cartoonists go in order to conceal the penis. Despite its stance on free expression and nudity, *Playboy* clearly feels there are some matters that are *not* fit for caricature!

(v) Pictorial Representation of the Body
Like the clothing category, pictorial representation of the body is particularly instructive about the role taken by female cartoon

characters. Three sub-divisions were devised: realistic, idealistic and freak. The idealistic sub-division featured caricatured depictions of conventionally desirable physical characteristics, whilst the freak sub-division was devised to accommodate abnormal and grotesque depictions of the cartoon characters.

Table 11.4 Sex by Body

	Realistic	Idealistic	Freak	
Female	21.9	73.6	4.5	$n = 1249$
Male	95.6	1.5	2.9	$n = 1161$

$x^2 = 1380.2$ DF = 0.2 $p < 0.05$ Missing cases = 2

Nearly three-quarters (73.6 per cent) of the cartoon depictions of women conformed to the caricature stereotype, whereas a very large majority of men (95.4 per cent) were depicted realistically. This is probably the single most striking piece of evidence in support of the objectification of female cartoon characters in purely sexual terms. The pictorial representation of the female is so caricatured that we instantly read large breasts, curvacious hips and protruding bottoms as symbols of sexual intent and/or availability. Thus, so far we have the image of the *Playboy* female cartoon character as young, sexily clothed and idealistically depicted whereas the male is more likely to be young to old, fully clothed and realistically drawn. The majority of female freaks can be accounted for by the old woman caricature previously discussed. She was portrayed in a ridiculed manner with large drooping breasts, knock-knees and scrawny body. Further analysis shows that whereas 77.5 per cent of old females were depicted as freaks, only 10 per cent of old males were so depicted.

(vi) Heterosexuality and Homosexuality
The overwhelming majority of cases were heterosexual. This at first sight may seem strange as homosexuality is a common theme of

Table 11.5 Sex by Heterosexual or Homosexual

	Heterosexual	Homosexual	
Female	98.6	1.4	$n = 1248$
Male	98.5	1.5	$n = 1162$

$x^2 = 0.04$ DF = 1 $p < 0.05$ Missing cases = 2

many jokes. Despite the liberal stance that *Playboy* editorials take towards homosexuality, cartoon humour on the subject is markedly restricted. Also, *Playboy* is an aggressively heterosexual magazine and one would expect the editorials, pictures, jokes and cartoons to reflect this. Homosexuality is thus not a general topic of interest in the magazine. This finding underlines the earlier argument concerning the consonance between editorial values and the values expressed through cartoons. Given the energetically heterosexual character of *Playboy* combined with its determinedly liberal stance, it is not surprising that homosexuality figures so little in the cartoons. If there is one thing that *Playboy* editors know for sure about their regular readers, it is that they are not gay.

(vii) Success of Sexual Activity
The consummation category was sub-divided in order to ascertain the extent of successful cartoon sex and the reasons for its failure.

Table 11.6 Sex by Consummation or Non-Consummation of Sex Act

	Non-consummation due to inability to sustain erection or due to inadequate size of penis or premature ejaculation	*Non-consummation due to female avoidance of sex*	*Non-consummation due to male avoidance of sex*	*Con-sum-mation*	*Cartoon did not give enough information*	
Female	2.7	6.2	4.8	41.3	45.0	$n \times 1248$
Male	2.9	6.4	5.3	37.9	47.5	$n \times 1162$

$x^2 = 10.9$ $DF = 0.1$ $p < 0.05$ Missing cases $= 2$

A large number of cases could not be coded because the cartoon did not give enough information concerning consummation. This was usually due to the depicted sex still being in progress. Consummation was the next largest sub-division, with the remaining sub-divisions which deal with sexual dysfunction and the wish to avoid sex containing quite small numbers. What this shows is that sexual dysfunction is a subject more appropriate to the serious sections of the magazine, whilst avoidance of sex is clearly a minority pattern, the very opposite of the healthy heterosexuality that *Playboy* conceives of as the norm.

(viii) Type of Sex Act

This category was devised in order to investigate the variety of sexual activity depicted in the cartoons.

Table 11.7 Sex by Sex Act

	Sexual inter-course	Group sex	Oral sex	Sadism	Bestia-lity	Exhibi-tionism	Proposi-tioning	
Female	58.3	12.2	3.7	2.5	4.4	8.6	10.3	$n = 1231$
Male	60.5	11.7	3.7	2.5	2.2	8.4	11.0	$n = 1138$

$\chi^2 = 9.3$ DF = 0.6 $p < 0.05$ Missing cases = 43

The most conventional of all sex acts, intercourse, was the predominant form of sexual activity depicted. This is somewhat surprising given that *Playboy* sees itself as a magazine dedicated to breaking down sexual myths and taboos. Rather more substantial frequencies for the alternatives to intercourse might have been expected. One explanation could be that sexual intercourse allows other elements of the cartoon scene or characters, such as adultery, age, discrepant relationship or office sex, to form the core of the humour. It is possible that depictions of less orthodox sexual activities tend to restrict the joke to the activity (e.g. bestiality) itself, crowding out other humorous possibilities. Intercourse presents a more open scenario.

(ix) Cartoon Characters and Age Discrepant Relationships

This category, together with the age of cartoon characters, furnishes the reader with information regarding the age stereotypes employed in *Playboy* cartoons. It also provides a useful tool for the comparison of male and female stereotypes.

The stereotype of the older male, younger woman occurs in just under one third of *Playboy* sex cartoons. We find, however, little evidence of the older female/younger male stereotype. Such a

Table 11.8 Sex by Age Discrepant Relationship

	Older man/ younger woman	Older woman/ younger man	Equal ages	
Female	29.4	3.5	67.1	$n = 1248$
Male	31.9	3.8	64.3	$n = 1163$

$\chi^2 = 514.1$ DF = 0.2 $p < 0.05$ Missing cases = 1

finding fits in with the *Playboy* view that the young woman is the only sexually desirable type. Males however are not sexually limited by age but rather continue to be active throughout the life cycle. Because the female is cast as the commodity and the male as the user, cartoon males can choose the most desirable on offer irrespective of their own age.

(x) Activity and Passivity in the Sexual Relationship
One important factor often omitted in content analysis studies of cartoons is data concerning the mood and motives of cartoon characters. In the cartoons under investigation these features can be conceptualised on a continuum between 'seducing' through 'willing' and 'resigned' to 'preventing' the sex act. The two extremes represent an active attitude to the relationship while the two intermediary sub-divisions are evidence of passivity.

Table 11.9 Sex by Activity or Passivity in Relationship

	Seducing	*Willing*	*Resigned*	*Preventing*	
Female	29.2	51.4	10.2	9.2	$n = 1165$
Male	51.5	39.3	3.0	6.2	$n = 1041$

$\chi^2 = 135$ DF = 0.3 $p < 0.05$ Missing cases = 206

Here we find some interesting differences between male and female depictions. The largest single sub-division for males was seducing which involves the cartoon character taking an active role. The largest single sub-division for women, however, was willing which is essentially a passive role. While these figures show that males are generally depicted as playing a more active sexual role, females are shown in four-fifths (80.6 per cent) of cases to be sexually available to man (i.e. seducing and willing). Whether these women are wives, secretaries, sex partners, prostitutes or strangers, they have one thing in common: they are generally agreeable to male sexual advances. Their own desires, aims and wants are subordinate to those of the male. *Playboy* cartoons thus depict a male fantasy world where a bevy of young, beautiful, sexily clad females are sexually available to old, young, dressed, undressed males, be they employers, husbands or whatever. The very essence of women is reduced to an existence which is principally described in terms of male sexual desire. This is the ultimate sexist caricature.

CONCLUSION

Clearly there are other formats available for the cartoon expression of sexual humour than that offered by *Playboy*. There is, for example, a striking contrast between the pervasive sexual anomie evident in *Playboy* cartoons and the firm sense of the stability of family life and the binding nature of marital ties that Orwell identified in the seaside postcards of Donald McGill (Orwell, 1942). At present, however, *Playboy* sex cartoons seem to be locked into a narrow range of stereotypes that are recycled month after month.

Our content analysis of *Playboy* sex cartoons suggests that female characters are more extensively depicted in a caricatured style than males. The 'idealised' female character is young, dressed in a sexually provocative manner if not completely undressed, and possesses a body featuring large breasts, curvacious hips, a protruding bottom and long legs. Irrespectve of setting – home, office, street – this female has one major function, that of sexual plaything. She is generally shown as passive and available. Her wants and needs are subservient to the male character's sexual desire. The converse of this image is the old aggressive predator who is ridiculed and rejected. The basis of these portrayals, rather than being peculiar to *Playboy*, is merely an exaggerated form of existing sexual stereotypes: in our society sexual aggressiveness by males and sexual provocativeness by females are widely accepted forms of conduct (cf. Lemert, 1972). To be sure, the mediation of these stereotypes by the cartoon frame makes for systematic ambiguities in the reader's perception of them. In the end, however, we suggest that these cartoons, like pornography more generally, should be seen as an aspect of the 'regime by which sexuality is organised and expressed in our culture' (Coward, 1982).

This chapter has attempted to locate the study of *Playboy* sex cartoons within the growing body of literature on images of women in the media. The work encompasses a wide range of theoretical and methodological approaches. The study has been restricted to content analysis, but we recognise its shortcomings and the potential value of semiotic approaches in this area (Sumner, 1979; Burgelin, 1968). The great merit of content analysis is that it permits the systematic investigation of a large quantity of material (cf. Woollacott, 1982) and is thus highly appropriate for an initial foray into the relatively unexplored area of *Playboy* sex cartoons.

REFERENCES

Berger, John, *Ways of Seeing* (London: British Broadcasting Corporation and Penguin Books, 1972).

Bogardus, Emory S., 'Sociology of the cartoon', *Sociology and Social Research*, vol. 30 (1945) pp. 139–47.

Brady, Frank, *Hefner* (New York: Macmillan, 1974).

Burgelin, Olivier, 'Structural analysis and mass communication', (orig. 1968) in Denis McQuail (ed.) *Sociology of Mass Communications: Selected Readings* (Harmondsworth: Penguin, 1972).

Cantor, Joanne R., 'What is funny to whom? The role of gender', *Journal of Communication*, vol. 26 (1976) pp. 164–72.

Cantor, Joanne R., 'Tendentious humour in the mass media', in A. J. Chapman and H. C. Foot (eds) *It's a Funny Thing, Humour* (Oxford: Pergamon Press, 1977).

Coward, Rosalind, 'Sexual violence and sexuality', *Feminist Review*, no. 11 (1982), cited in Jane Root, *Pictures of Women: Sexuality* (London: Pandora Press, 1984).

Dworkin, Andrea, *Pornography: Men Possessing Women* (London: Women's Press, 1981).

Emerson, Joan P., 'Negotiating the serious import of humour', *Sociometry*, vol. 32 (1969) pp. 169–81.

Fine, Gary Alan, 'Sociological approaches to the study of humor', in Paul E. McGhee and Jeffrey H. Goldstein (eds) *Handbook of Humor Research: Vol. I Basic Issues* (New York: Springer-Verlag, 1983).

Fry, William F., Jr, *Sweet Madness: A Study of Humor* (Palo Alto, California: Pacific Books, 1968).

Glassner, Barry and Jay Corzine, 'Library research as fieldwork: A strategy for qualitative content analysis', *Sociology and Social Research*, vol. 66 (1982) pp. 305–19.

Goffman, Erving, *Frame Analysis: An Essay on the Organization of Experience* (Harmondsworth: Penguin, 1975).

Goffman, Erving, *Gender Advertisements* (London: Macmillan, 1979).

Greenberg, Bradley and Sandra Kahn, 'Blacks in *Playboy* cartoons', *Journalism Quarterly*, vol. 47 (1970) pp. 557–60.

Harrison, Randall P., *The Cartoon: Communication to the Quick* (Beverley Hills, California: Sage, 1981).

Hines, Edna, 'Cartoons as a means of social control', *Sociology and Social Research*, vol. 17 (1933) pp. 454–64.

Johnson, Isabel Simeral, 'Cartoons', *Public Opinion Quarterly*, vol. 1 (1937) pp. 21–44.

Jones, James M., Gary Alan Fine and Robert G. Brust, 'Interaction effects of picture and caption on humor ratings of cartoons', *The Journal of Social Psychology*, vol. 108 (1979) pp. 193–8.

King, Josephine and Mary Stott (eds) *Is This Your Life?: Images of Women in the Media* (London: Virago, 1977).

Kris, Ernst and E. H. Gombrich, 'The principles of caricature', in Ernst Kris, *Psychoanalytic Explorations in Art* (New York: International University Press, 1962).

Lederer, Laura (ed.) *Take Back the Night: Women on Pornography* (New York: Morrow, 1980).

Lemert, Edwin C., *Human Deviance, Social Problems and Social Control* (Englewood Cliffs, New Jersey: Prentice-Hall, 1972).

McKay, Timothy D. and Marcia E. McKay, 'Captioned and non-captioned cartoons: effects of structural properties on ratings of humour', *Perceptual and Motor Skills*, vol. 54 (1982) pp. 143–6.

Marcus, Steven, 'Pornotopia' *Encounter* (1966) pp. 9–18.

Michaelson, Peter, 'How to make the world safe for pornography', in Philip Nobile (ed.) *The New Eroticism: Theories, Vogues and Canons* (New York: Random House, 1970).

Miller, Russell, *Bunny: The Real Story of Playboy* (London: Michael Joseph, 1984).

Moye, Andy, 'Pornography', in Andy Metcalf and Martin Humphries (eds) *The Sexuality of Men* (London: Pluto Press, 1985).

Orwell, George, 'The Art of Donald McGill', in Sonia Orwell and Ian Angus, *The Collected Essays, Journalism and Letters of George Orwell, Vol. II: My Country Right or Left* (London: Secker and Warburg, 1968).

Palmer, C. Eddie, 'Pornographic comics: a content analysis', *Journal of Sex Research*, vol. 15 (1979) pp. 285–98.

Platt, Jennifer, 'Evidence and proof in documentary research, parts 1 and 2', *Sociological Review*, vol. 29 (1981) pp. 31–66.

Posner, Judith, 'Dirty old women: Buck Brown's cartoons', *Canadian Review of Sociology and Anthropology*, vol. 12 (1975) pp. 471–3.

Root, Jane, *Pictures of Women: Sexuality* (London: Pandora Press, 1984).

Sacks, Harvey, 'Some technical considerations of a dirty joke', in Jim Schenkein (ed.) *Studies in the Organization of Conversational Interaction* (New York: Academic Press, 1978).

Sewell, Edward H., Jr, 'Appreciation of cartoons with profanity in captions', *Psychological Reports*, vol. 54 (1984) pp. 583–7.

Seymour-Ure, Colin, 'How special are cartoonists?' in Anon., *Getting Them in Line* (University of Kent at Canterbury: Centre for the Study of Cartoons and Caricature, 1975).

Stauffer, John and Richard Frost, 'Male and female interest in sexually-oriented magazines', *Journal of Communication*, ol. 26 (1976) pp. 25–30.

Stephenson, Richard M., 'Conflict and control functions of humor', *American Journal of Sociology*, vol. 56 (1951) pp. 569–74.

Sumner, Colin, *Reading Ideologies: An Investigation into the Marxist Theory of Ideology and Law* (London: Academic Press, 1979).

Tuchman, Gaye and Arlene Kaplan Daniels, *Hearth and Home: Images of Women in the Mass Media* (Oxford: Oxford University Press, 1978).

Weyr, Thomas, *Reaching for Paradise: The Playboy Vision of America* (New York: Times Books, 1978).

Wilson, Christopher P., *Jokes: Form, Content, Use and Function* (London: Academic Press, 1979).

Woollacott, Janet, 'Messages and meanings', in Michael Gurevitch, Tony Bennett, James Curran and Janet Woollacott (eds) *Culture, Society and the Media* (London: Methuen, 1982).

Zidjerveld, Anton C., 'Jokes and their relation to social reality', *Social Research*, vol. 35 (1968) pp. 286–311.

12 In Search of Literature on the Sociology of Humour: A Sociobibliographical Afterword

George E. C. Paton

Initial attempts to search for and locate sources in the sociological literature which discuss humour as a sociocultural phenomenon are about as fruitful and as frustrating as the search for the Holy Grail. At best, the two major sociological journals which deign to periodically index subjects as well as authors – the *American Journal of Sociology* and the *American Sociological Review* – under the respective headings of 'Humour, functions of' and 'Humour' throw up a total of only five articles up to 1965 and 1960 respectively.[1] This basic categorisation, however, fails to trawl other articles in these journals relevant for the study of humour which omit the word from their titles.[2] Similarly, diligent searches of article titles and bibliographies indicate that in the 1950s and 1960s such established social science or sociological journals as *Sociometry, Human Relations, Journal of Social Issues, Sociological Inquiry* and *Social Research* published one or more articles on sociological aspects of humour, albeit employing keywords such as 'jokes' or 'comedians' rather than humour in their titles.[3] In terms of the British sociological literature the first traceable paper devoted to the sociological aspects of humour does not appear until 1982 with the publication in the *British Journal of Sociology* of a paper by Christie Davies.[4] Nevertheless, it is possible to concur with Goldstein's observation made in the mid-1970s that, 'within the past ten years psychologists and sociologists have written more on the topics of humour and laughter than from the beginning of this century to 1967'.[5]

Not surprisingly, of the two, the psychology of humour is much the best documented bibliography and particularly so since the holding of

the First International Conference on Humour and Laughter in Cardiff in July 1976.[6] However, the first comprehensive annotated bibliography of nearly 400 published items on humour in the research literature and an analysis of trends for the period 1900 to 1971 was published in 1972 as an appendix to their edited book of readings by the American psychologists Goldstein and McGhee.[7] Although the vast majority of their references are culled from psychological and psychoanalytical literature, there are some also from anthropological and philosophical literature as well as items from sociology journals other than those cited above. Thus such sources are important for the sociologist as a touchstone for determining and explicating what is more distinctly a sociological approach to humour. The overlap especially with social psychology, in terms of the functions and intersubjective nature of humour in small group settings, immediately suggests its relevance as does the latter's centrality to ethno-methodological studies of humour which appeared in the 1970s.[8]

The anthropology of humour is perhaps the best established source of literature for comparative purposes and for suggesting research topics for fieldwork, especially with regard to joking relationships in a variety of societies and cultures. This applies not only to establishing the universality of humour and its varied expression as a non-material culture trait, but also in its application to ethnographic studies in advanced societies where the technique of participant observation can and has been used to advantage in studying the uses of humour in a variety of work situations.[9] Likewise, the necessary ground-clearing exercise which the sociologist needs to engage in to clarify the variety of sociocultural meanings of humour and its synonyms, and derivative sociocultural forms, stresses the importance of philosophical analyses of humour to establish its inter-subjective as distinct from subjective or psychological significance for social actors. As histori-cally the earliest analyses of humour and comedy date from the writers of Ancient Greece and every philosopher of note since appears to have written on the subject, there is a formidable intellectual pedigree to contend with and the best short-cut to establish relevance for more strictly sociological purposes is to take a time-honoured remedy and resort to encyclopaedia resumés by experts.[10]

There is also a parallel need to heed the long-established tradition in literary criticism, by no means solely restricted to English literature, to discuss the nature of comedy and the comic in such art forms.[11] Again, this is not only concerned with the perennial nature

of literary humour and its various genres, but, as importantly for the sociologist, contains analyses of changes and innovations therein over time as reflecting and articulating responses to social worlds and behaviours of social actors in fictive form.[12] The use of such sources clearly assumes particular importance for students of humour and its institutionalised form of comedy[13] in the burgeoning field of the sociology of literature, and more indirectly for sociologists studying popular culture. Here again authors in the adjacent field of social history can provide invaluable and stimulating insights and material of a diachronic nature for the sociologist studying humour to help him or her establish benchmarks of significant changes in a society and the functions of humorous expressions at such times.[14]

These preliminary excursions at this stage in the development of the sociology of humour serve merely to indicate the sociological relevance of some of the literature and methods developed by authors in adjacent disciplines to sociology *per se*. This hardly constitutes, however, a conceptual framework or model for a sociology of humour as consciously developed by sociologists utilising the discipline's own concepts, theories and methods in a systematic way to analyse and explain the sociocultural meanings of humour in society. At best what few contributions have been made to date by sociologists, at either a micro or macro level of analysis, merely reflect attempts by authors to illustrate the functions of humour in a particular arena or milieu, e.g. a work situation, for the social actors involved in terms of social control, resistance to such control or social facilitation.[15] It is, therefore, perhaps best to initially set out a basic taxonomic framework of areas of interest to the sociologist which is more or less exhaustive of the relevant literature published to date. This permits both the initiate and the old hand to the sociological study of humour to engage in a more productive form of intellectual mapping in formulating his or her area of interest for expository and/ or investigatory purposes.

The following classificatory schema has been evolved by the author in the course of collecting and recording literature relating to the sociology of humour over the past decade. Whilst it is readily conceded that there is some possible overlap in a number of the following categories the more definitive classificatory schema precludes this to a large extent. It is accordingly expected that refinements of and within each sub-category will be made as and when the publication of a comprehensive annotated bibliography is made possible.

1. The Comic Muse/Vision: mythological, philosophical and archetypal aspects of humour/comedy.
2. Social Historical/Civilisational Perspectives on and Sociocultural Developments in Humour/Comedy (including charivari, carnivals, mystery plays).
3. Institutionalised Forms of Vernacular Humour and Popular Culture: folk and oral traditions (including music hall, circus, cartoons, film, radio, television).
4. Humour and Learned/High Culture (including literature, drama, classical music, fine arts).
5. Comic Figures/Practitioners of Humour: the role of the fool, comedian, humorist, etc.
6. Humorous Language/Speech in Human Communication (including jokes, riddles, puns, joke-telling).
7. Social Contexts/Themes of Humour (including national, ethnic, sex differences, joking relationships).
8. The Social Functions of Humour: micro- and macro-sociological.
9. The Analysis of and Theories about Forms and Types of Humour (including satire, irony, farce).

Some literature, of course, will be classifiable under one or more sub-categories. To this end it is proposed that a full annotated bibliography of works in the sociology of humour would be greatly enhanced by incorporating into each of the above categories the symbolic annotation used by Goldstein and McGhee in their pioneering work cited above. The omissions from this would be in connection with their symbols F and T respectively covering functions of humour, either in a cultural, social, personality, or physiological context, and original theory or theoretical developments, as these are either irrelevant for strictly sociological purposes or are here covered in our schema by categories 8 and 9 above. Similarly, their subscript Dx is omitted for whilst it is in keeping with psychological experimental studies of humour it has little or no relevance for sociological research studies which, of course, are strictly speaking of a non-experimental nature.

D   Paper contains original data.
c   (Subscript) Data are of a correlational nature. Included here are also factor and content analyses.
Ch   Paper deals in some way with humour in children.
M   Paper is methodological in nature, or presents significant methodological techniques for the study of humour.
R   Review of the humour literature or some specific part of it.

G   General discussion of humour. Also included are papers which do not conveniently fit any of the above categories.

S   Studies included in the preceding methodology survey.

This procedure still requires further refinement, of course, to be of use to the researcher in that he or she requires to start with a keyword[16] or set of keywords to extract from the mass of literature the material for the task in hand and to establish in which of the broad categories and theoretical/investigative perspectives therein is likely to be found literature of sociological import. This is particularly important in not only up-dating any Bibliography but also in determining the current state of the art in any given category of sociological study of humour.

The successful carrying out of this task has been greatly facilitated by the continuous and cumulative bibliographical compilations of the American Institute for Scientific Information (ISI) which both in its weekly and annual published forms of *Current Contents*[17] furnish the most comprehensive worldwide coverage of research and practice in the social and behavioural sciences as well as the arts and humanities. Thus the two volumes most germane to sociological investigations of humour are entitled 'Social & Behavioural Sciences' and 'Arts & Humanities' which abstract the article title, author and journal reference from more than 1300 and 1200 journals respectively in the course of a year. Furthermore, the former is in its fifteenth volume and the latter is of more recent origin dating back to 1977. There is also some overlap in the case of the arts and humanities with respect to the monthly *Humanities Index* (*HI*), published also by ISI since 1975, in which subject fields covered include archaeology and classical studies, area studies, folklore, history, language and literature, literary and political criticism, performing arts, philosophy, religion and theology, and related subjects, all of which can and do periodically deal with aspects of humour of sociological relevance.

The principle keywords for search purposes located in the subject index of the above abstracts are 'humour', 'humorous';[18] 'comedy', 'comic', 'comedian'; 'jokes', 'joking', 'laughter', 'satire', 'satirical' (including sub-heads in *HI* of 'caricature', 'caricatures-cartoons', 'grotesque', 'irony', 'parody', 'wit and humour'). Other derivative terms such as, for example 'pun', 'nonsense', 'farce', etc., readily suggest themselves as possible keywords throwing up connections with sociological and cultural phenomena in such sources.

Whilst these bibliographical sources effectively comb the vast

output of relevant periodicals there are still, of course, considerable numbers of books published annually on every facet of humour and comedy. There appears to be no comparable abstract of book titles under subject areas such as those listed above which concern us here in the sociology of humour.[19] At best the researcher is reduced to examining the annual catalogues of book publishers which are known to regularly publish books on humour and which suggest that sociological and cultural aspects of the topic are being discussed. Again such books contain bibliographies which may throw up valuable sources of other books and articles escaping the above abstracting nets. This, of course, applies particularly to older published sources many of which are no longer in print but which can be located in libraries, and especially by inter-library loan services available at least to university researchers.

Book reviews in sociological, arts and humanities journals also furnish other possibilities for locating material in book form. Indeed, the extended reviews themselves in such notable review journals as *The New York Review of Books, Times Literary Supplement, London Review of Books*, etc. are often of themselves excellent summaries and exigeses on the current state of research and scholarship in a particular facet of the study of humour.[20] Their critical comment and acumen, even if not that of the professional sociologist, is frequently suggestive of areas of research which can fruitfully be undertaken to improve our sociological knowledge of humour and its manifestations in social contexts and forms. Similarly, more extended critical articles by literary and arts reviewers and critics in the so-called quality press, especially the *Sunday Times* and *Observer* in Britain, where they deal with humorists, comic novelists, comic actors, etc., are suggestive of leads and themes for the sociology of humour. The weekly publications *New Society* and *The Listener* are particularly invaluable sources of contemporary literature, especially on popular cultural aspects of humour, the latter publication often reproducing radio talks by experts on various facets of humour and comedy, nationally and internationally. In addition the weekly editions of *Radio Times* and *TV Times* frequently contain articles on current star comedians, comedy scriptwriters and sitcoms which give insights into facets of the comic art of performers and the social and cultural contexts in which various styles and types of humour develop and flourish.

Connected with these multifarious written forms of commentary and analysis of humour and comedy is the increasing preservation of

comic performance in aural and visual forms, principally on the traditional recording disc and now on audio and video cassettes. The compilation of the recorded output of particular comedians and popular comedy programmes on radio and television has led to the creation of neologisms such as 'discography', 'filmography', 'tele-ography', etc., all of which should be consulted by sociologists researching particular comic artists to flesh out more descriptive and autobiographical material and to furnish cues for interpreting the sociological and cultural significance of their humour and comedy.[21]

The importance of establishing the coherent intellectual para-meters of literature extant in any given sub-discipline, let alone a discipline, especially a new and burgeoning one such as the sociology of humour, is, as indicated above, far from easy and as a dynamic cognitive system is subject over time to change, differing emphases and new developments. The publications explosion long recognised in the physical and life sciences has in the past twenty years or so been more than matched by that in the social and behavioural sciences. This has both complicated and drawn attention to the problems inherent in recognising, establishing and delineating new knowledge systems. Accordingly, for the proper dialectical relation-ship between practitioners in the new field to emerge to articulate and substantiate the intellectual base and eventual superstructure of the sociological study of humour to guide and incorporate social research into this area, there is the primary imperative to join social and bibliographical research into a new form of inquiry which Ilse Bry has termed 'sociobibliography'.[22] This would, in her words, 'bring bibliographic data to bear on social studies and would modify the aims and methods of bibliography in the light of social research'.

She further sees the problem posed for such a sociobibliography, which is precisely highlighted in our case by the sociology of humour, as being twofold: '(1) the prevailing bibliographic organisation of the literature of the social sciences does not provide a reasonably complete, much less an integrative access to knowledge on most of the significant issues of our times; and (2) there are no bibliographic methods and systems that can reflect progress in the social sciences as a still evolving and expanding major area of knowledge'.[23]

To achieve this intellectual reorientation she underlines three basic principles which sociobibliography incorporates and which are derived from important scientific and social perspectives of our time. Whilst she is concerned with the more macro perspectives of the social sciences in general, the first of these directs its main pioneer

effort to the detection and bibliographic presentation of novel concepts, incipient trends, and germinal ideas, and these, of course, as demonstrated in this paper apply aptly to such a topic as humour.[24] The second principle relates to the concept of optimal growth of scientific literature and the premise that the scientific community exerts its own controls on growth through the processes of selection and rejection aimed at avoiding 'malignant growth'. Thirdly, sociobibliography strengthens the application of the human intellect by conserving intellectual resources through 'the recycling and reuse of the competent work already done throughout the stages that lead to the formation of the scientific literature'.

All of these principles, then, clearly are salient to our initial and modest endeavours here to establish the parameters of the emerging sub-discipline of the sociology of humour. That they should also guide the practice and particularly the future development of the sociological study of humour is self-evident and, if not a guarantee that any sociologist drawn to the field will find the Holy Grail, he or she will, in pioneering and following sociobibliographic principles, establish it as a justifiably serious-minded look at a funny subject.

APPENDIX

Select list of journals which regularly contain articles on various sociological aspects of humour as described in the above schema.

American Quarterly
American Speech
Anglia
Apollo
Apropos

Comparative Literature
Eighteenth Century Studies
English Literature in Transition 1880–1920
Folklore
Gazette Des Beaux-Arts
German Life and Letters

Journal of American Culture
Journal of Broadcasting and Electronic Media (formerly *Journal of Broadcasting*)
Journal of Communication

New Society
Nineteenth Century Theatre Research
PMLA
Radio Times
Restoration and 18th Century Theatre Research
Scholia Satyrica
Screen (formerly *Screen Education*)
Semiotica

Speculum
Studies in Contemporary Satire
Studies in English Literature 1500–1900
Television Quarterly
Thalia

The America Imago

Journal of Contemporary History   *The Chaucer Review*
Journal of the History of Ideas   *The Drama Review*
Journal of Popular Culture   *The Listener*
Literature and Society   *The Modern Languages Review*
Maledicta   *The Sewanee Review*
Medium Aevum   *Theatre Quarterly*
Modern Drama   *Theatre Studies*
Modern Languages Quarterly   *TV Times*
Modern Philology   *Victorian Studies*
Mosaic   *Western Folklore*

NOTES

1. *Cumulative Index to the American Journal of Sociology* (prepared
   under the editorship of Peter M. Blau), Volumes 1–70 (1895–1965)
   (Chicago: University of Chicago Press, 1966); *Index to the American
   Sociological Review*, Volumes 1–25 (1936–1960) (New York: American Sociological Association, 1961). The major contribution to
   remedying this glaring aphasia of the sociological imagination is the
   recently published extended review article, including an extensive
   annotated bibliography, by Anton Zijderveld entitled 'The Sociology
   of Humour and Laughter', *Current Sociology*, vol. 31, no. 3 (Winter
   1983). See also a rejoinder essay by Christie Davies entitled
   'Commentary on Anton C. Zijderveld's Trend Report on "The
   Sociology of Humour and Laughter" ', *Current Sociology*, vol. 32, no.
   1 (Spring 1984) pp. 142–57.
2. See, for example, O. Klapp, 'The Fool as a Social Type', *American
   Journal of Sociology*, vol. 55 (1950) pp. 157–62; T. Burns, 'Friends,
   Enemies and Polite Fiction', *American Sociological Review*, vol. 18
   (1953) pp. 654–62.
3. See for example, J. Emerson, 'Negotiating the serious import of
   humour', *Sociometry*, vol. 32 (1969) pp. 169–81; P. Bradney, 'The
   joking relationship in industry', *Human Relations*, vol. 10 (1957) pp.
   179–87; M. Salutin, 'The Impression Management Techniques of the
   Burlesque Comedian', *Sociological Inquiry*, vol. 43 (1973) pp. 159–68;
   A. Zijderveld, 'Jokes and Their Relation to Social Reality', *Social
   Research*, vol. 35 (1968) pp. 286–311. Further evidence of the
   difficulties of locating such texts is furnished by checking such sources
   under the headings and sub-headings in *Sociological Abstracts*. Thus,
   for example, Zijderveld's paper is listed under 0200 Sociology: history
   and theory: 07 Theories, ideas and systems; and Salutin's under 1000
   Social Differentiation. 20. Sociology of occupations and professions!
4. C. Davies, 'Ethnic Jokes, Moral Values and Social Boundaries',
   British Journal of Sociology, vol. 33 (1982) pp. 383–403. Perhaps the
   first notable paper on humour by a sociologist, however, is that of the
   Belgian author E. Dupreel, 'Le problem sociologique du rire', *Revue
   philosophique*, vol. 106 (1928) pp. 213–60.

5. J. Goldstein, 'Theoretical Notes on Humour', *Journal of Communication* (Summer 1976) p. 105.

6. The papers, or abstracts of papers, delivered at the conference are reproduced in A. Chapman and H. Foot (eds) *It's A Funny Thing, Humour* (Oxford: Pergamon Press, 1977). Since 1982, WHIM (Western Humor and Irony Membership) based on Arizona State University has held annual conferences, the proceedings of which are published as serial yearbooks (WHIMSY) under the editorship of Don L. F. Nilsen, English Department, Arizona State University, Tempe, Arizona 85287, USA.

7. J. Goldstein and P. McGhee (eds) *The Psychology of Humour* (New York: Academic Press, 1972). A particularly wide ranging and rich bibliographical source for students of American humour is *American Humor: An Interdisciplinary Newsletter (AH:IN)*, the first volume of which dates from Spring 1974 (edited by Lawrence E. Mintz, American Studies Department, University of Maryland, College Park, MD 20742, USA). The most up-to-date and comprehensive bibliography which is especially useful for psychological and sociological research on comedians and their world is in S. Fisher, and R. Fisher, *Pretend the World is Funny and Forever: A Psychological Analysis of Comedians, Clowns, and Actors* (New Jersey: Lawrence Earlbaum Associates, 1981).

8. See, for example, H. Sacks, 'An Analysis of the Course of a Joke's Telling in Conversation', in R. Bauman and J. Sherzer (eds) *Explorations in the Ethnography of Speaking* (Cambridge: Cambridge University Press, 1974); G. Jefferson, 'A Technique for Inviting Laughter and its Subsequent Acceptance Declination', in G. Psathas (ed.) *Everyday Language: Studies in Ethnomethodology* (New York: Irvington Publishers, 1979).

9. See, for example, P. Bradney, 'The Joking Relationship in Industry', *Human Relations*, vol. 10 (1957) pp. 179–87; R. Coser, 'Some Social Functions of Laughter', *Human Relations*, vol. 12 (1959) pp. 171–82; A. Sykes, 'Joking Relationships in an Industrial Setting', *American Anthropologist*, vol. 68 (1966) pp. 188–93.

10. See, for example, M. Adler and C. Van Doren, *Great Treasury of Western Thought: A Compendium of Important Statements on Man and his Institutions by the Great Thinkers in Western History* (New York: R. R. Bowker, 1977) Section 16.4 'Tragedy and Comedy', pp. 1039–52; E. Ballard, 'Sense of the Comic', in P. Wiener (ed.) *Dictionary of the History of Ideas, Vol. 1* (New York: Scribners, 1978/ 83); W. Kaiser, 'Wisdom of the Fool', in P. Wiener, (ed.) *Dictionary of the History of Ideas, Vol. 4* (New York: Scribners, 1978/83); J. Stolnitz, 'Notes on Comedy and Tragedy', *Philosophy and Phenomenological Research*, vol. 16 (1955) pp. 45–60; D. Monro, 'Humour', in *The Encyclopaedia of Philosophy, Vol. 4* (New York: The Free Press, 1967).

11. The most immediately suggestive sources written by sociologists are those of H. Duncan, *Communication and Social Order* (London: Oxford University Press, 1970); L. Lowenthal, *Literature, Popular*

Culture and Society (Englewood Cliffs, NJ: Prentice-Hall, 1961). The best surveys of sources by literary critics or historians of comic genres are R. Heilman, *The Ways of the World: Comedy and Society* (Seattle/London: University of Washington Press, 1978) and R. A. Wellek, *History of Modern Criticism 1750–1950. Vol. 2 The Romantic Age* (Cambridge: Cambridge University Press, 1955).

12. See, for example, E. Burns and T. Burns (eds) *Sociology of Literature and Drama: Selected Readings* (Harmondsworth: Penguin, 1973), esp. Introduction and Part 3 'The Fictive and the Social World'.

13. Sinclair Goodlad has perceptively dubbed and discussed comedy as 'institutionalised humour' in his 'On the Social Significance of Television Comedy' in C. Bigsby, (ed.) *Approaches to Popular Culture in Early Modern Europe* (London: Temple Smith, 1978) p. 216.

14. K. Thomas, 'The Place of Laughter in Tudor and Stewart England', *Times Literary Supplement*, 21 January 1977, pp. 77, 81; T. Zeldin, *France: 1848–1945. Vol. 2* (Oxford: Clarendon Press, 1977) Part 2, Chap. 13 'Happiness and Humour'. Perhaps the earliest and so far unexplored contribution by a major sociologist to the diachronic study of humorous expression in a variety of cultures is that of W. Sumner, in his classic book *Folkways* (New York: Mentor Books, n.d.) Chap. 7 'Popular Sports, Exhibitions, and Drama'.

15. The social facilitation aspect of humour, which has yet to be fully expounded and investigated for its contribution to our understanding of the sociology of humour, especially for inter-subjective tension management at the group level and beyond, is based on a concept originally propounded by the social psychologist Zajonc. See, for example, P. McGhee, 'Birth Order and Social Facilitation of Humour', *Psychological Reports*, vol. 33 (1973) pp. 105–6.

16. Raymond Williams has usefully suggested that the term 'keywords' be used in two connected senses, viz. 'they are significant, binding words in certain activities and their interpretation; they are significant, indicative words in certain forms of thought'. See his *Keywords: A Vocabulary of Culture and Society* (London: Fontana/Croom Helm, 1976) p. 13.

17. *Current Contents* is published by H. W. Wilson, New York.

18. I have here anglicised the American 'humor' for stylistic and consistency purposes.

19. The exception to this generalisation is the monthly publication *Cumulative Book Index: A World List of Books in the English Language* which is also published by H. W. Wilson, New York. Even this, however, is clearly dependent on notifications from publishers themselves and a number of minor publishers in Britain, for example, of important humour books, especially in paperback, do not appear on inspection to be represented in their monthly listings. Again, it is necessary to look under sub-heads such as 'comedy', 'comic', 'humour', etc., to discover recently published books relevant to sociological analysis of humour.

20. Indeed, the author has come across promising material in the form of

book reviews and articles even in such a source as the weekly published *Times Higher Education Supplement*!

21. For a model filmography in the realm of comedy and for particular film comedians see, for example, that compiled by Maryann Chach in T. Dardis, *Keaton: The Man Who Wouldn't Lie Down* (London: Deutsch, 1979) pp. 285–317. For a model teleography see, for example, that of Lucy Tuck in J. Cook, (ed.) *Television Sitcom*, BFI Dossier 17 (London: British Film Institute, 1982) pp. 88–100.

22. *The Collected Essays of Ilse Bry*, edited and compiled by Lois Afflerbach and Marga Franck (Westport, CT.: Greenwood Press, 1977) p. 150.

23. Ibid., p. 239.

24. Ibid., p. 244. One such germinal idea which has been suggested, and in very rare cases pursued, is that of linking irony with social science perspectives in analysing modern society. Thus, Ernest Gellner has highlighted what he considers to be a very important general trait of modern societies, viz. the emergence of 'ironic cultures'. See his *Legitimation of Belief* (Cambridge: Cambridge University Press, 1974) p. 193. Duncan has similarly pointed to Veblen's role as a 'comic artist' in his use of the 'rhetoric of ironic appeal' in his attacks on the businessman, and the use of irony as the 'comedy of reason' by writers down the ages (Duncan, pp. 198, 385–6). Margaret Rose has importantly also drawn attention to the way in which the young Marx used parody to free himself from the terminology and presuppositions of the authors he cited and criticised in his works. See her *Reading the Young Marx and Engels: Poetry, Parody and the Censor* (London: Croom Helm, 1978). The author of this paper has in train a sociobibliographic project to relate the seminal ideas of Pitirim Sorokin in terms of his ideational and sensate sociocultural systems to various periods or eras in a given society's history with a view to testing the *'fin-de-siècle'* syndrome in relation to the emergence of a strong satirical movement in that society.

General Index

Index of Authors

277

W